EAST ASIAN COOPERATION: SEARCHING FOR AN INTEGRATED APPROACH

东亚合作:寻求协调一致的方式

**Edited by
Zhang Yunling**

张蕴岭 主编

World Affairs Press
世界知识出版社

Cataloging-in-Publication Data

East Asian Cooperation: Searching for an Integrated Approach
Edited by Zhang Yunling/June 2004
ISBN: 7-5012-2298-3
Copyright © 2004 by World Affairs Press

图书在版编目(CIP)数据

东亚合作：寻求协调一致的方式/张蕴岭主编．—北京：世界知识出版社，2004.6
 ISBN 7-5012-2298-3
 Ⅰ.东… Ⅱ.张… Ⅲ.地区经济-经济合作-东亚-文集-英文 Ⅳ.F114.46-53
 中国版本图书馆 CIP 数据核字(2004)第 055418 号

责任编辑：王江洪鸿　　责任出版：夏凤仙
特约编辑：毛　悦　　　　责任校对：何　莉
封面设计：林　昶

EAST ASIAN COOPERATION: SEARCHING FOR AN INTEGRATED APPROACH
东亚合作：寻求协调一致的方式

世界知识出版社出版发行
(北京市东城区干面胡同 51 号　邮政编码：100010)
网址：http://www.wap1934.com
北京市朝阳展望印刷厂照排印刷　新华书店经销
850×1168 毫米　1/32　印张：10　字数：260 千
2004 年 6 月第一版　2004 年 6 月第一次印刷　印数：1—1000 册
ISBN 7-5012-2298-3/F·129　定价：35.00 元

版权所有　翻印必究

Contents

Foreword (1)

Building an East Asian Economic Community
　　　　　　　　　　　　　　　Hadi Soesastro (1)

East Asian Economic Cooperation: Retrospect and Prospect
　　　　　　　　Thomas J. P. Voon and Edward K. Y. Chen (31)

ASEAN Plus Three: A New Formal Regionalism in East Asia
　　　　　　　　　　　　　　　Ratanak Hav (59)

A Road Map to the East Asia Community
　　　　　　　　　　　　　Daisuke Hiratsuka (85)

An East Asian FTA: Recent Progress and Policy Implications
　　　　　　　　　　　　　　　Inkyo Cheong (108)

Thai Perception on East Asian Cooperation
　　　　　　　　　　　Nattapong Thongpakde, et. al. (139)

The East Asia Free Trade Agreement: An ASEAN Perspective
　　　　　　　　　　　　　　Mohd Haflah Piei (173)

East Asian Cooperation: The ASEAN View
Gloria O. Pasadilla (217)

Making ASEAN as a Close Partner: Comparing China and Japan
Zhang Yunling (248)

The Economic Rise of China: A Catalyst for East Asian Economic Integration   *John Wong* (265)

Emerging East Asian Identification: A Cultural Perspective
Yu Xintian (293)

Foreword

As stated by East Asian Vision Group in its report to leaders: East Asia is moving from a region of nations to a *bona fide* regional community with share challenges, common aspirations, and a parallel destiny. ① It seems that East Asian cooperation emerges as an East Asian regionalism. There are three key words relating to this East Asian regionalism: Why, What and How.

Why does East Asia need a regionalism? East Asia emerged as an integrated region based on closer economic linkages. Economic integration not just created more interrelated interests, but also requires more regional arrangements friendly for exchanges and business. The financial crisis in 1997 gave another impetus by calling for an immediate action to deal with the crisis, which set a foundation for "10 + 3" dialogue, i. e. between ASEAN and China, Japan and the Republic of Korea (ROK). The progress of "10+3" process (annual leaders' meeting, regular ministers' meeting, etc) helps to enforce an East Asian identity. This was well reflected in the report of East Asian Vision Group by calling for an East Asian Community building. However, the East Asian identity still needs time to be accepted and enriched.

What should and could be done for an East Asian identity? An East Asian FTA (EAFTA) is the first thing to be considered since an integrated and open market seems a core in any regional economic cooperation. The key issue is how to converge the current diversified FTA efforts into an integrated approach toward an EAFTA. The financial cooperation is another area. Chiang

---

① *Towards an East Asian Community: Region of Peace, Prosperity and Progress*, East Asian Vision Group Report, p. 1.

Mai Initiative made a good start, but the question still remains: Does the region need an East Asian Monetary Fund (EAMF) and a regional currency in the long run? Further more, as a process of regionalism, its institutional building in the political as well as security areas should not be excluded. Thus, political and security cooperation needs to be strengthened.

How can East Asian region achieve its goal for a community building? East Asian regionalism has its own unique feature different from Europe and America. East Asian cooperation and its regionalism must find its own way. Diversity in economic development levels, political systems and security concerns makes East Asian integration process must be gradual on the one hand, and the regional institutional building moderate by nature on the other hand. From beginning, ASEAN played an active role in bringing 13 parties together. However, a key factor is how to make China and Japan really together to promote East Asian integration process, either for EAFTA, EAMF or a security forum.

We have witnessed fast progress of East Asian cooperation in recent years. Nevertheless, it is crucial to search for an integrated approach, i.e. how to converge diversified efforts into a well coordinated approach toward an East Asian regional identity.

In September 11—12, 2003, an international conference was held in Beijing by Institute of Asia—Pacific Studies and Center for APEC and East Asian Cooperation, Chinese Academy of Social Sciences on "East Asian cooperation: Searching for an integrated approach" with the participation of more than 30 scholars and experts from East Asia. This book contends 11 papers written by those participants.

My gratitude should be given to The Ford Foundation for its valuable financial support for the conference and publication of this book. My special acknowledgement goes to Ms. Mao Yue who helped me greatly in editing this book and Ms. Li Mo who did an important job in coordinating the conference and paper contributors.

> Zhang Yunling
> Professor, Director
> Institute of Asia—Pacific Studies
> Center for APEC and East Asian Cooperation
> Chinese Academy of Social Sciences

> January 8, 2004
> Beijing

Building an East Asian Economic Community

Hadi Soesastro[1]

Introduction

The vision for an East Asian community has been articulated by the East Asian Vision Group (EAVG) in its Report, "Towards an East Asian Community", submitted to the ASEAN Plus Three (APT) Leaders at their Fifth Summit in Brunei Darussalam in November 2001. The vision is of an East Asia that moves "from a region of nations to a *bona fide* regional community with shared challenges, common aspirations, and a parallel destiny." Furthermore, the Report also stated that " the economic field, including trade, investment, and finance, is expected to serve as the catalyst in the comprehensive community-building process."

In the field of economic cooperation, the vision is that of a progressive integration of the East Asian economy, ultimately leading to an East Asian economic community. Economic integration is to be pursued through the liberalization of trade and investment, development and technological cooperation, and information technology development.

---

[1] Hadi Soesastro, Executive Director, Center for Strategic and International Studies, Jakarta, Indonesia.

In trade, it recommended the formation of an East Asia Free Trade Area (EAFTA), and the liberalization of trade should be well ahead of the Bogor Goal set by APEC. In investment, it proposed the establishment of an East Asian Investment Area (EAIA) by expanding the Framework Agreement on ASEAN Investment Area (AIA) to cover East Asia as a whole. In the area of finance, the recommendation towards greater financial integration was to adopt a staged, two-track approach, namely for the establishment of a self-help arrangement (e. g. an East Asian Monetary Fund) and for coordinating a suitable exchange rate mechanism amongst countries in the region.

The EAVG has also listed the various motivations for the development of an East Asian community. A great deal has been written on this. Three considerations have stood out. First, the need to establish a regional (institutional) identity, in view of the fact that other regions (Europe and the Americas) have established or are developing their own regional arrangement. Second, it is needed to amplify an East Asian voice on regional and global issues, in view of East Asia's increased stakes in regional and global developments. Third, the need to promote regional peace and prosperity through cooperation, in view of the region's own internal political dynamics.

Despite this compelling rationale, difficulties and obstacles in creating an East Asian community have also been recognized. Three problems have been identified. First, there are great diversities amongst countries in the region, and especially the large gaps in levels of economic development. Second, there is a lack of a mechanism (and tradition) for regional cooperation in Northeast Asia. Third, it is the prevailing political security problems in the region (China-Taiwan[①], the Korean Peninsula,

---

[①] Taiwan in this book refers to Chinese Taipei. Hong Kong refers to Hong Kong SAR. ——Editor

and to a much lesser extent the South China Sea).

I. The ASEAN Plus Three Process

With the development of the ASEAN Plus Three (APT) process, it can be said that ASEAN has taken the lead in establishing the foundation for eventual East Asian economic integration. This process, as suggested by its name, is supposed to be driven by ASEAN. In fact, if ASEAN had not taken the lead, this process may not have emerged. A Japanese or Chinese initiative and leadership would have killed it. Until today the main APT meetings take place in conjunction with ASEAN meetings. Some see this as a possible obstacle to the creation of a truly East Asian regional arrangement (Jayasuriya, 2000).

The APT process began as a modest undertaking. Foreign Ministers from the three Northeast Asian countries initially came for an informal meeting over lunch during an ASEAN meeting. There was no specific agenda for those meetings. This process attracted the involvement of the heads of state. The first (informal) APT Summit was held in December 1997 in Kuala Lumpur. The Asian financial crisis appears to have provided the impetus for this Summit. The APT process became more serious. Although the process has been and is essentially driven by ASEAN, the agenda setting was not monopolized by ASEAN.

In the Second APT Summit in Hanoi in November 1998, ROK President, Kim Dae-jung, made his remark by proposing the establishment of an East Asia Vision Group (EAVG) to craft out a mid-to long-term vision for the cooperation. The Third APT Summit in Manila in November 1999 was held under the banner of "East Asian Cooperation". The meeting discussed various ways to promote cooperation and to cope with the new challenges of the 21st Century. APT heads of state adopted the "Joint Statement on East Asian Cooperation "suggesting cooperative measures in various areas including security, economy, culture, and development strategy. This agreement led to the launching since 2000 of a series of APT meetings of finance and economic ministers, in addition to those of foreign ministers.

In May 2000, at the APT Finance Ministers Meeting, discussions on the need to build a regional financial framework led to the adoption of the so-called Chiang Mai Initiative (CMI). This initiative aims at creating a network out of existing currency swap arrangements of ASEAN and bilaterally between ASEAN members and the other Three countries.

In the Fourth APT Summit in Singapore in November 2000, Chinese Prime Minister Zhu Rongji came up with suggestions that the APT should focus on the following areas of cooperation: the development of Mekong River Basin transportation and communication infrastructure, IT (information technology), human resources development, agriculture, and tourism. China also took the initiative to convene an APT meeting of agriculture and forestry ministers, and offered to host an agricultural technology and cooperation business forum. ROK President Kim Dae-jung proposed the establishment of an East Asia Study Group (EASG), consisting of officials, with the mandate to assess the recommendations of the EAVG, and from that assessment, sort out a practical number of concrete measures that should be given high priority and are relatively easy to carry out. Its other task is to explore the idea and implications of an East Asian Summit.

The Singapore Summit concluded with a public statement by Prime Minister Goh Chok Tong, highlighting the "two big ideas" that emerged from the discussion, namely the development of institutional links between Southeast Asia and Northeast Asia, and the setting up of a working group to study the merits of an East Asian free trade and investment area. In response to suggestions of transforming the APT Summit into some kind of East Asia Summit, he recommended a gradual evolution. He noted, however, that what was important was that the leaders of the thirteen countries were starting to think as "East Asian".

At the Fifth APT Summit in Brunei Darussalam in November 2001, leaders endorsed the Report by the EAVG, including the development towards an East Asian Economic Community, among other means through the creation of an East Asian Free Trade Area. However, this meeting and the agreements reached were overshadowed by China's "surprising" proposal for an ASEAN-China Free Trade Agreement. Global terrorism issues as well as the signing of the Framework Agreement on ASEAN-China Comprehensive Economic Cooperation, which provided the basis for negotiating an ASEAN-China Free Trade Agreement (ACFTA), also overshadowed the Sixth APT Summit in Phnom Penh in November 2002. In addition, the leaders of ASEAN and Japan also issued a Joint Declaration on the Comprehensive Economic Partnership between ASEAN and Japan, which may include an FTA element.

The above development shows that the APT process appears to have moved its main attention away from financial cooperation to developing FTAs in the region, seen as building blocks for an eventual region-wide free trade area, the East Asian Free Trade Area (EAFTA). Indeed, the EAVG Report made the suggestion that adopting a building block approach, and consolidating the existing bilateral and sub-regional FTAs in the region could achieve the establishment of an EAFTA.

II. Trade Integration or Fragmentation?

It has been speculated that the ASEAN-China initiative was largely politically motivated. Strengthening of ASEAN-China relations is indeed a critical element in the development of an East Asian community. The search for an institutional identity in East Asia, as in other regions, tends to be dominated by ideas about regional trade structures, in particular FTAs. In a region as diverse as East Asia it will not be easy to establish a regional-wide free trade arrangement. There are suggestions that perhaps such a regional arrangement can result from the development of bilateral or sub-regional trading arrangements as its building blocks. Recent initiatives to form bilateral FTAs may be inspired by that idea.

There are various possible routes to develop an East Asian institutional identity (Soesastro, 2001). One possible route is through the formation of a Northeast Asian subregional FTA that subsequently could be linked to the one already in existence in Southeast Asia (AFTA), resulting in an East Asian Free Trade Area (EAFTA). A modified version of this is to extend AFTA's CEPT (common effective preferential tariffs) to the other Three. The other option, focusing on development cooperation, is to develop an OECD-type institution. This will require establishing and operating large resources, and takes away much of the limelight from the political leaders. This option is a desirable one but not likely to be pursued in East Asia.

Still another route, as will be examined later, is through financial cooperation. The route that is currently being taken, namely along the pragmatic, develop-as-you-go approach, is perhaps the politically preferred one. However, there needs to be a clear vision and strategy as to how the APT process can be strengthened by the bilateral initiatives.

The ASEAN-China agreement and the ASEAN-Japan initiative will now take the center stage. The ASEAN bureaucracies will devote a great deal of energies and attention to these initiatives. ASEAN will effectively become a "hub". In September 2002, a Joint Ministerial Declaration on Closer Economic Partnership (CEP) has been signed between ASEAN and the CER countries (Australia and New Zealand). In late October 2002, at the occasion of the APEC meeting in Mexico, President Bush also proposed the "Enterprise for ASEAN Initiatives" that will provide a framework for the US to negotiate both bilateral and regional free-trade agreements with Southeast Asia. At the First ASEAN-India Summit in November 2002, India too has offered to start free trade talks and to have a free trade agreement (FTA) working within 10 years. Australia has also courted ASEAN to have an ASEAN-Australia Summit.

Can one conclude that the region has effectively embarked on bilateral agreements as building blocks towards an East Asian Community? ASEAN appears to have become more inclined to develop bilateral initiatives. A region-wide initiative does not seem to be the preferred option. Perhaps there are concerns in ASEAN that in a region-wide arrangement it would be overwhelmed by the much larger Northeast Asian region. The combined GDP of the three Northeast Asian countries is currently about 13 times larger than ASEAN's GDP. At the ASEAN Economic Ministers Meeting in September 2002, Singapore Trade and Industry Minister, George Yeo, stated "it has long been a position of ASEAN that we deal separately with China, with Japan, with ROK in order to secure a certain position for ourselves." (*The Sunday Times*, 15 September 2002). It is not immediately clear what this statement exactly means, but the preference for bilateral initiatives is unmistakable.

Indeed, ASEAN's strategy seems to have been reinforced by the favorable response from a number of its economic partners. All of a sudden ASEAN has been brought to the limelight (again). ASEAN will definitely exploit this opportunity in order to be able to come out from the back stage, where it has been pushed to since the financial crisis. As has been reported, Singapore's Prime Minister Goh Chok Tong is now talking about "the ASEAN jumbo jet [that] has one wing in the making in the East, through agreements with China and Japan. India's proposal provides the second wing. With this, we can take off." (*The

Strait Times, 6 November 2002). In fact, an ASEAN-US initiative will be much more significant for ASEAN. Singapore officials have also speculated that ROK, which has not offered to enter an FTA with ASEAN, may get into the act next year (*The Straits Times*, 6 November 2002). This may be the case. At the APT Economic Ministers Meeting in September 2002 in Brunei Darussalam, it was reported that ROK Trade Minister Hwang Doo-yun stated that his country was doing a study on the pros and cons of entering into such an agreement with ASEAN (*The Sunday Times*, 15 September 2002). Lee Yock Suan, a minister in the office of the Singapore Prime Minister, believes that " slowly but surely, we are seeing the emergence of an East Asian community." (*International Herald Tribune*, 4 November 2002).

In addition to going bilateral, it appears that there has emerged an ASEAN understanding that any economic cooperation arrangement today, be it bilateral, sub-regional or inter-regional cannot have a narrow agenda. Any FTA initiative today will have to be of a "new age" type. It can be given any label, FTA, CEP (Closer Economic Partnership) or EPA (Economic Partnership Arrangement), but whatever it is called it is going to have a broad, comprehensive agenda that covers a host of non-border measures in addition to border liberalization efforts.

III. ASEAN's Role

As ASEAN has come to the center stage, and as it emerges as a potential "hub", the big question is whether ASEAN can effectively manage the process. Prime Minister Goh of Singapore rightly asked the question of whether ASEAN could sustain the interests of its partners (*The Straits Times*, 6 November 2002). It is clear that ASEAN has to put its home in order first. It has to formulate a comprehensive and coherent AFTA Plus as the basis for developing external, bilateral, and inter-regional linkages. He has proposed to accelerate ASEAN's economic integration towards an ASEAN Economic Community (AEC) as a common market, along the lines of the European Economic Community, by 2020. This, it is argued, is simply a "logical extension of AFTA".

There is as yet insufficient confidence in the region itself that ASEAN can effectively take up this new agenda. Comments refer to the fact that ASEAN "remains so fragmented that any meaningful package within the region seems elusive" (*The Jakarta Post*, 6 November 2002). The outgoing ASEAN Secretary General, Severino, in his report to the ASEAN Summit called for political commitment within ASEAN to achieve economic integration. He suggested that ASEAN "seems to have become stuck in framework agreements, work programs and master plans", and it needs to translate them into concrete actions.

ASEAN must have a strategy for creating both an ASEAN Economic Community and the East Asian community. They have to be pursued in parallel. In essence, it needs to assure that: (a) bilateral initiatives become building blocks towards an East Asian community; (b) the various bilateral and sub-regional arrangements will strengthen economic reform efforts within the ASEAN economies. This strategy has to be supported by other East Asian countries. In fact, it should be adopted as an East Asian strategy.

Elements (and principles) of such a strategy have been formulated first by a high-level Task Force on an AFTA-CER FTA, which was headed by Cesar Virata. In addition to WTO consistency, the elements include:

(a) *Comprehensiveness*: it must cover trade in all goods, services (covering all modes of supply), investment, technical barriers to trade, and mutual recognition agreements (MRAs);

(b) *Speed*: the pace of liberalization should proceed faster than that of APEC;

(c) *Flexibility*: some elements of the agreement can be achieved earlier than others (Early Harvest);

(d) *Simplicity*: the rules of origin in relation to the FTA element must be as liberal as possible and should be simplified and standardized;

(e) *Facilitation*: trade and investment facilitation are to be pursued continuously;

(f) *Capacity building* is an integral part of the arrangement.

Comprehensive coverage is illustrated by the Singapore-Japan New Age Partnership (JSEPA), which was signed in January 2002. It has two main components. The first is *liberalization and facilitation*. This component covers: trade in goods (including elimination of tariffs), rules of origin, MRAs, trade in services, investment, movement of natural persons, intellectual property rights, paperless trading, competition policy, government procurement, and customs procedures. The second is *closer economic partnership*, which includes: ICT, human resources development, trade and investment promotion, SMEs, tourism, financial services, science and technology, and broadcasting.

The ASEAN-Japan bilateral initiative, as proposed by Prime Minister Koizumi in January 2002, has also led to a Joint Declaration on Comprehensive Economic Partnership, signed at the Sixth APT Summit in November 2002. The declaration proposed the comprehensiveness not only of sectors but also of *countries*, although allowing for the development of bilateral economic partnerships between Japan and individual ASEAN countries. In addition, it stipulated the following guiding principles: reciprocity and mutual benefits, special and differential treatment (and additional flexibility to the new ASEAN members), to begin in areas where implementation is feasible. The declaration stated that the Partnership agreement would include "elements of a possible free trade area" that "should be completed as soon as possible within 10 years, taking into account the economic levels and sensitive sectors in each country". A framework agreement is to be endorsed by the leaders in 2003.

It may well be that the ASEAN-Japan Framework Agreement be modeled and expand on the Framework Agreement on Comprehensive Economic Cooperation between ASEAN and China, signed in Phnom Penh on 4 November 2002. The Agreement consists of 16 Articles. Article 2 lists the measures for comprehensive economic cooperation to establish an ASEAN-China FTA within 10 years. These include:

(a) Progressive elimination of tariffs and non-tariff barriers in substantially all trade in goods;

(b) Progressive liberalization of trade in services with substantial sectoral coverage;

(c) Establishment of an open and competitive investment regime that facilitates and promotes investment within the ASEAN-China FTA;

(d) Provision of special and differential treatment and flexibility to the newer ASEAN members;

(e) Provision of flexibility in the negotiations to address their sensitive areas in the goods, services and investment sectors with such flexibility to be negotiated and mutually agreed based on the principle of reciprocity and mutual benefits;

(f) Establishment of effective trade and investment facilitation measures, including, but not limited to, simplification of customs procedures and development of mutual recognition arrangements;

(g) Expansion of economic cooperation in areas as may be mutually agreed upon that will complement the deepening of trade and investment links and formulation of action plans and programs in order to implement the agreed sectors/areas of cooperation; and

(h) Establishment of appropriate mechanisms for the purposes of effective implementation of the Agreement.

Substantive articles in the Agreement are: Article 3 on Trade in Goods and Article 6 on Early Harvest. Negotiations in the area of goods trade will involve a gradual reduction or elimination of substantially all products. In the *Normal Track*, the listed products will have their respective applied MFN tariff rates gradually reduced or eliminated in accordance with specified schedules and rates (to be mutually agreed upon) over a period from 1 January 2005 to 2010 for ASEAN 6 and China, and from 1 January 2005 to 2015 in the case of the newer ASEAN members. In regard to the *Sensitive Track*, the respective MFN tariff rates will be reduced (and eliminated) in accordance with the mutually agreed end rates and end dates or timeframes. The number of products in the Sensitive Track is subject to a maximum ceiling. The negotiations will also cover other detailed rules, e.g. reciprocity; rules of origin; treatment of out-of-quota rates; non-tariff measures; safeguards; subsidies and countervailing measures and anti-dumping measures; as well as facilitation and promotion of effective and adequate protection of TRIPs.

An Early Harvest program has been agreed upon. The products covered by this program include all agricultural products (chapters 01 to 08) at the 8/9-digit level (HS Code), except those in the Exclusion List. Additional, specific products, negotiated bilaterally, have also been included in the program (a number of ASEAN countries have not concluded their negotiations). Products under this program are divided into 3 categories for tariff reduction and elimination:

a) Category 1: products with MFN tariff rates higher than 15% for China and ASEAN 6, and 30%, or higher for the newer ASEAN members.

b) Category 2: products with MFN tariff rates between 5%

and 15% for China and ASEAN 6, and between 15% and 30% for the newer ASEAN members.

c) Category 3: products with MFN tariff rates lower than 5% for China and ASEAN 6, and lower than 15% for the newer ASEAN members.

Table 1 China-ASEAN 6 Early Harvest Timeframes

Product Category	Not later than 1/1/04	Not later than 1/1/05	Not later than 1/1/06
1	10%	5%	0%
2	5%	0%	0%
3	0%	0%	0%

For the newer ASEAN members the timeframe is stretched out to 1 January 2010. Vietnam will begin the process before 1 January 2004, while Laos, Myanmar and Cambodia before 1 January 2006. Cambodia's elimination of tariffs will be one year slower than that by Laos and Myanmar.

Many observers have expected that the Early Harvest program will be more substantial than finally agreed upon. The program covers about 10% of all tariff lines, involving 600 products that belong to the following categories: live animals, meat and edible meat offal, fish, dairy produce, other animal products, live trees, edible vegetables, edible fruits and nuts. Trade between ASEAN and China in products covered by the program amounted only to about 860,000 US $ in 2001.

The fact that the Early Harvest program was not a major "bang" suggests how difficult the follow-up negotiations will be. ASEAN-China Trade Negotiation Committee (ASEAN-China TNC) will conduct future negotiations. One wonders whether the Committee has the ability to deal with the total package covered by the Framework Agreement so as not to get bogged down in the FTA negotiations and yet still be able to produce a significant outcome. This is why the broad-based, comprehensive agreement is so critical to the success of the undertaking. The institutional arrangement must match this task.

The initiative by China to negotiate an FTA with ASEAN, which was politically attractive to ASEAN, could be the deciding factor in ASEAN's decision to go into such bilateral agreements. China is the first country that concluded a framework agreement with ASEAN as a group. This could provide a strong incentive for ASEAN to act as a group in developing similar agreements with Japan and ROK or other countries. If ASEAN can become a strong hub and introduce some consistency in its various bilateral agreements, it can turn them into a comprehensive, region-wide agreement. This will make the bilateral a redundancy. It is one way to make the building block approach operational.

It is puzzling and also rather disturbing that several ASEAN countries have embarked on bilateral FTA negotiations with the same country that ASEAN has concluded or will conclude an agreement. Thailand is negotiating a bilateral FTA with China, the Philippines, Thailand, and Malaysia respectively are also interested in concluding a bilateral FTA with Japan. Thus a further fragmentation is currently being observed in East Asia.

IV. Financial Cooperation and Integration

East Asia may become an interesting laboratory to test whether monetary and financial, rather than trade and investment cooperation can become the main drivers for regional economic integration. The prevailing wisdom, inspired mainly by the European experience, suggests sequencing with trade cooperation far preceding monetary and financial cooperation. As surveyed by Rana (2002), the argument for focusing on trade cooperation is that the benefits from monetary and financial cooperation increase with the level of trade integration. The counter argument is that joining a monetary union could have significant multiplier effects on trade. This argument is supported by a study that shows that trade between countries that share a common currency is on average more than three times what would be predicted from a gravity model of trade.

Proponents of monetary and financial cooperation argued that this kind of cooperation does not require potentially de-stabilizing socio-political measures that accompany more traditional forms of regionalism. They also suggest that monetary and financial cooperation provide members who participate more opportunities for "win-win" situations, since it does not involve loss of competitiveness vis-à-vis trading partners and trade diversion as could cooperation in trade and investment (Rana, 2002).

Higgot (2000) enthusiastically argued that a "new monetary regionalism" is emerging in East Asia, which may well become "the first region that builds a grouping based on monetary and financial co-operation rather than increased inter-regional trade concentration". The origins of the new monetary regionalism in East Asia can be found in the debate on the creation of an Asian Monetary Fund (AMF) in late 1997 and the agreement between the ten ASEAN countries and China, Japan and ROK to adopt the so-called Chiang Mai Initiative (CMI) in May 2000. These two initiatives, one aborted and the other one taking off, were both a response to the Asian financial crisis. Monetary regionalism aims at enhancing the region's ability to weather financial crises. This could be seen as the region's response to the challenges of globalization.

Before the financial crisis, economic integration was essentially market-led. As a response to the crisis, are we seeing the gathering of a momentum for a policy-led integration? (Wang, 2002). The crisis was definitely a major catalyst in East Asia's search for an institutional identity. As observed by Stubbs (2002), the crisis has added to the sense of common history that has emerged in the region: "⋯nearly every government in East Asia felt its reverberations and had to deal with the fallout of the crisis". It also demonstrated the ineffectiveness of APEC and ASEAN as neither was in the position to help the crisis-hit countries. Furthermore, there was resentment with the way the International Monetary Fund (IMF), in conjunction with the US government, handled the crisis by imposing a set of solutions that only served to exacerbate the situation.

Countries in East Asia thus looked to the emerging ASEAN Plus Three (APT) process as the best vehicle for developing a strategy for dealing with future crises. In May 2000, on the sidelines of the annual meeting of the Asian Development Bank (ADB) in Chiang Mai, the Finance Ministers of the APT agreed to pool their hard currency resources. The hope is that this Chiang Mai Initiative (CMI) will become the cornerstone of East Asian cooperation. Can the region build on the CMI to promote further financial cooperation and integration? In turn can monetary and financial cooperation become the driver for regional economic integration?

Ito (1999?) has not come to a conclusion whether monetary and financial integration can precede trade integration. His hunch is that it may not. More importantly, he is also not convinced that the APT is the right grouping. At present, region-wide processes in East Asia are undertaken mostly under the APT framework. The APT is all what the region has.

The EAVG Report did not single out financial cooperation as a core activity towards the establishment of an East Asian Community. It is one of the six areas of cooperation that the Vision Group has recommended. In total, it recommended 57 concrete measures encompassing the six areas of cooperation. The EASG recommended 26 "implementable" concrete measures, composed of 17 measures for possible immediate implementation and 9 measures for possible implementation in the medium-term or long-term.

In the area of financial cooperation, the EAVG proposed

that East Asian governments adopt a staged, two-track approach towards greater financial integration: one track for establishing a self-help financing arrangement and the other for coordinating a suitable exchange rate mechanism among countries in the region. Key recommendations by the Group included the following:

- Establishment of a self-help regional facility for financial cooperation.
- Adoption of a better exchange rate coordination mechanism consistent with both financial stability and economic development.
- Strengthening of the regional monitoring and surveillance process within East Asia to supplement IMF global surveillance and Article IV consultation measures.

Recommendations by the EASG may become official policy. Financial cooperation is placed amongst the medium-term and long-term measures. The Group selected two measures, namely to undertake further study (with high priority) on (a) the establishment of a regional financing facility; and (b) the pursuance of a more closely coordinated regional exchange rate mechanism.

The EASG left out the Vision Group's recommendation to strengthen the regional surveillance and monitoring process perhaps because such a process is already in place as manifested in the APT Economic Review and Policy Dialogue Process. Indeed, the past few years have seen a number of initiatives to promote financial cooperation and integration in East Asia by groups such as ASEAN, the APT, and ASEM (Asia Europe Meeting).

In his survey, Rana (2002) identified the two main areas of financial cooperation in East Asia, namely: (a) information exchange and surveillance processes; and (b) resource provision mechanisms. The former is seen as a weaker form of cooperation, allowing individual countries to make policy choices in a more informed environment. The latter is in contrast with a stronger form of cooperation, ranging from the negotiation of bilateral swaps to the creation of a permanent common reserve pool administered by a secretariat.

Surveillance

The first regional surveillance process was established in November 1997, the Manila Framework Group (MFG). Higgot (2000) saw this as a significant exercise in the recognition of the "East Asian-ness" of the region. The Agreement to "Enhance Asian Regional Cooperation to Promote Financial Stability" was "very much part of the wider exercise of soul searching that took place both within ASEAN and between ASEAN and its other East Asian partners." The Group, consisting of deputies from the finance ministries and central banks of 14 Asia Pacific countries, meets twice a year. The ADB, IMF and World Bank provide surveillance reports to these meetings. In addition to surveillance, the Framework included other initiatives: (a) economic and technical cooperation in the financial area ("financial ecotech"); (b) measures to strengthen the IMF's capacity to respond to financial crises; and (c) development of cooperative financing arrangements to supplement the resources of the IMF and other international financial institutions. In its meeting in December 2001 the MFG discussed the proposal by a working group (led by Australia) to establish a "regional financing facility" under this Group.

Some observers see the MFG as the preeminent forum for regional surveillance and peer pressure. Wang (2002) is of the view that the MFG has not been very successful as a mechanism for regional financial cooperation. First, the MFG has not yet clearly specified the objectives of information exchange and surveillance. Second, there is no actual peer review process in the MFG. Third, issues related to financial sector reform are only discussed cursorily.

In its response to the crisis, ASEAN held a special meeting of finance ministers in Kuala Lumpur in December 1997. The ministers did not come up with any ASEAN financing agreement to assist crisis-affected members. They agreed to renew the ASEAN Swap Arrangement that was due to lapse in August 1999, but did not appear to have examined the reasons why this arrangement had not been used during the early stages of the crisis. Another meeting of ASEAN finance ministers was held in Jakarta in February 1998. The most concrete step taken was to agree on the establishment of a regional surveillance mechanism within ASEAN. It was only in October 1998, eight months after it was agreed on, when the ASEAN Finance Ministers signed a Terms of Understanding that established the ASEAN Surveillance Process. In fact, the agreement to develop a surveillance mechanism was watered down to a surveillance process. This process is based on the principles of peer review and mutual interest. ASEAN finance ministers meet twice a year for policy coordination under this Process. The ADB provided the surveillance report, but the report and the results of the meeting are kept confidential. The effectiveness of the surveillance process has been questioned.

Under the APT process, a peer review meeting, the Economic Review and Policy Dialogue Process, was first held in May 2000 in the sidelines of the ADB annual meeting. This process is similar to the ASEAN Surveillance Process. Finance Ministers of the 13 countries also meet twice a year for policy coordination. A template to monitor short-term capital flows has been finalized and implemented by several countries under a Japan-ASEAN technical assistance. In May 2001, a study group was established to enhance the process. It recommended a two-phase approach: the first phase is to strengthen the existing process by organizing an additional informal meeting of the APT deputies, and in the second phase an independent surveillance unit is to be established.

The latest development is the establishment of an APT Early Warning System (EWS). This was agreed upon at the APT finance ministers meeting in Honolulu in May 2001. An EWS is being developed with the assistance of the ADB.

Regional Financing Facility

The idea of a regional financing facility was first proposed by Japan. The financial crisis provided an occasion for Japan to play an important role in the creation of new mechanisms in East Asia through a mix of policies, including financial assistance (Kikuchi, 2002). It was Japan that proposed to ASEAN to hold an ASEAN-Japan summit to commemorate the thirtieth anniversary of ASEAN in 1997. ASEAN responded with a proposal to invite the leaders of China and ROK, and this became the first APT (informal) summit. When the crisis hit Thailand, Japan attempted to respond with emergency assistance through the existing framework centering on the IMF. Thailand's liquidity shortfall was estimated at US $ 14 billion. The IMF and Japan provided US $ 4 billion each, but through additional bilateral support, the total package reached US $ 17.2 billion. These additional funds came from multilateral institutions (such as the ADB) and countries in Asia (including Australia). This showed that the countries in Asia could work together to deal with this kind of crisis. This recognition led to the stepping up of moves within the Japanese government to build a mechanism for a regional financing facility.

The idea of a regional mechanism to stabilize Asian currencies began to be launched in Japan in the autumn of 1996, before the crisis struck. This arose from the 1994 Mexican crisis. The view in the Japanese ministry of finance (MOF) was that if a similar crisis would occur in Asia, the US and the IMF might not respond as swiftly as they did in the Mexican case. With their combined foreign reserves, countries in Asia could respond to such a crisis if a mechanism exists. A tentative proposal was drafted but before it could be discussed with other countries in the region, the Thai crisis struck (Kikuchi, 2002).

It was at the ASEM finance ministers meeting in September 1997 that Japan's concept of an Asian Monetary Fund (AMF) was first discussed. It was also informally discussed at the joint annual meeting of the IMF and the World Bank in Hong Kong in that same month. The finance ministers of Indonesia, Malaysia and Thailand immediately supported the idea of an AMF, which would have a nucleus of US $ 10 billion in capital from the Japanese government. Opposition to this idea came from the United States, China, and the IMF. As a result Japan was unwilling to pursue the idea further. Instead, the Manila Framework, adopted by a subset of APEC economies in November 1997, was seen as a substitute for the setting up of a regional monetary institution.

As the crisis unfolded, the Japanese government provided large amounts of funds to the crisis-affected countries, mainly through bilateral arrangements. By November 1998 the amount of this funding reached US $ 44 billion. As its regional approach failed to materialize, Japan stepped up on its bilateral cooperation through the New Miyazawa Initiative that was launched in October 1998. The main elements of this Initiative are as follows: (a) US $ 15 billion in short-term support for Asian countries; (b) US $ 15 billion in funds to meet their medium-to long-term financial needs; (c) provision of credits by the Exim Bank of Japan; (d) purchase by the Exim Bank of Japan of bonds issued by Asian governments; and (e) provision of concessional yen loans by the Japanese government. As part of this Initiative, Japan entered into currency swap arrangements with Malaysia and ROK, which guaranteed the provision of foreign currency reserves in the case of a crisis but without any linkage to IMF conditionality. The second phase of this New Miyazawa Initiative was announced in May 1999. One of its elements is the active use of private sector funds. Another element is to build a regional fund-raising system. Proposals for a regional monetary fund did not die down. They were raised not only from within East Asia, but also by Europeans and even from the US (Rana, 2002).

The desire to develop mechanisms for resource provision within the region led to the adoption of the Chiang Mai Initiative (CMI) by the APT Finance Ministers in May 2000. In addition to reiterating the need for strengthened policy dialogues and regional cooperation activities, the CMI called for:

• • An expanded ASEAN Swap Arrangements (ASA) that would include all ASEAN countries and a network of bilateral swap and repurchase agreement (BSA) facilities among ASEAN countries, China, Japan, and ROK.

• • Use of the APT framework to promote the exchange of consistent and timely data and information on capital flows.

• • Establishment of a regional financing arrangement to supplement existing international facilities.

• • Establishment of an appropriate mechanism (the EWS) that could enhance the ability to provide sufficient and timely financial stability in the East Asian region.

The ASEAN Swap Arrangement (ASA) was expanded in November 2000 to cover all ASEAN members and the total amount was increased from US $ 200 million to US $ 1 billion. The contribution of ASEAN-6 (Brunei, Indonesia, Malaysia, the Philippines, Singapore and Thailand) amounts to US $ 150 million each. That of the rest varies: Vietnam US $ 60 million, Myanmar US $ 20 million, Cambodia US $ 15 million, and Laos US $ 5 million. The maximum drawdown amount by each participating member is limited to twice its committed amount under the ASA. The swap transactions have maturity not exceeding 6 months, subject to rollover for a period not exceeding 6 months.

The network of Bilateral Swaps and Repurchase Agreements (BSA) is designed to provide short-term liquidity assistance in the form of swaps of US dollars with the domestic currencies of a participating country. Participating countries can draw on the BSA for a period of 90 days. The first drawing may be renewed seven times. The interest rate applicable to the drawing is the LIBOR plus a premium of 150 basis points for the first and the first renewal drawings. Thereafter, the premium is increased by an additional 50 points for every two renewals, but not exceeding 300 basis points.

The disbursement of funds under the BSA is tied to IMF conditionality. However, it allows for automatic disbursement of up to 10 percent of the maximum amount of the drawing without any linkage to an IMF program or conditionality. This limit will be increased as the region develops its own surveillance capacity. The BSA will be reviewed in 2003 (or 2004), with Malaysia's objection to the IMF conditionality as one of the issues likely to be on the agenda. APT members may also decide to make it permanent or even to multilateralize it.

As of end of February 2003, 12 BSAs have been concluded with a total amount of US $ 31.5 billion. A few others are still under negotiations (See Table 2). Japan has been playing a leading role in terms of both number and amount. As stated in the EASG Report, the CMI is seen as a significant step as it is the first concrete agreement among ASEAN countries, China, Japan, and ROK to strengthen cooperation in the financial area. The CMI is also seen as a launch pad from which to broaden and deepen their cooperation and coordination to ensure financial stability.

East Asia has definitely moved ahead rather significantly in terms of monetary and financial cooperation. The APT has established semi-annual peer review meetings of finance ministers, efforts to establish an EWS are under way, and through the CMI East Asian countries have begun to develop mechanisms to share resources among each other.

Under the APT framework, the region has developed two of the three pillars of regional financial cooperation, namely mutual surveillance and liquidity assistance. The one pillar it has not developed is exchange rate coordination. Both the EAVG and the EASG have recommended that the region pursue a more closely coordinated regional exchange rate mechanism. This item has been put on East Asia's agenda.

Table 2 Progress on the Chiang Mai Initiative
(as of end of February 2003)

BSA	Currencies	Conclusion Date	Amount
Japan-ROK	USD/Won	July 4, 2001	US$ 7 b(*)
Japan-Thailand	USD/Baht	July 30, 2001	US$ 3 b
Japan-Philippines	USD/Peso	August 7, 2001	US$ 3 b
Japan-Malaysia	USD/Ringgit	October 5, 2001	US$ 3.5 b(*)
Japan-China	Yen/Renminbi	March 28, 2002	US$ 3 b equivalent
Japan-Singapore		under negotiation	
Japan-Indonesia	USD/Rp	Feb. 17, 2003	US$ 3 b
China-Thailand	USD/Baht	December 6, 2001	US$ 2 b
China-ROK	Won/Renminbi	June 24, 2002	US$ 2 b
China-Malaysia	USD/Ringgit	October 9, 2002	US$ 1.5 b
China-Philippines		under negotiation	
China-Indonesia		under negotiation	
ROK-Thailand	USD/Baht	June 25, 2002	US$ 1 b
ROK-Malaysia	USD/Ringgit	July 26, 2002	US$ 1 b
ROK-Philippines	USD/Peso	August 9, 2002	US$ 1 b
ROK-Indonesia		under negotiation	

Note: (*) The US dollar amount includes the amounts committed under the New Miyazawa Initiative, US$ 5 Billion for ROK and US$ 2.5 billion for Malaysia.

Despite great progress, the region has not as yet established the network of institutions to evolve into what Bergsten (2000) has suggested: an East Asian economic bloc.

As clearly described by Wang (2002), regional financial institutions range along a spectrum from simple information exchange and informal consultation forums to a supranational entity like the EMU. At the early stage of no institutional integration, governments take note of the policies of other governments without making any attempt to influence them. In view of potential policy spillovers it may still be useful for governments to exchange information and consult with each other.

ASEAN has moved beyond this stage when they agreed to institute surveillance based on a peer review process, to monitor "developments in ASEAN member countries and in the international economy that could affect individual ASEAN economies and the region". For ASEAN this was the first instance in which ASEAN members will make comment on internal developments. This was seen as a first step in ASEAN's transformation as a regional organization (Soesastro, 1998). However, the ASEAN Surveillance Process has been poorly implemented thus far.

In the next stage, when mutual liquidity provision is introduced, it is imperative that monitoring and surveillance mechanisms are in place to control the moral hazard involved. This is the reason why the CMI relies on the IMF and may develop its own independent surveillance mechanism. The final stage, involving exchange rate coordination, would require monetary policy coordination. Wang (2002) also noted that in the absence of exchange rate coordination, incentives for mutual surveillance would be limited because a member country facing a speculative attack may be free to float its exchange rate vis-à-vis those of other neighboring countries. Under the current APT framework, the purpose of the CMI and mutual surveillance is mainly to prevent the occurrence of financial crises and contagion in the region.

How will and can the region move ahead? Wang (2002) believes that the APT framework is the appropriate grouping for regional financial cooperation because this group has begun to develop a common vision for East Asia. The annual APT summits provide a basis for strong political support. In addition, through the ASEM framework, in January 2001 the finance ministers have launched the so-called Kobe Research Project. The project is designed to facilitate inter-regional research cooperation on issues of monetary and financial cooperation in East Asia, taking into account the lessons learned from the European integration experience.

Strengthening the surveillance mechanism is a key task for further financial cooperation and integration. As reviewed before, the next major task for the APT finance ministers is to develop an early warning system (EWS). As argued by Wang (2002), it may be difficult to construct a credible EWS given the lack of reliable statistics in most developing countries. An EWS consists of leading indicators that signal in advance the onset of a crisis. However, not all crises are alike, and thus a "one size fits all" system will not be useful. The MFG and the APT Surveillance Process need to be strengthened. In the MFG, which is based on information provided by the IMF, the World Bank and the ADB, no new or region-specific analysis is presented beyond what is readily available. The process is also felt to be dominated by the US and the IMF. Similarly, discussions in the APT Surveillance Process do not focus on issues of concern and emerging problems.

Malaysia's opposition to linking the CMI to the IMF has led to the establishment of a Study Group to examine how the CMI can develop an independent monitoring and surveillance mechanism. The first meeting of the APT Study Group proposed a two-phased action agenda. The first phase enhances the existing APT process of economic reviews and policy dialogues. The second phase constructs a new strengthened policy dialogue mechanism. The second meeting of the APT Study Group, held in

Myanmar in April 2002, failed to reach an agreement on the surveillance issues, except for institutionalizing the APT meetings of deputies for informal policy reviews and dialogues. There is not likely to be an effective surveillance mechanism soon.

The issue of leadership is a critical one in the region. As shown before, Japan has provided a *de facto* leadership in the implementation of the CMI as a key provider of financial resources. If the CMI is to become the launch pad for further cooperation, the number and amounts of the BSAs need to be increased. Japan is the only party that has agreed to increase the amounts of the bilateral swaps in order to make the CMI a more credible financing scheme. However, Japan needs to be given greater assurances that their short-term lending will be repaid. As a minimum condition for expansion of the BSAs, Japan wants to see the development of an effective surveillance mechanism in which it can exercise its influence commensurate with its financial contribution. Japan and China have not been able to agree on a number of operational issues, including the surveillance mechanism. China may not want to grant leadership to Japan in any regional initiative in East Asia. This may be the most serious roadblock to the further development of the CMI (Wang, 2002) as well as to the APT process in general (Stubbs, 2002). There is also this strong underlying competition between China and Japan also in developing bilateral trade arrangements with ASEAN. The region's preoccupation with the large number of FTAs definitely diverts attention away from the efforts to promote monetary and financial cooperation and integration. More importantly, however, they may also divert governments from the task of developing the APT process and the building of an East Asian community.

Conclusion

The development of an Asian Bond Market has given impetus for strengthening cooperation among East Asian countries in the financial field. A further elaboration of the Early Harvest component of the ASEAN-China Comprehensive Economic Cooperation Agreement in Bali in early October 2003 as well as the signing of a similar framework agreement between ASEAN and Japan has strengthened the atmosphere of cooperation in East Asia.

What is still missing is the institutional set-up that will drive the cooperation process at the East Asian-wide level and will give coherence to many regional initiatives. East Asia is not likely to immediately move ahead on a region-wide FTA. Thus, the region's institutional arrangement cannot be built on an FTA framework. What is more likely is an array of region-wide economic and development cooperation activities. This could be promoted through an institutional arrangement that begin with studies and policy recommendations on an on-going manner. It should not rely on the process of senior officials meetings (SOM or SEOM). The idea of an OECD for East Asia is worth exploring. However, the region is very allergic to having large multilateral organizations that could turn into a supranational body. But a small Secretariat alone will not suffice.

The proposal advanced here is for East Asia to have a decentralized OECD for East Asia. An East Asian Secretariat could be established in Kuala Lumpur to act as a clearinghouse. An East Asian Institute of Monetary and Financial Cooperation could be set up in Tokyo. An East Asian Institute of Trade and Investment Cooperation could be established in Seoul, and an East Asian Institute of Development Cooperation could be formed in Beijing. These regional bodies should operate as semi-governmental organizations in that they will be established and fully funded by governments but staffed by individuals from the region on a competitive basis. These regional bodies will drive the process of regional cooperation and integration through the conduct of studies and consultative processes that are participative and involving representatives from various walks of life, not confined only to government officials. These institutional characteristics may distinguish East Asia cooperation from that in other regions of the world. On this basis, an authentic East Asian model might emerge.

References

Bergsten, C. Fred (2000), "Towards a Tripartite World", The Economist, 15 July, pp. 20-2.

East Asia Study Group (2002), *Final Report of the East Asia Study Group*, submitted to the ASEAN Plus Three Summit in Phnom Penh, Cambodia, on 4 November 2002.

East Asia Vision Group (2001), *Towards an East Asian Community—Region of Peace, Prosperity and Progress*, Report submitted to the ASEAN Plus Three Summit in Brunei Darussalam, 31 October 2001.

Higgot, Richard (2000), "ASEM and the Evolving Global Order", in Chong-wha Lee (ed.), *The Seoul 2000 Summit: The Way Ahead for the Asia-Europe Partnership*, Korea Institute for International Economic Policy, Seoul, pp. 11-47.

Ito, Takatoshi (1999?), "Regional Cooperation in Asia: Theoretical Framework, Recent Movements and Prospects", presentation at the Convention of the East Asian Economic Association, Singapore.

Jayasuriya, Kanishka (2000), "Asia-Pacific Regionalism in the Form of 'Minilateralism'", *The Strait Times*, Singapore, 18 November.

Kikuchi, Tsutomu (2002), "East Asian Regionalism: A Look at the 'ASEAN plus Three' Framework", *Japan Review of International Affairs*, Spring, pp. 1-23.

Rana, Pradumna B. (2002), "Monetary and Financial Cooperation in East Asia: A Survey", *Panorama*, a publication of the Konrad-Adenauer-Stiftung's "Regional Program for Southeast Asia", Singapore, No. 2/2002, pp. 17-34.

Soesastro, Hadi (1998), "ASEAN during the Crisis", *ASEAN Economic Bulletin*, Vol. 15, No. 3, December, pp. 373-81.

Soesastro, Hadi (2001), "Towards an East Asian Regional Trading Arrangement", in Simon SC Tay, Jesus Estanislao, Hadi Soesastro (eds.), *Reinventing ASEAN* (Singapore: Institute of Southeast Asian Studies), pp. 226-42.

Stubbs, Richard (2002), "ASEAN Plus Three: Emerging East Asian Regionalism?", *Asian Survey*, Vol. 42, No. 3, May/June, pp. 440-55.

Wang, Yungjong (2002), "Prospects for Financial and Monetary Cooperation in East Asia", *Panorama*, Singapore, No. 2/2002, pp. 35-53.

East Asian Economic Cooperation: Retrospect and Prospect

Thomas J. P. Voon and
Edward K. Y. Chen[1]

Introduction

East Asia is witnessing a new era in regional cooperation with the emergence of a new and growing body, ASEAN-10 Plus Japan, ROK and China (hereafter ASEAN Plus Three or APT). This occurs at about the same time when the principal regional organizations in East Asia and Asia-Pacific, ASEAN and APEC, are declining in importance (see Webber 2001, Ravenhill 2000). The change in the pattern of Asia-Pacific regionalism is propelled by a host of factors, of which the Asian financial crisis (AFC) appears to be the immediate cause. The AFC in particular has exposed the impotence of ASEAN and APEC in restoring their regional economic strength. No doubt that the Asia Pacific Economic Cooperation (APEC) deserves the merit of bringing together the APEC economies in many cooperative ways in the last decade or so through the so-called APEC process. But the actual impacts on policy have been limited.

The rise of APT is attributed to several factors, aside from

---

[1] Thomas J. P. Voon, Associate Professor, Department of Economics, Lingnan University; Edward K. Y. Chen, President, Lingnan University.

the unprecedented onset of the AFC. For example, the statistical trend shows that merchandise trade between Southeast Asia and Northeast Asia has grown at a rate much faster than their trade with the rest of the world, pointing, *inter alia*, to the role of integration for these two geographical regions that made up of APT. Other factors propitious to the rise of APT include: the frustration of the regions with the slow pace of liberalization; resentments against the US as a leader and role model for the Asia-Pacific organization; the emergence of China as an economic power and the regional engine of growth; the changing role of Japan; the evolution of the European Union (EU), and the North American Free Trade Area (NAFTA) and Free Trade Areas of the Americas (FTAA) into bigger and stronger discriminatory trading blocs; the growing complementary relationship between Southeast and Northeast Asia (as opposed to their relations with the US for instance); emergence of unilateralism and bilateralism in East Asia; reduction in economic rivalry and the possibility of tension resolution in the region; and so on. These changing trends and developments in the region, which may foretell the prospect of East Asian regionalism, will be discussed in this paper.

APT is still at the early stage of development. It is currently fraught with some problems, which may impede the development of the organization and hence slow down the pace of integration to the detriment of East Asia. For example, the evolution of APT may be hampered by: the absence of a dominant leader state such as the US; the geopolitical tension (e.g. territorial dispute over the South Seas); and the economic rivalry among the APT members. There are possibly other obstacles, which remain to be identified and resolved. Given both the strengths and weaknesses inherent in the development of East Asian regionalism, should the regions proceed with their aspiration for more cooperation? What is the prospect of the APT developing into an effective regional cooperative organization capable of integrating and prospering the East Asian economies? We attempt to answer such questions by performing an analysis that may assist us in weighing and gauging all the possible factors that favor or disfavor the development of APT and upon which a reasonably sound judgment may be made. Our analytical framework is based on two premises. First, we gauge the prospect of the development against a set of criteria, which may be used to more objectively determine the probability of success and failure of such a development. Second, we gauge the prospect of the development by looking at the current trends or directions of the development that may extrapolate into the future. This is analogous to the theory of revealed preferences in economics.

This paper initially examines the historical developments and epochal events that had led to the birth of a regional integration concept and subsequently to the inception of a complex organization such as APEC. Attempts have been made to explain how APEC has "failed" in recent years and eventually paved a way for the evolution of the APT. Since the emergence of APT follows from past events, a retrospective analysis would be a useful starting point. We then provide a prospective analysis on the development of East Asian integration in light of (a) some of the important criteria that determine the success and failure of a regional organization and (b) the events that have been developing and potentially shaping into a particular or predictable form of regionalism. From a casual observance, APT hitherto is very different from APEC: notably it is smaller in size and in membership, less diverse, does not include US (and other advanced Pacific nations) as its core members, and currently at an infancy stage of development without proper organizational structure and a secretariat. Attempts have also been made in this paper to analyze how the weaknesses and strengths inherent in the APT may be ameliorated and fortified, respectively, in order to maximize the benefits accruable from closer East Asian integration and cooperation. Our analysis has important policy implications for business in the region.

I. Progress of East Asian Integration

East Asian integration used to be as part of the process of Asia-Pacific integration, which has evolved slowly, and several milestones have been achieved over the last four decades or so. Interestingly, very few, if any, of the regional organizations that have evolved so far are uniquely East Asian (embodying only Southeast and Northeast Asian states). The pattern of the historical evolution of Asia Pacific regionalism is depicted as follows:

PAFTA

The concept of Asia-Pacific cooperation was widely accepted to be the brainchild of Kojima (Kojima 2002). Kojima suggested the establishment of a Pacific Free Trade Area (PAFTA) in 1965, which consisted of five advanced countries, namely Japan, the US, Canada, Australia and New Zealand. Kojima proposed that these countries pooled the gains from their trade expansion into a monetary fund, which could be used to promote development of the developing countries of East Asia (Kojima 2002). The developing countries that eventually gained from PAFTA were then encouraged to join the organization accordingly.

PAFTAD

PAFTA did not materialize into a functional regional organization because of the predominance of developed countries, though the concept appeared to be plausible at that time. Nevertheless, it gave rise to the formation in 1968 of the Pacific Trade and Development Conference (PAFTAD) in Tokyo. PAFTAD, with its secretariat in Canberra, has since organized meetings on an annual basis in order to advance the cause of Asia Pacific cooperation by providing avenues for the presentation of the research findings. The close link between some academics and the business and government sectors had produced considerable impact on the official acceptance of the importance of regional cooperation. PAFTAD was a forerunner of PECC. Prior to the establishment of PAFTAD, it should be noted that the Association of Southeast Asian Nations (ASEAN) came into being in 1967, pointing to the need for a rigorous development of cooperation in the region at that time. However, at the earliest stage, ASEAN's objectives were primarily related to regional security rather than economic development.

PECC

The concept of Asia Pacific cooperation had evolved into a more advanced form of integration with the inauguration of the Pacific Economic Cooperation Conference (later Council) (PECC) in 1980. The Council is tripartite in nature, involving business, government as well as academics from different countries. PECC's activities were mainly research and discussion of policy proposals by several task forces under the jurisdiction of the Council. Trade policy in the Pacific region appeared to be the main focus of PECC. Studies have been conducted on trade liberalization and facilitation, agricultural products, energy, fisheries, livestock, grain, forestry, capital transfers, private direct investment, technological transfer, and so on (Kojima 2002). More recently, emphasis is also placed on eco-tech and capacity building. PECC has also encouraged more economic cooperation with other nations and regions, in line with the concept of open regionalism.

APEC

The force of economic cooperation and the formation of an economic community within the Asia Pacific region were accelerated by the successful establishment of the Asia Pacific Economic Cooperation (APEC) in 1989. APEC is perceived to be primarily an Australian initiative. Japan has also contributed to the formation of APEC (Harris 2000). At first, APEC comprised the same members of PECC, but without China. The initial members of the 1989 APEC meeting include the ASEAN-6 (Malaysia, Singapore, Thailand, Indonesia, Philippines and Brunei), ROK, Japan, The US, Canada, Australia and New Zealand. China was later admitted together with Taiwan and Hong Kong. China accepted Taiwan as a member of APEC also because at that time China was anxious to rejoin the international community after the Tiananmen Square incident. APEC has hitherto been a development-oriented community, engaging mainly in capacity building as well as economic and technical cooperation. The attempts in trade and investment liberation and facilitation were of limited success. It has not met the requirements of GATT Article 24, and therefore, has not been recognized as an institution of formal economic integration like the EU and NAFTA.

Areas of cooperation designed by APEC include human resource development, capital markets, economic infrastructure, technical development, environment, and small and medium enterprises. The November 2000 meeting of APEC Leaders in Brunei stressed the importance of capacity building, infrastructure, and the improvements of policies, institutions, skill, and technology (including information technology and the internet). It seems that liberalizing cross-border trade and investment in the pace and manner enshrined by the World Trade Organization

(WTO) is not the major agenda for APEC. Rather than targeting zero tariffs across countries within the shortest possible period of time, APEC has pursued an integration that entails member economies to reform industrial structure, method and technology of production and management of firms, and even economic, political and social institutions of the nation states.

ASEAN-10 Plus 3

Since the formation of APEC, the idea of an East Asian bloc has been promulgated. Kojima (2002) has recently proposed the formation of a core group of the Asian Economic Community (AEC) consisting of all the ten members of ASEAN (the original Five plus Brunei, Cambodia, Laos, Myanmar and Vietnam) and three Northeast Asian economies (Japan, China and ROK). The above entity is essentially ASEAN-10 Plus Three (or APT), formed in 1997. Letiche (2000) proposed an East Asian Monetary Authority akin to the European Economic and Monetary Union (see also Dutta 2000). The above initiative appears to be directed at forming a pure East Asian replica of an Asian Pacific organization such as APEC or PECC. AEC or APT is similar to the concept of East Asia Economic Caucus (EAEC) proposed by Prime Minister Mahathir of Malaysia in 1990, though it was strongly objected by the US and therefore Japan at that time. Now, with NAFTAD and FTAA in place, it is difficult for the US to take the same stance. Also with the rise of China as an economic power and potentially as a leader of APT, the US considerations have to be different.

In the third APT summit in November 1999, a joint statement on East Asian cooperation was released. On the basis of the previous agreements reached, the fourth summit held in Singapore in 2000 was hailed to be a significant step toward regional cooperation. The most notable development was the Chiang Mai

Agreement reached in May 2002 during the APT finance ministers meeting. It involves a network of swap arrangements among the ASEAN states, China, Japan and ROK. The APT initiative has since been promoted actively by China. Chinese leaders' worry about the deterioration (or the possibility of it) in Sino-US relations, and the potential danger of the "containment" of China by Western countries has been an important motivation for their promotion of East Asian regionalism through the APT route (Cheng 2001).

ASEAN-10 Plus 1

Some countries in the region, such as Japan, Singapore, Malaysia, ROK and even China seem to be frustrated with the slow pace of liberalization and the stagnancy of trade negotiation within APEC. Members opting for faster liberalization may choose to form regional free trade areas (FTA) that are smaller, hence more tractable and flexible. A watershed in the history of East Asian regionalism is perhaps the establishment of the ASEAN-10 + 1 (APO) in November 2002. The initiative has been successfully implemented without vehement objections from the US and Japan.

Bilateral Free Trade Agreement (FTA)

As a consequence of the failure of the December 1999 Seattle WTO negotiations, bilateral free trade agreements (FTAs) and regional trading arrangements (RTAs) have proliferated. A quickest way for two or more countries to achieve trade liberalization together is via bilateral trade negotiations or free trade arrangements among two or more countries. Japan, for instance, has a large number of bilateral trade arrangements with other countries, reflecting among other things its aspiration for more liberalization than what has been pursued via APEC. Japan signed an agreement with Singapore in January 2002. It has formed or proposed bilateral FTA with ROK, Chile, Mexico, Canada, Australia, New Zealand, and Thailand. ROK is also negotiating with Chile, New Zealand, Mexico, Thailand, as well as Japan. Singapore and New Zealand signed an agreement in November 2000. Singapore is negotiating with Australia, Canada, Mexico, and India. Even Hong Kong has an FTA with New Zealand, and now with Mainland China. Hence, in the East Asian region, Japan, Singapore and ROK are actively involved in bilateral negotiations (see Harvey and Lee 2002). Bilateral relations can provide a quicker liberalization since many difficult issues (particularly those related to agriculture and textile), as well as some bureaucratic red tapes, can be effectively averted or resolved. Bilateral agreements can focus on issues specific to the countries concerned that may be non-WTO and non-conventional. In addition, a deeper form of integration and cooperation may be achieved more efficiently. In the past few years, there was a proliferation of literature on FTA, RTA and their implications for the multilateral trading system advocated under the WTO.

Generalization and Implications

There are several lessons and implications that we could derive or observe from the historical development of the Asia Pacific regionalism. First, a full-fledged discriminatory trading bloc typical of the EC and NAFTA has never materialized. The process has also been a slow and evolutionary one. This is largely due to the fact that the Asia Pacific member countries are too diverse in nature. Also, they opt to operate on the principle of open regionalism, which implies that member countries are allowed to promote unilateral or bilateral arrangements inside the region while applying the same non-discriminative trade policies and concessions to the third countries. However, the pace has become faster as a response to recent events.

Second, Asians are for a long time also more inclined to build informal rather than formal regional organizations. The cooperative efforts have never been formal (unlike the EU and NAFTA). Cooperation in East Asia is at the lower level of integration with EU presumably at the highest. The cooperation is often directed at providing a type of cooperation rather than integration involving mutual research, discussions and forums.

But, the cooperative efforts have recently become increasingly more sophisticated, from a regional cooperative concept PAFTA to the formation of APEC that bears a complicated structure encompassing a great range of members. However, since the formation of APEC, the cooperative efforts have somehow become less complex but more institutionalized with the subsequent formations of the APT and the bilateral FTA. Many East Asian countries now seem to prefer more unilateral and bilateral liberalization rather than being bound by the liberalization rules and requirements embodied in GATT/WTO or APEC. East Asian countries opt for more liberalization on the understanding that (a) any adverse contagion emanating from future crisis could be contained (for example in the form of currency swap arrangement) and (b) members can follow their own pace and level of liberalization (many countries in East Asia do not want to liberalize hurriedly in the same degree and speed of progress called for by the US and the WTO). With the formation of the APT and the APO, the ASEAN free trade area (AFTA) cutting the tariffs to 5% or less, and the emergence of a host of bilateral trading arrangements involving the same countries in the region (for example between ASEAN and Northeast Asian countries), more liberalization would be achieved at a faster pace than the time frame stipulated by APEC.

Third, the US and other advanced Pacific countries have always been the partners of East Asia until the recent formations of the APT as well as the APO. In other words, the cooperation has recently become more and more uniquely East Asian. China appears currently to be a dominating member in the evolving East Asian regional organizations. This is in sharp contrast to the situation when China was initially excluded from APEC membership in 1989. China has even become a leader in some of the evolving cooperative arrangements (as in the case of the APO).

II. Prospect of East Asian Integration

The prospect for integration in East Asia and formation of a regional cooperative organization, for example the APT, is espoused in this paper using a framework which uses a set of established criteria for gauging and determining the success and failure of closer integration (*the criteria for success* approach). In addition to the criteria, we study the prospect of East Asian regionalism by examining (a) the past developments, which provide the implications for the future developments, and (b) the current developments, which may drive their existing trends of developments in particular directions into the future (the *development trend* approach). By examining both the past and the present development trends, we are able to derive reasonable conclusions from the analysis. The extrapolation of a current trend into the future could be a subjective exercise. However, the observation of multiple developmental trends would provide a more objective measure for judging the size of the benefit that potentially drive or derail, naturally or coercively, a future development plan. This type of analysis may also enable us to examine how a particular trend may be offset or diluted in such a way as to maximize the net gains.

We aim to answer two fundamental questions. The first is:

Would the APT evolve into a more formal and closer regional cooperative organization given that it is currently not based on any treaty or formal binding agreement between the participating states, and has no central secretariat? The second is: How likely would East Asia or the APT develop into full-fledged discriminatory trading blocs exemplified by the EU or NAFTA? In the following analysis, we will gauge the prospect by using the framework elucidated above.

The Criteria for Success Approach

Prospect for Regional Integration

Mattli (1999) has identified two critical (economic and political) preconditions of successful integration: first, a strong market pressure for integration, which will arise if there is considerable economic gain accruable from the integration; and second, an undisputed leadership, which serves to coordinate rules, regulations and policies, and to resolve distributional conflicts of the participating countries. If these two strong criteria were sufficient for gauging the success of a regional integration outcome, as claimed by Mattli, then the outcome for East Asia would be ambiguous because the presence of strong market pressure for East Asian integration (since the economic gains accruable from East Asian integration seem to be huge, given the enormous increase in trade flow between the Southeast and Northeast Asian regions) appears to be offset by the lack of an undisputed leader (since it is not clear if China or Japan, or a coalition of states, should provide the necessary leadership). But, economic complementarity in the Asian region should be understood with the following in mind. Before the emergence of China as a huge market, economic cooperation in this region has always been on the basis of pooling resources rather than sharing markets. Even today the importance of East Asian exports to the rest of the world is still significant. This also explains why open regionalism is a guiding principle underlying East Asian economic cooperation. In future, the opening of the China market would make a difference. Also the economic complementarity cannot be fully revealed by an analysis at the one or two-digit SITC level. A study of intra-industry trade and intra-regional trade at a more disaggregate level shows that East Asian competition in production and trade is much less than commonly envisaged. This explains why export orientation in East Asia has for a long time not been a zero-sum game. This is of course an illustration of the flying geese pattern of industrialization in which a sophisticated sub-regional division of labour is practised.

Most observers judge East Asian economic integration or cooperation as a success since a number of economies, particularly the five ASEAN members (Malaysia, Singapore, Thailand, Indonesia and The Philippines) and the three Northeast Asian economies (Japan, China and ROK) grew very rapidly and prosperously subsequent to their cooperative endeavors. Economic growth of these countries has been spurred, among other things, by trade facilitation, cost reductions, shared resources, FDI flows, and the division of labor resulting from their cooperation. The benefits of economic growth in the forms of poverty reduction and enhanced living standards are enormous, especially before the onset of the AFC. Admittedly, the benefits had diminished somewhat as a result of the AFC. However, many economies like ROK, Thailand and Malaysia have since recovered from the downturn wrought by the AFC. The East Asian economies still have a large labor productivity gap with the leading OECD countries and substantial scope for further rapid catch-up growth (Crafts 1999).

It is expected that China will continue to provide ample room for its East Asian partners to reap the opportunity generated by China. The synergistic relationships between China and its regional neighbors and among the APT states will generate competition and substantial efficiency gains in terms of total factor productivity (TFP) growth. At present, many economists believe that TFP growth is small for most of the Asian economies and their economic growth was driven mostly by input accumulations (see the review by Voon and Chen 2003). If their findings are credible (see Felipe 1999), then the contribution of TFP growth accruable from East Asia integration will be important in sustaining the economic growth, which will in turn provide the incentive for more integration in East Asia.

However, Sino-Japanese rivalry could be an insidious obstacle to closer East Asian integration. For example, in China's view, Japan has not apologized for the period of the Japanese invasion and occupation of China from 1937 to 1945. There remain at present some differences in political ideologies between China and Japan. The triangular relationship among China, Japan and the US is also delicate. On the one hand, according to some observers, Japan, being less threatening to the region now, possesses a potential hegemonic power and means to mediate and resolve distributional conflicts in the region. On the other, a serious limitation on Japanese regional leadership is its own domestic economy: Japan has not been able to provide a domestic market for imports from the regions during periods of regional economic retraction, and if the present rates of economic growth (and the growth of military prowess) in China continue into the future, China will eclipse Japan in terms of the capacity for regional leadership in East Asia (Weber 2001). Another pertinent question is: Can ASEAN take over the leadership role? However, in view of political realities, both China and Japan would for the time being prefer to dodge the issue of leadership in as much as an unchallenged leadership has not yet emerged. Both countries understand that a working relationship has to be built up first.

Last but not least, how will the US react to the APT from which it is excluded? Will the US in due course oppose it as much as it did to the EAEC in 1990? It seems that the Clinton administration had displayed a more relaxed attitude to East Asian regional integration (Asia Week 2000). The Bush Administration seems to be preoccupied with the problems inherent the domestic economy, the Middle East, the war on terrorism, and the process of promoting North/South American integration and its ties with Mexico. It has remained relatively quiet and not vied for leadership or membership within the APT thus far.

In the long run, governments in the region perhaps should make an attempt to resolve the leadership issue if cooperation and long-term integration are to continue smoothly. At present, it appears that the pressure from the economic gains outweighs the leadership dilemma, hence potentially driving the leaders to reconciliation and resolution in the foreseeable future.

Prospect for Trade Bloc

Of the set of established criteria failure of EU-or-NAFTA-typed trading bloc (see Noland 1994; Voon and Nguyen 1992), commonalities in institutions, culture, history, etc. appear to be the most critical criterion. Asia Pacific countries differ tremendously from each other in size, levels of development, political culture and institutions, domestic economic structure, and geographical location. These tend to limit them from developing into a full-fledged trading bloc envisaged by the EU or NAFTA, which entails a deeper form of political and economic union. Openness is another important criterion. This means that if the countries in the region adopt a common goal of pursuing outward-looking policies, they are unlikely to evolve into a discriminatory bloc, typical of EU or NAFTA. Most of the East Asian countries are open to trade, investment and liberalization. They have continued to pursue a policy of open regionalism; for example, trade concessions are not confined to the members but also to "outsiders". Thus, East Asian countries are very unlikely to evolve into EU-style trade bloc. However, countries within the APT are fewer and perhaps not as diverse as those within APEC. This means that the APT will probably develop into a closer entity than that within APEC. East Asian regionalism depends to some extent on the development of ASEAN. The widening of the ASEAN from ASEAN-5 to ASEAN-10 for instance has broadened the diversity and hence lessened the possibility of a closer and formal East Asia bloc that bears the characteristics of EU. The widening has posed an obstacle to its deepening.

The Development Trend Approach

The past and current development trends can be used as yardsticks for gauging the shapes of the future development outcomes. A retrospective assessment of the past development trends in East Asia was provided in Section 2. In what follows, we provide a prospective assessment using the current trends.

Growth of Intra-regional Trade

The degree of regional integration is often measured by the growth in the level of intra-regional trade. Hence, East Asian integration is likely to continue in view of the growing importance of the intra-regional trade (as opposed to its trade with the EU and with NAFTA). For instance, intra-Asia trade constituted 53.1% in 1997 and has increased very rapidly since the recovery of the region from the AFC (Rugman 2001). A recent study shows that the major part of Asian trade (in absolute terms) is with Asia and is several times that with the US (Agarwala and

Prakash 2002), suggesting that greater attention should be given to improve trade facilitation within Asia than trade with the US. Another study showed that ASEAN integration did not increase intra-ASEAN trade, but an increase in trade occurred with members of a wider APEC group (Sharma and Chua 2000).

The growth trend of East Asia is confirmed by a recent study demonstrating that ASEAN trade with their Northeast Asian counterparts has expanded at a higher rate than intra-ASEAN trade (Tho 2002). Conversely, the Northeast Asian economies have expanded their manufactured exports to the ASEAN market at a faster rate than to the rest of the world. Tho (2002) conjectured that while AFTA is contributing to the stability of ASEAN, its effects on the development of these countries are not as important as the dynamic interdependence between ASEAN and other East Asian countries. This view is shared by Cheng (2001), reiterating that domestic difficulties in the ASEAN states in the wake of the AFC prompted their leaders to turn to Northeast Asia, and at the same time, the Northeast Asian countries were seeking ways to exploit the evolution of AFTA. The above studies point unequivocally to the need for more integration in East Asia.

Growth in Threats from Other Regions

East Asian countries have been discriminated against and threatened by the two giant regional trading blocs, namely the EC and NAFTA. The discrimination comes in the form of higher tariff and non-tariff barriers (e.g. export subsidies, agricultural protection, vested interests, etc). With the EC developing into a currency union and NAFTA predicting to expand successfully into Free Trade Areas of the Americas (FTAA), the threats posed by these discriminatory blocs have become more distinctive. This is because the economies of East Asia are now facing a proliferation of regionalism in both Europe and in the Americas, making the task of further expanding exports to these key markets increasingly difficult. This could continue to drive East Asia into developing its own geographical region demarcated for instance by the formation of the APT in order to counter the threats by becoming more competitive regionally and internationally. And one way to become more competitive regionally is by closer integration and cooperation.

Emergence of China

China has now become an increasingly important trading partner for nearly all the East Asian countries. The emergence of China, with its hyper-growth and its increasingly high domestic purchasing power, will definitely lead to more trade with the ASEAN countries, Japan and ROK. This again points to the growing regionalism in East Asia. China has already formed a closer partnership with ASEAN in terms of the formations of the APT as well as the APO. The growing importance of China over the next decade will continue to strengthen the growth of these regional organizations. It is likely that China will replace Japan and the US as the economic locomotive of Asia. China will also look increasingly to the Asian markets because of US and European protective trade policies.

Onsets of AFC and SARS

The onset of AFC has sent an important message to the community of East Asia that it could not withstand such abrupt and insidious forms of attack. This suggests that a stronger strain of cooperation involving integration of the financial markets would be essential for the region. To the extent that cross-border capital flows continue to increase as a result of the globalization of financial markets and given that East Asia now has huge official monetary reserves to protect itself against a financial crisis (Bergsten 2000), the incentives for closer regional monetary cooperation to combat currency instability are likely to rise. This will certainly enhance the prospect of closer East Asian integration.

The AFC has indeed exposed the weaknesses of the existing institutions like APEC and ASEAN, both of which are incapable of tackling the crisis. Neither APEC nor ASEAN is a financial institution and has access to funds that could be mobilized in the crisis, despite the region's large exchange reserves. The inability to build on a Japanese proposal, in a way that, given the right circumstances, would have contributed constructively to ameliorating the problem, was especially unfortunate. The AFC has inadvertently led to the declining importance of APEC and, correspondingly, to the formation and rise of the APT at which the currency-swap facility for the region has been initiated at Chiang Mai in Thailand in May 2000. Since then, East Asian cooperation via the APT and the APO has gained considerable momentum in a relatively short time (Alatas 2001). China, despite the drastic devaluation of currencies in some Asian countries, upheld the RMB exchange rate, thus receiving applauses from its neighbouring countries. On the contrary, the controversial IMF policies imposed on some Asian countries have raised serious concerns.

The recent onset of the sudden acute respiratory syndrome (SARS) and the fear of this recurring in the future will also lead to the strengthening of the regional organizations. China has already become more transparent and works ever more closely with countries in the region in order to avoid the pandemic and a huge economic loss resulting from the contagion.

Resentments Against the US

East Asian states have recently expressed their discontent with the US. There are a couple of reasons for this. First, the US has been accused of not living up to the leadership role in APEC. As mentioned already, there has been a concern with the failure of the International Monetary Fund (IMF), appointed by the US, to resolve the AFC. This is evident in Mahathir's persistent efforts to reduce dependence upon the West (particularly the US), which were illustrated by Malaysia's avoidance of IMF intervention in favor of alternative funding sources, notably Japan. Countries in East Asia felt that the Americans did not tackle the Asian crisis as much, and as readily, as they rushed in to assist in the Russian and Brazilian crises (cited in Weber 2001). A result of the resentment is the exclusion of the US from the APT and other regional bodies.

Second, a recent manifestation of the US's protectionist stance seems to be in conflict with its multilateral aspiration: on the one hand, it strives rapid liberalization within APEC, but on the other, it imposes extensive protection policies in the forms of export subsidies and other non-tariff barriers. In fact, given the size of its bargaining power both in APEC and the WTO, East Asian nations believe that APEC's targets of liberalization as well as reforms in the region could be manipulated by the US to the benefit of American business. Besides, negotiations within APEC or WTO have seen a movement of agendas toward issues that are of more interest to the US (Harvey and Lee 2002).

The above has led to the development of an exclusively East Asian organization such as the APT. The resentments would also have the effect of reducing East Asia's dependence on the US as their export destination while enhancing East Asian trade with one another. It is of interest that the Chinese Authorities, in view of the difficulties in Sino-American relations, now attach top priority to East Asian cooperation, following the formula of APT (Cheng 2001).

Emergence of RTA and Bilateral FTA

In response to the stagnation of global trade liberalization, epitomized by the collapse of the 1999 Seattle talks that intended to launch a new round of WTO trade negotiations, a number of bilateral trading arrangements within the East Asian region have recently emerged and proposed. For example, China has actively pursued bilateralism with ASEAN, as proposed by Premier Zhu Rongji in November 2001. Japan has also pursued a comprehensive economic partnership with ASEAN, as proposed by Prime Minister Koizumi in April 2002. Such a growth trend, depicted by the ubiquitous emergence of the bilateral FTA, is likely to promote freer trade and closer integration in East Asia. But the crucial question is still whether the current regionalism, sub-regionalism and bilateralism will eventually be a stepping-stone or a stumbling block to globalism and multilateralism.

The quest for more bilateralism may also be attributed to the inefficient functioning of APEC: the size of the institution (as opposed to a smaller regional body such as the APT) implies that it may be slow to respond to impending decisions, lack flexibility, and lack knowledge of the regional circumstances to make effective contribution to the problems at the regional level (Harris 2000). As East Asia aspires for more liberalization, one would expect the regional integration to grow stronger.

Infrastructure Developments

East Asian regionalism will also be strongly promoted by road, rail, and water transport links between China and the

ASEAN states. A Lancang-Mekong development project is underway, paving the way for commercial navigation on the Mekong River from Thailand to China (cited in Cheng 2001). China, together with Thailand and the Asian Development Bank, is ready to build the Laos section of the proposed Kunming-Bangkok highway. In addition, ASEAN leaders have endorsed the US $ 2.5 billion Trans-Asian railway project joining Kunming and Singapore (Cheng 2001). Such infrastructure developments will certainly give rise to closer economic integration.

East Asian Rivalry

China, with its cheap labor resources, may pose as a rivalry for some of East Asian countries that export similar products to similar export destinations (Voon and Ren 2003; Ho 2001). Another element that adds to the contention is the increasing concentration of FDI in China. The rivalry may also be accentuated by the perceived under-valuation of the RMB, which may hurt exports by the other East Asian countries (Business Week, July 2003). The most serious type of rivalry or tension could be geopolitical in nature, such as the territorial disputes in the region. Such phenomena, or development trends, admittedly, may impede the cooperative efforts toward a closer regional integration.

Conclusion

This paper reveals that the pattern of regionalism in Asia and the Pacific has dramatically changed, with the emergence of several regional cooperative bodies concomitant with the decline of the roles of APEC and ASEAN. A model is developed for gauging the prospect for closer integration in East Asia in light of the changing regionalism in East Asia. The model departs from the previous studies in that it employs two approaches for assessing the prospect for closer integration in East Asia. In addition to the "criteria for success" method, as in previous research, this paper identifies the changing development trends in the region that favor and disfavor the prospect for closer integration. Our model could give rise to a more comprehensive and a more objective analysis of East Asian regionalism.

Our study shows that closer East Asian integration could be impeded by the absence of undisputed leadership as well as the presence of geopolitical tension among the APT member states. However, the pressure for economic benefits is enormous in the region. This will potentially dilute the leadership polemic and drive the region into closer integration. Moreover, many other developments in the region have also provided credence and optimism to the changing regionalism in East Asia. The unprecedented growth in trade volume within East Asia rather than with other regions of the world implies that East Asia will become more closely integrated. The escalating threats by other regional blocs such as the EU and NAFTA have compelled the region to cooperate, and to remain competitive regionally and globally. The emergence of China as the economic and military power constitutes another powerful force driving ASEAN and other Northeast Asian states to trade and cooperate with China, hence coalescing East Asia into a more integrated region. With the onset of the AFC and SARS, East Asia is compelled to cooperate in order to counter the negative externality and the growth retrogression wrought by the contagion. The face of East Asian regionalism has also changed in favor of the development of the APT as a result of their resentments against the US. The region, aspiring for more liberalization, has also resorted to more bilateral trading arrangements, which would hopefully in the longer run engender freer regional and closer economic relations and integration. Last but not least, the physical infrastructure linking the various member states has been improving. This will facilitate trade and the flows of production factors, and hence contribute to closer integration in the region. All the developments above have clearly pointed to a favorable prospect for closer integration in East Asia. Notwithstanding this, East Asia is unlikely to develop into a full-fledged discriminatory trading bloc bearing the characteristics of EU or NAFTA in view of the region's diversity as well as its aspiration for more trade liberalization and openness.

As a whole, we are quite optimistic that East Asia will grow to be increasingly integrated. The regional cooperative bodies represented for instance by the APT (ASEAN Plus Three) are likely to grow in stature, which would then act as a catalyst for closer integration in East Asia. Some of the inherent problems or obstacles have been identified in this paper. However, it is not an overstatement to say that the existing problems in the region that may hamper the growth of APT into a regional organization may well be overshadowed or preempted by the huge and growing benefits accruable from the cooperation in the region as well as by the trends and evidence that have collectively and strongly pointed to the development of a more integrated region. Moreover, most of the identified problems appear to be tractable. For example, the rivalry between China and ASEAN as a result of their export competition in the same market could have been overstated and can be ameliorated by reducing their over-dependence on exports to the US: this is already happening given the remarkable expansion of the intra-regional trade. The fear of the RMB under-valuation threatening the region may not be real and may be allayed in the foreseeable future because China would just revalue its RMB in China's own interest (Voon and Li 2003).

It is of interest to note that East Asian cooperation started with a narrow focus on trade and investment so as to avoid the more controversial issues. But more recently, East Asian cooperation has extended from economics to much wider issues. Specifically, the following have increasingly become important items on the agenda of regional meetings.

First, the issue of cooperation in economic security has emerged after the Asian financial crisis. Economic security is not only confined to self-sufficiency in food and fuel but more importantly extended to capital flows and financial stability.

Second, regional security is also very much on the agenda. The geopolitical tension has extended from territorial claims in the South China Sea to the Korean Peninsular question and the question of Mainland-Taiwan relationships. Geopolitical considerations could be important underlying factors for economic cooperation.

Third, after the September 11th incident, the importance of social and civil security issues has given rise to cooperative efforts in coping with the worldwide spread of terrorism. The Huntington hypothesis of the clash of civilizations and the dominance of local conflicts has taken a new dimension.

Lastly, the SARS outbreak in many parts of Asia Pacific has also raised the concern of health security. Globalization has caused the transmission of the virus very difficult to control. Such health hazard with devastating economic effects has to be contained at the regional or even international level. East Asian cooperation can no longer be confined to trade and investment. It is however too early to tell whether such widening of cooperation makes cooperation in this region easier or more difficult.

References

Agarwala, R. and Prakash, B. (2002), "Regional Cooperation in Asia: Long-term Progress, Recent Retrogression, and the Way Forward", *ERD Working Paper Series*, No. 28, Economics and Research Department, Asian Development Bank.

Alatas, A. (2001) "ASEAN-Plus-Three Equals Peace Plus Prosperity", Institute of Southeast Asian Studies, Singapore, *Working Paper Series*, No. 2.

Asia Week (2000), "Southeast Asia Adrift", 1 September, pp. 45-6.

Balassa, B. and Noland, M. (1994), "Prospects of Trade and Regional Cooperation of the Industrializing Economies of East Asia", in S. C. Yang (ed.), *Manufactured Exports of East Asian Industrializing Economies: Possible Regional Cooperation*, M. E. Sharpe, New York.

Bergsten, F. (2000), "The New Asian Challenge", *Working Paper*, No. 00/4, Institute for International Economics, Washington D. C..

Cheng, J. Y. S. (2001), "Sino-ASEAN Relations in the Early Twenty-first Century", *Contemporary Southeast Asia*, 23 (3), 420-51.

Crafts, N. (1999), "Implications of Financial Crisis for East Asian Trend Growth", *Oxford Review of Economic Policy*, 15 (3), 110-31.

Dutta, M. (2000), "The Euro Revolution and the European Union: Monetary and Economic Cooperation in the Asia Pacific Region", *Journal of Asian Economics*, 11, 65-88.

Drysdale, P. and Vines, D. " Europe, East Asia and APEC: A Shared Global Agenda", Drysdale and Vines (eds.), Cambridge MA: Cambridge University Press.

Felipe, J. (1999), "Total Factor Productivity Growth in East Asia: A Critical Survey", *The Journal of Development Studies*, 35 (4), 1-41.

Harris, S. (2000), "Asian Multilateral Institutions and Their Response to the Asian Economic Crisis: The Regional and Global Implications", *The Pacific Review*, 13 (3), 495-516.

Harvey, C. and Lee, H. H. (2002), "New Regionalism in

East Asia: How Does it Relate to the East Asian Economic Development Model?" *ASEAN Economic Bulletin*, 19 (2), 123-40.

Ho, K. L. (2001), "Rituals, Risks and Rivalries: China and ASEAN in the Coming Decades", *Journal of Contemporary China*, 10 (29), 683-94.

Kojima, K. (2002), "Asian Economic Integration for the 21st Century", *East Asian Economic Perspectives*, 13, 1-38.

Letiche, J. (2000), "Lessons from the Euro Zone for the East Asian Economies", *Journal of Asian Economics*, 11, 275-300.

Mattli, W. (1999), "The Logic of Regional Integration: Europe and Beyond", Cambridge University Press, Cambridge/New York/Melbourne.

Ravenhill, J. (2000), "APEC Adrift: Implications for Economic Regionalism in Asia and the Pacific", *The Pacific Review*, 13 (2), 319-33.

Rugman, A. M. (2001), "The Myth of Global Strategy", *AIB Newsletter*, Second Quarter, 11-4.

Sharma, S. C. and Chia, S. Y. (2000), "ASEAN: Economic Integration and Intra-regional Trade", *Applied Economics Letters*, 7, 165-9.

Tho, T. V. (2002), "AFTA in the Dynamic Perspective of Asian Trade: Towards a Closer Cooperation among ASEAN+3 Countries", *The Journal of The Korean Economy*, 3 (1), 151-79.

Voon, J. P. and Li, G. Z. (2003), "The Effects of Exchange Rate Misalignment and Volatility on Chinese Commodity Exports", *Lingnan University Research Paper Series*, Tuen Mun, New Territory, Hong Kong.

Voon, J. P. and Nguyen, D. T. (1992), "Prospects for Trading Blocs in Asia and the Pacific: Implications for Business", in Oliver H. M. Yau and William F. Shepherd (eds.), *Problems and Prospects in International Business*, University of Southern Queensland Press, pp. 36-40,1992.

Voon, J. P and Chen, E. K. Y. (2003), "The Contributions of Capital Stock Quality Improvement to Economic Growth; The Case of Hong Kong", *Journal of Asian Economics* (Forthcoming).

Voon, J. P. and Ren, Y. (2003), "China-ASEAN Export Rivalry in the US Market: The Importance of the HK-China Production Synergy and the Asian Financial Crisis", *Journal of Asia Pacific Economy*", 8 (2), 157-79.

Webber, Douglas. (2001), "Two Funerals and a Wedding? The Ups and Downs of Regionalism in East Asia and Asia-Pacific after the Asian Crisis", *The Pacific Review*, 14(3), 339-72.

Yusuf, S. (2002), "Remodeling East Asian Development", *ASEAN Economic Bulletin*, 19 (1), 6-26.

ASEAN Plus Three:
A New Formal Regionalism in East Asia

Ratanak Hav[1]

Introduction

In the post-World War II period, given a number of issues such as the legacy of Japanese imperialism, internal strife and a series of wars resulting from de-colonization, historical animosities, the great diversity of the region, the gap in socio-economic developments among nations and the continuing security problems, economic regionalism in East Asia was almost totally absent. It was not until the mid-1980s, following the success of Japan as an economic superpower, the emergence of the newly industrializing countries (NICs), and the rise of China, that East Asia emerged as a *de facto* economic regionalism.

Given the changes in the global trading system, the dynamic growth of this region and its increased interdependence, it can be argued that there is a need to have a regional institution to coordinate economic cooperation. However, a formal institution for East Asian regionalism has not been established. The present

---

[1] Ratanak Hav, Deputy Director, Department of Economic Integration and ASEAN, Ministry of Economy and Finance, Cambodia. The views expressed in this paper are entirely the writer's own and should not be taken as bearing the government's view.

situation is that regionalism in East Asia has developed informally. The question now is whether this informal regionalism will develop into a formal regionalism for East Asia. In this paper, the formal regionalism refers to a regional integration based on institutions, rules and regimes, which could help address problems in economic and political integration and reduce market failures if necessary.

The concept of regionalism in East Asia was influenced by the growth of regional blocs elsewhere in the world. The trend towards increased protectionism, the expansion of regional integration in Europe (EU), and the formation of a free trade area in North America (NAFTA) stimulated the concept of East Asian regionalism. However, apart from Dr. Mahathir's less expected proposal to establish an East Asian Economic Group in 1990, the concept of East Asian regionalism revives only in the aftermath of the Asian financial crisis[1] 1997—1998. In other words, the Crisis brought East Asian countries closer together and prompted them to seek an enhanced institutional identity. In this sense, the ASEAN Plus Three (APT)[2] was institutionalized. This grouping provides the potential for the establishment of a more formal regionalism for East Asia following the ASEAN+3 summit at the end of 1999 since its cooperation has significantly advanced in many fields.

Therefore, this paper aims to investigate whether cooperation within the ASEAN+3 framework will advance to the next stage and develop into a new formal regionalism in East Asia and how it will be achieved.

The paper is divided into three parts. Part One examines the concept and practice of regionalism in East Asia. Part Two looks

---

[1] The terms Asian financial crisis and the Crisis will be used interchangeably in this paper.

[2] The terms APT (ASEAN Plus Three) and ASEAN+3 will be used interchangeably in this paper.

into the ASEAN+3 vis-à-vis the increased bilateral/sub-regional free trade arrangements (FTAs) by focusing on the question of building block/stumbling block, and on the implication of the increased FTAs for the ASEAN newer members. Part Three investigates the likelihood of ASEAN + 3 as a new formal East Asian regionalism. Finally, the findings will show that ASEAN +3 will likely become a new formal regionalism in East Asia if each of the plus three countries will willingly promote their negotiations of FTA with ASEAN as a group and then the sub-regional FTAs between ASEAN and the respective plus three country would work as building blocks for the eventual East Asian free trade area (EAFTA).

I. Regionalism in East Asia: Concept and Practice

In East Asia, the trend toward economic regionalism accelerated in the mid-1980s, largely in response to the beginning of the US-Canada negotiations on forming a free trade area in North America and to the passing of the Single European Act in 1986. Japan intensified its own efforts to create and lead a regional economy in East Asia, fearing exclusion from both of those regional market blocs, promoted Asian Pacific regionalism. ①Then a phenomenon of an economic regionalism began to appear. In this sense, Gilpin sees the phenomenon of this East Asian regionalism is principally driven by market force. ②

However, there is no single perspective that can explain regionalism in East Asia. There are contending analytical perspec-

---

① Andrew Wyatt-Walter, "Regionalism in Theoretical Perspective", in Louise Fawcett and Andrew Hurrell (eds.), *Regionalism in World Politics: Regional organization and International Order* (New York: Oxford University Press, 1995), p. 83.

② Robert Gilpin, *Global Political Economy: Understanding the International Economic Order* (New Jersey: Princeton University Press, 2001), p. 342.

tives on regionalism, especially between state-driven, market-driven, and network-driven perspectives.

From state-driven perspective, regional cooperation or integration is not market-driven, but determined by the nature of the legal and institutional framework, which is formed through coordination among nation-states. In other words, it is the sum of state interests that dictates the patterns of regional economic conflict and cooperation. Formal coordination among government authorities becomes an essential prerequisite for regional economic cooperation. [1]

In this respect, the state-driven school observes that the dynamics of economic development and regional cooperation in East Asia have given significance to the role of the state in its institutional arrangement and strategic actions. As Chung-in Moon puts it, "the East Asian model can be defined as the developmental state paradigm which is composed of a collection of theories, descriptions, and assertions that relate economic performance to institutional arrangements centered around the state."[2] This gives support to proponents of the theory of the "Developmental State", who argue that the outstanding economic success of Japan and other East Asian countries was due to their adoption of the developmental state model in which the state had to play the central role in guiding economic development and had to lead rather than follow the market.[3] In this sense, the principal actors in regional economic cooperation are governments, not firms.

However, the "network-driven" perspective argues that regionalism in East Asia operates through complex networks that form through commodity chains, movement of capital, and,

---

[1] Chung-in Moon, "Political Economy of East Asia Development and Pacific Economic Cooperation", *The Pacific Review*, Vol. 12, 1999, pp. 202-3.
[2] Ibid., p. 207.
[3] Robert Gilpin, pp. 316-20.

more importantly, human networks. There are two business networks of particular significance. One is the Japanese-led production network, and the other is the ethnic Chinese connection. While Japan's assertive foreign direct investments in East and Southeast Asian countries have cultivated dense production networks, ties among overseas Chinese merchants have created new forms of production and capital networks in Asia.[1] As a result, these networks have fostered greater economic cooperation and integration in the region.

In practice, the phenomenon of East Asian regionalism did not become evident until the mid-1980s, especially when Japan's foreign direct investment (FDI) began to accelerate vigorously. East Asian regionalism has emerged and developed through networks led by FDI.

The change was accelerated by the breakdown fixed exchange rate of the Bretton Woods monetary system in 1971. At that time Japanese capital became very important to Asian regional development. As the yen appreciated in value[2], the corresponding costs of land and labor in other parts of the world fell dramatically in yen terms. Japanese FDI increased substantially, especially after the sharp yen appreciation following the Plaza Accord of 1985. Japanese companies moved certain production bases to East Asian countries in order to take advantage of the latter's cheap labor, rent and export quotas to the US. Japanese FDI to East Asia rose from $ 1.19 billion out of a total Japanese FDI of $ 4.69 billion in 1980 to $ 2.33 billion of a $ 22.32 billion total in 1986; $ 8.24 billion of a $ 67.54 billion total in 1989. In 1997, Japanese FDI to East Asia rose to a new height of

---

[1] Chung-in Moon, "Political Economy of East Asia", pp. 203-4.

[2] The Japanese yen, fixed at Y360 to the US dollar from 1947 until 1971 had appreciated to about Y80 vis-à-vis the US dollar in 1995.

$12.22 billion out of the total of $54.06 billion Japanese FDI. ① As Japanese investment rose sharply, the production networks expanded rapidly.

The Japanese FDI has resulted in regional production networks (RPN). In East Asia, these networks not only exist, but have also become a major means of economic integration. They have forged strong linkages among the East Asian countries in the absence of formal integrative mechanisms. ②

Significantly, the Japanese RPN helped launch, first, the East Asian newly industrialized and then those of the ASEAN Four (Thailand, Malaysia, Indonesia and the Philippines) and China. As a matter of fact, by mid-1993, Asia accounted for 19 per cent of Japan's outstanding FDI. The bulk of Japan's actual investment went to NIEs and Southeast Asia. ③ The ASEAN Four became heavily reliant on the Japanese FDI.

At this point, the expansion of Japanese FDI in East Asia since the mid-1980s has resulted in the expansion of regional division of labor and increasing regional economic integration centered around Japan.

However, Japan and its companies were not alone in expanding their Asian investment. Hong Kong, Taiwan, and ROK were not only receiving Japanese FDI in more advanced industries and service sectors but also moving their labor-and-land-intensive industries offshore through their FDI, especially to China. ④

Following the Plaza Accord, the consequent devaluation of

---

① Dajin Peng, "The Changing Nature of East Asia as an Economic Region", *Pacific Affairs*, Vancouver, Summer 2000, p. 6.

② Ibid. , pp. 2-3.

③ T. J. Pempel, "International Finance and Asian Regionalism", pp. 63-5.

④ Kevin G. Cai, "The Political Economy of Economic Regionalism in Northeast Asia: A Unique and Dynamic Pattern", *An International Quarterly*, Vol. 17, No. 2, Summer, 1999, p. 8.

the US dollar and China's devaluation of its currency by about 50% had implications in particular for NIEs. For example, this gave companies in ROK, Hong Kong and Taiwan a strong incentive to move their production facilities abroad to cheaper locations. Between 1979 and 1995, Hong Kong's investment accounted for roughly 30% of the total FDI in China. In the same period, Taiwan invested $ 30 billion in China against about $ 21 billion from Japan. [1]Between 1986 and 1993, Japan ranked only fourth among China's foreign investors. Then, China's development depended less on Japanese FDI. Instead, about 70—80 percent of the foreign capital in China came from overseas Chinese. This means that China relies more on another mechanism of regional integration: overseas Chinese business networks. [2] As a result, overseas Chinese business networks have created a new layer of division of labor and become another powerful mechanism for regional integration, which challenges the dominance of Japan-led production networks of integration in East Asia.

In some ways, the nature of East Asian regionalism has changed. However, overall, the regional production networks, whether Japanese-led or ethnic Chinese, characterize the pattern of economic integration in East Asia. Thus, unlike the other two regions, Western Europe and North America, which are economically institutionalized by the EU and NAFTA, East Asia is not a well-defined economic region yet. East Asia has no comparable regional arrangement.

There has been an attempt to institutionalize East Asia as regional bloc or so-called "closed form of regionalism". Dating back to 1990, in reaction to the moves towards economic integration in Europe and North America, Prime Minister Mahathir of

---

[1] T. J. Pempel, "International Finance and Asian Regionalism", pp. 66-7.

[2] Dajin Peng, "The Changing Nature of East Asia as an Economic Region", p. 9.

Malaysia called for the creation of an economic bloc in the form of East Asian Economic Group (EAEG), which was intended to be a formal preferential trading area, to include all countries in Northeast and Southeast Asia (ASEAN). Then, the EAEG initiative emerged to give negotiating strength for bargaining vis-à-vis other blocs. However, Prime Minister Mahathir's initiative appears to have less expected progress since it has been transformed into a so-called "East Asian Economic Caucus (EAEC)".

Generally, East Asia did little to foster regionalism until the Asian financial crisis erupted in 1997—1998. The Crisis had an impact on the whole region. It severely affected many ASEAN members as well as ROK, and Japan's recession deepened as a consequence. Among other factors, the Crisis made East Asians realize that closer regional cooperation is indispensable to prevent such an occurrence in the future. This was a turning point for a rising sense of regionalism in East Asia, including Japan, China, ROK and the members of ASEAN. In taking action, the ASEAN Plus Three has been institutionalized in 1998 to pave the way for a possible formal regionalism in East Asia, which is still absent to date.

In sum, the theoretical concept and practice show that East Asian regionalism is an informal integration, which is a combination of state-driven, market-driven and network-driven processes. From state-driven perspective, the state is supposed to play an important role in guiding economic development and cooperation rather than follow the market. Hence, the so-called "soft regionalism" of East Asia is not only state-driven but incorporates market and network features.

II. ASEAN Plus Three vis-à-vis Bilateral/ Sub-regional Trading Arrangements

The Institutionalization of ASEAN Plus Three

The Asian economic and financial crisis during 1997—1998 and the response that emerged during the crisis time were widely accepted as the foremost factor of driving force for East Asian regionalism. As *The Economist* highlights, the financial crisis of 1997 — 1998 is "the single greatest catalyst for the new East Asian regionalism."[①] As a result, the ASEAN+3 was institutionalized during the 6th ASEAN Summit in December 1998 in Hanoi.

Since a regional integration in East Asia has not been formalized for many decades, the institutionalization of the ASEAN+3 process appears as a turning point for East Asian cooperation. From 1999, ASEAN+3 process has been deepened, at the same time, a new sense of East Asian regionalism has revived.

At their meeting in November 1999, the leaders of the ASEAN+3 adopted a "Joint Statement on East Asia Cooperation" which has served as the first blue print for guiding the ASEAN+3 cooperation. Within this framework, there has been notable development in the ASEAN+3 cooperation, particularly significant progress has been made in the field of financial cooperation. Under the "Chiang Mai Initiative" (CMI) adopted by the ASEAN+3 Finance Ministers in May 2000, a network of 12 bilateral swap arrangements (BSAs) between China, Japan, and ROK and several of the ASEAN members has been established with a combined size of US $ 31.5 billion. Four more BSAs are being negotiated. These innovative finance mechanisms are expected to help avert crises that may arise from short-term liquidity problems among the partners. Many see this move as a way of strengthening East Asia's self-help mechanisms to maintain financial stability in East Asia.

Recently, the "Asian Bond Markets Initiative (ABMI)" was

[①] "Towards a Tripartite World", *The Economist (US)*, Vol. 356, No. 8179, July 15, 2000.

adopted at the ASEAN+3 informal session in December 2002 in Chiang Mai. Taking advantages of that many countries in Asia have long enjoyed high savings rates, and have accumulated a substantial amount of foreign reserves in recent years, fostering bond markets in Asia has been advocated as a major challenge for the region to tackle collaboratively in order to attain sustainable economic development as well as to prevent recurrence of currency and financial crisis. And now the process is well underway. Three working groups were established to study (i) creation of security debt instruments; (ii) establishment of the Asian Credit Guarantee Facility; and (iii) establishment of an Asian Credit Rating Board. So, the Asian Bond Market Initiative (ABMI) also holds significant promise as useful instruments to promote close cooperation in the region. Especially, it is expected to enable countries in the region to be able to better utilize aggregate savings and minimize the risk of maturity and currency mismatches.

Generally, the ASEAN+3 process has been matured. At the ASEAN+3 Summit in Phnom Penh in November 2002, the leaders agreed to expand cooperation to include regional political and security issues such as the fight against terrorism and transnational crime.

Despite the above development, it is worth noting that there is an existing vision for the evolution of ASEAN+3 process. The East Asia Vision Group (EAVG)[1] is the first initiative to look into the possibility of creating an East Asian community. Among the 57 concrete measures of recommendations, two big

---

[1] EAVG was introduced by the President of the Republic of Korea, Kim Dae-Jung at the ASEAN+3 Summit held in Hanoi in December 1998. Its establishment was agreed by all ASEAN leaders in order to explore ways and possibility for cooperation among the 13 countries in the fields of politics, economic and socio-economic in the medium and long run. The EAVG put forward a set of 57 recommendations at the 5th ASEAN+3 Summit on 5th Nov 2001 in Brunei.

ideas were recommended by the EAVG namely the feasibility and the implications of developing ASEAN+3 into a new formal regional grouping with a regular East Asia Summit (EAS); and the possibility of a Free Trade Zone for East Asia. Given the importance of the future of East Asian cooperation, the ASEAN+3 leaders at their ASEAN+3 Summit in Singapore in 2000, decided to establish the East Asia Study Group (EASG)[1] to assess the EAVG recommendations including the assessment of the implications of an East Asian summit. Taking into account state of discussions on the implications of an East Asian Summit stated in the EASG final report presented to the Leaders of ASEAN+3 in Phnom Penh last November, "Leaders agreed with the ROK's vision for ASEAN+3 summits to evolve in the long term into East Asian summits and eventually an East Asian Free Trade Area"[2]. Thus, there is a general consensus that the two big ideas are the long-term objective of the ASEAN+3 cooperation.

The Increased Bilateral/Sub-regional Trading Arrangements: Building Block or Stumbling Block For A New Formal East Asian Regionalism?

While Members of ASEAN+3 agreed that evolution of an EAS should proceed in a gradual and balanced way, members also agreed on a building-block approach as the best way forward. As a result, there are increased sub-regional and bilateral free trade arrangements within East Asian region. Main economic players in the region have come up with their own initiative to move ASEAN+3 cooperation forward.

---

[1] EASG was initiated by the President of the Republic of Korea, Kim Dae-Jung at 4th ASEAN+3, 2000.
[2] Press Statement by the Chairman of the 8th ASEAN Summit, the 6th ASEAN+3 Summit, 4 Nov. 2002.

China's Approach to ASEAN

Notably, China is the first country in the region, which has been moving faster than others to establish a free trade area with ASEAN while the ROK's vision of EAS and EAFTA was under the study. In pursuing its vision for strengthened ties with ASEAN, China put forward the initiative to establish an ASEAN-China Free Trade Area within the next decade at the 7th ASEAN Summit in Brunei Darussalam in 2001. Despite some reservations raised then by some members, in acknowledging the important and growing role of China in regional and world affairs, at the 8th ASEAN Summit in Phnom Penh, the ASEAN and Chinese leaders signed the Framework Agreement on ASEAN-China Comprehensive Economic Cooperation to establish an FTA by 2010 for the older ASEAN members and 2015 for the newer members. This framework has paved the way for the start of negotiations on FTA between ASEAN and China.

A market of 1.8 billion population of ASEAN-China FTA has brought attention not only from inside the region but also outside the region. This move can be explained in two ways: firstly, China has its own vision for ASEAN+3 cooperation and trade liberalization in East Asia. Secondly, this FTA has sent a message to outside world as China's reaction to the growing sub-regional arrangements in the Western hemisphere particularly the expansion of North American Free Trade Area (NAFTA) into free trade area of America (FTAA) by 2005 and the expansion of the EU in Europe.

Japan's Approach to ASEAN

To deepen and widen the scope of cooperation in East Asia for the future, during his visits to five ASEAN member countries in January 2002, Prime Minister Junichiro Koizumi proposed five initiatives, among others, namely the Initiative for Development in East Asia (IDEA), and Japan-ASEAN Comprehensive Economic Partnership (CEP).

Japan's approach somehow explained its reaction to the outside world as the Joint Declaration on CEP recognizes that "rapid progress of regional economic integration, especially in Europe and North America, has been promoting the liberalization of world trade in stimulating regional dynamism"[①].

In regional context, Japanese proposals can be also seen as the Japanese reaction to the ASEAN-China FTA. At the beginning many ASEAN + 3 members had a concern over Japan's IDEA to become a new mechanism that would duplicate the existing ASEAN+3 framework. Through consultations, IDEA is part of the ASEAN+3 framework and a testimony of long-term political commitment of Japan to Southeast Asia and East Asia as a whole. In addition, Japan pledged to continue its support for ASEAN in implementing the IDEA by "stressing the close links between ODA, FDI and trade facilitation for developing countries"[②].

As mentioned above, China is the fastest mover to initiate ASEAN-China FTA in November 2001 and received great support of the ASEAN leaders. Originally, Japan had not initiated FTA with all ASEAN members, but started bilateral negotiation on FTA only with Singapore. Hence, Japan's approach to ASEAN is seen as its reaction to China's move. To advance its vision, Japan signed with ASEAN the Joint Declaration on the CEP to develop a concrete framework to realize the economic partnership, including "elements of a free-trade area, should be

---

① Press Statement by the Chairman of the ASEAN-Japan Summit, 5 Nov. 2002.

② Ibid.

fully implemented as soon as possible within 10 years"[1] during the ASEAN-Japan Summit in November 2002. The draft framework for CEP between ASEAN and Japan was endorsed recently at the 35th ASEAN Economic Ministers Meeting (AEM) on 2nd September 2003 in Phnom Penh, and is expected to sign by the Leaders at the ASEAN-Japan Summit in Bali in October 2003.

However, Japan's approach to ASEAN is different from China. In the light of different levels of economic development of ASEAN member countries, Japan initially proposed bilateral arrangements as a strategy in negotiating ASEAN-Japan CEP. Obviously, the discussion on the framework for CEP between ASEAN and Japan was preceded by the successful conclusion of Japan-Singapore economic partnership agreement.[2] To date, Japan has been consulting similar CEP with the Philippines, Malaysia and Thailand, whose processes have been moving close to the start of formal negotiations. The four CEP/FTAs (Japan-Singapore, Japan-Thailand, Japan-Philippines, Japan-Malaysia) would account about 70% of Japan's trade with ASEAN.

So, at this stage, Japan's approach to CEP somehow shows its emphasis more on bilateral FTA with some ASEAN members than on a sub-regional CEP/FTA agreement between ASEAN and Japan as a whole.

ROK's Complementary Approach to ASEAN

The Republic of Korea (ROK) is the first country that initiated the study of ASEAN+3/East Asian vision. Given the views that EAFTA remains one of the long-term objectives in economic cooperation in East Asia and in reaction to China and Japan's free

---

[1] Press Statement by the Chairman of the ASEAN-Japan Summit, 5 Nov. 2002.

[2] Japan and Singapore signed a New Age Economic Partnership Agreement (JSEPA) in January 2002 during Koizumi's visit.

trade arrangements with ASEAN, ROK also advocates the building block approach and now looking into modalities to establish ASEAN-ROK FTA, or a comprehensive economic partnership or a closer economic partnership with ASEAN.

Building Block or Stumbling Block?

The given trend has raised a question of whether the increased bilateral and sub-regional FTAs will constitute as building block or stumbling block for the evolution of ASEAN+3 towards long-term goal of EAS and EAFTA? So far, in theory, it is argued that bilateral/sub-regional FTAs would play as building-block approach to regionalism and global trade liberalization. Yet, in practice there is no proof.

The new bilateral/sub-regional FTAs in East Asia, on one hand, could be a stumbling block for the ultimate objective of EAFTA. On the other hand, they could play a positive role in the future of EAFTA as a building block providing an alternative path toward free and open trade and investment in the region. However, there is no clear-cut as in nature regional trading arrangements (RTAs) can give rise to trade diversion as well as trade creation, because this issue derives from the discrimination between members and non-members that is inherent in the preference of regional trading arrangements (RTAs). [1]

The hypothesis here is whether ASEAN+3 will develop as a new regionalism in East Asia. According to the 1995 OECD report, which stressed that, "hub-and-spoke agreements have a damaging effect on the multilateral system because they multiply

---

[1] Robert Scollay & John P. Gilbert, *New Regional Trading Arrangements in the Asia Pacific*, (May 2001), p. 10 (Chapter I).

the number of different trade regimes". ① Seen in this light, there is hub-and-spoke issue in East Asia. One country as the hub has many different bilateral arrangements with many individual countries as spokes. To point out, Japan-ASEAN trading arrangement shows that Japan is a hub in relation to individual ASEAN members as spokes. This hub-and-spoke issue can also apply to China-ASEAN, and likewise to ROK-ASEAN. However, hub-and-spoke issue in East Asia is two-way since ASEAN as a group can also be a hub vis-à-vis China, Japan, ROK as spokes. Therefore, as hub-and-spoke problem in East Asia is a two-way issue, it is possible to assume that there is no clear-cut, whether the increased bilateral/sub-regional FTAs in East Asia can work both as stumbling blocks or building blocks for EAFTA.

To agree with the building block theory, EAFTA is likely to happen as we can see, particularly, on the economic and financial front there have been many developments. Some ASEAN members have established bilateral Swap arrangements with China, Japan and ROK. The Asian Bond Markets have been fostered. ASEAN also entered into the arrangements to develop a "comprehensive" economic relationship leading to an ASEAN-China free trade area with China and to forge a "comprehensive economic partnership" with Japan and possibly with ROK. These arrangements will create a new configuration of economic cooperation in East Asia. ②

However, since each plus three country, namely China, Japan, and ROK respectively has its own vision and strategy for

---

① Geun Woo Ryu, "A View of Regionalism and Subregionalism in the APEC Context", in John Ingleson (ed.), *Regionalism, Subregionalism and APEC*, Monash Asia Institute, Clayton, Vic., 1997, pp. 160-2.

② Key Note Address by Samdech Hun Sen, Prime Minister of the Royal Government of Cambodia, *"Cambodia: Fully Engaged in the ASEAN Community"*, 36th AMM, 16 June 2003, Phnom Penh.

free trade with ASEAN group, this would likely to create many standards of free trade arrangements in East Asia in terms of coverage, trade and investment regime, and especially different sets of rules of origin. Consequently, it would be very difficult to hammer out negotiations for a common standard. This would not be just constrains but become obstacles to the establishment of EAFTA, although it is understood as long-term objective. In fact, it is likely the evolution of the ASEAN + 3 into an East Asian regionalism as long as ASEAN-China, ASEAN-Japan, and other country bilateral agreements serve as the building blocks as they perceived in their concept, and not as the stumbling-block to a wider East Asia cooperation. Nonetheless, since some countries especially the plus three countries are approaching East Asian cooperation differently, there is concern if the stumbling block would become the issue rather than the perceived building block as each of bilateral FTAs will have its own set of rules of origin, which could become impediments for the regional integration.

It is worth recalling that a major thrust in the aftermath of the Asian financial crisis is to establish a formal integrated East Asian regionalism as each member was of view that East Asia must have its own institution to prevent and deal with a future crisis. In this regard, if we continue to have many standards and layers in bilateral/sub-regional arrangements, ASEAN + 3 can hardly achieve a formal regional integration with regime-based institution as other regions have, such as NAFTA or EU. Then, ASEAN+3 will remain an informal regionalism with many bilateral/sub-regional arrangements.

Moreover, the building block approach raises a reservation for its success, given that East Asia has its own specific nature in terms of regional geopolitics, geo-economics and historical animosity. The strategic rivalry, business network competition and historical and cultural differences between China and Japan may explain why each key player has its own vision and strategy in relation to ASEAN in the context of ASEAN+3 cooperation. In this regard, in achieving a formal East Asian institution, the question perhaps, remains who will take leadership or who can influence the process. One of the answers that could come is when they can achieve equilibrium of power relationships, and no one would lose face to the other.

If this is the case, a full EAFTA will remain long-term objective with indefinite time frame. As a repercussion, ASEAN+3 may lose out in the global competition in the long run as the vision of EAFTA has taken into account the fact that the EU is expanding, the US is reaching out to Latin America to form the Free Trade Area of Americas (FTAA) by 2005.

In a nutshell, the concept of building block is the optimistic view. Although there is no explicit answer or proof to say that bilateral/sub-regional FTAs will work as building block for the success of EAFTA/EAS and eventually East Asian regionalism, the sub-regional FTAs between ASEAN and the respective plus three countries, somehow, serve as an option of strategy toward the realization of the East Asian vision.

Implications for the Newer Members of ASEAN

Based on the assessment of the implications of an East Asian Summit conducted by the EASG, East Asia has come to be regarded as one of the three major economic regions in the world and one of the world's current leading centers of growth. Statistics reveal the tremendous potential for growth in this region and the rationale for creating a broader cooperative regional framework as East Asia represents 23% of the world's GDP and 40% of its foreign reserves. Moreover, East Asia constitutes roughly one third of the world's population, which bears the potential size of the growing East Asian market.

Despite the potential revealed, there is a consensus that "evolution of [the annual summit meetings of ASEAN+3 into] an East Asian Summit should proceed in a gradual and balanced way, and a building block approach is the best way forward". [1] This approach has been taken due to some concerns, among others, namely: (i) ASEAN should remain the driving force of East Asian cooperation; (ii) To avoid marginalization of ASEAN upon the creation of EAS. In this context, the ASEAN+3 Leaders also agreed that an East Asian Free Trade Area is eventually established when the EAS is created.

However, approaches to establish FTA with ASEAN, which is taken by key economic players in East Asia, have different implications on ASEAN especially on the newer members namely, Cambodia, Laos and Myanmar. So far, we have two versions of FTA within the framework of East Asian cooperation.

China's Version of FTA with ASEAN

To establish ASEAN-China FTA, China and ASEAN agreed to a framework that set modalities for regional negotiation between China and ASEAN as a whole. Now, the ASEAN-China negotiations are well in progress. Being as a group, on one hand, ASEAN can maintain its driving force in the East Asian cooperation process. On the other hand, China's version is well in consistent with AFTA process as they agree to establish the FTA by 2010 for older ASEAN members and 2015 for the newer members with flexibility on sensitive commodities. Moreover, China's version is also supportive to the newer members of ASEAN. While the framework was signed, China agreed to help the newer members by granting special and preferential tariff

---

[1] *Final Report of the East Asia Study Group*, p. 60.

treatment to Cambodia, Laos, and Myanmar. In this sense, China's version has positive impact given that ASEAN members including the newer members are not marginalized in the process.

Japan's Version of FTA with ASEAN

Japan has pursued "dual track" modality to create CEPs/FTAs with ASEAN. As discussed earlier, Japan concluded the CEP Agreement with Singapore in January 2002. Pending the CEP framework for regional negotiation with ASEAN, Japan has started consultations with the Philippines, Malaysia and Thailand to establish the similar CEP. By now those processes have been moving close to a start of their respective formal negotiations. This explains that the process is irreversibly going. Then, the concern was that Japan's "dual track" with ASEAN might weaken ASEAN's driving force in the ASEAN+3 process. As consequence, each member certainly will have its own standard of agreement with Japan particularly in terms of coverage, trade and investment regime, and rules of origin. By starting bilateral FTAs rather than a regional ASEAN-Japan FTA, the newer members of ASEAN would be left behind. Since their economies are less developed compared with the older members, bilateral FTAs will create different speeds of trade liberalization among ASEAN members vis-à-vis Japan. And when ASEAN and Japan start their regional negotiation, the newer members will have less options to accept conditions that have had been agreed bilaterally between Japan and the other more developed economies of ASEAN, whereby the newer members were not party to. Naturally, member countries that have bilateral FTAs, would focus more on their bilateral FTAs. Eventually, the newer members of ASEAN which have no bilateral FTAs might be marginalized or lose out somehow.

However, this is not the end of the story for the ASEAN newer members. The successful conclusion of the 35th AEM on 2nd September in Phnom Penh gave an indication that the framework for CEP between ASEAN and Japan is expected to sign at the ASEAN-Japan Summit in October 2003. The Economic Ministers agreed to recommend to the Leaders that "ASEAN and Japan should proceed with the implementation of the elements of the CEP as soon as possible by 2012, taking into account the economic levels and sensitive sectors of each country, including allowing additional five years for the newer ASEAN member countries". [1]

In this regard, Japan's version would have positive impact on ASEAN newer members likewise China's version. And the newer members of ASEAN will not be left out in the process if ASEAN and Japan would start consultations and negotiations on a CEP agreement between ASEAN and Japan as a whole, including elements of a possible free trade area as soon as possible.

III. The Likelihood of ASEAN+3 as a Formal New East Asian Regionalism

The likelihood of a new East Asian regionalism depends on whether the ASEAN FTA (AFTA), the China-ASEAN FTA, Japan-ASEAN CEP/FTA and the possible ROK-ASEAN FTA will constitute as building blocks and synergy for East Asian cooperation. As discussed earlier, China's version of FTA with ASEAN is complementary for EAFTA as both sides agreed on regional negotiation framework and now their negotiations are in good progress. However, ASEAN-Japan CEP remains an issue since Japan opted a "dual track" to start bilateral CEPs/FTAs with some ASEAN members prior to the beginning of a regional

---

[1] Joint Media Statement, 35th ASEAN Economic Ministers Meeting, 2nd September 2003, Phnom Penh.

negotiation on CEP/FTA between ASEAN and Japan as a whole.

In fact, some ASEAN members sought bilateral free trade negotiations with Japan by taking into account the trend outside the region, specifically FTA negotiations between the US and some countries in Latin America. There is an existing perception "to follow the big guys, otherwise one will lose out in global trade competition". However, as we may know, any big player would favor bilateral negotiation.

So for the interest of ASEAN, ASEAN members had better deal with Japan as a group, because FTAs are good for all if they simultaneously implement at full speed.

ASEAN has its own FTA called "AFTA". If members are sidetracking and resort to other bilateral FTAs within the region and outside the region, then the proliferation of bilateral FTAs may distract their focus on internal ASEAN integration. They will naturally focus more on their bilateral FTAs. As a result, ASEAN would wither and eventually be marginalized if intra-regional trade is not substantially boosted.

The "dual track" of Japan's strategy with ASEAN members has raised a concern, whether the bilateral standards of negotiations with Japan could be compromised for a common standard for ASEAN-Japan CEP. It is possible that the newer members will have less choice and have to follow the other more developed members if regional negotiations on the CEP including the FTA between ASEAN and Japan cannot start as early as possible. In this sense, ASEAN's driving force in the ASEAN+3 process is likely to be weakened in relation to Japan. The newer members would likely be marginalized in the context of East Asian integration.

ASEAN in fact has a common goal to achieve. At the 8th ASEAN Summit in Phnom Penh last November, the leaders considered the idea of an ASEAN Economic Community (AEC) as an end goal for the Roadmap for the integration of ASEAN and Vision 2020. The concept of AEC is expected to adopt at the coming Summit in Indonesia. To materialize this vision, it is needed to take into account the findings of McKinsey and Company's study on ASEAN Competitiveness that "improving productivity is the key to enhancing national and regional competitiveness in ASEAN", which can be done through enhanced regional integration. And a deeper integration of ASEAN will boost ASEAN companies' productivity. He also points out that the main challenge for ASEAN is to change investors' thinking, as so far they perceive ASEAN as 10 separate markets not as one integrated regional market. Therefore, ASEAN needs to break this perception. ① Thus, to achieve the end goal of ASEAN integration, ASEAN should act as an entity as it is indispensable for ASEAN.

However, if ASEAN withers away and cannot act as an entity, the evolution of ASEAN+ 3 into an EAS will not be materialized. Without solidarity as a group, East Asia cannot be strong. Eventually, the impetus and thrust toward an East Asian regionalism arising in the aftermath of the Asian economic and financial crisis during 1997 — 1998 will lose its take-off ground. In this regard, ASEAN members should come to realize that their best prospect for sustainable growth lies in regional arrangements, especially as the region is now confronting new challenges arising from economic globalization and IT revolution. And the Plus Three countries should deal with ASEAN as a whole regional group if they really desire to achieve a new and strong regionalism for East Asia. A repercussion is simple, if there is no strong ASEAN, there would be no strong ASEAN+

---

① Dr. Roland Villinger, McKinsey and Company, *Perspectives on National and Regional Competitiveness*, Paper presented to the Seminar on ASEAN-Japan: Partners in Regional Integration, Bangkok, 29 May 2003.

3/East Asia as well.

Conclusion

The Asian economic and financial crisis is the foremost factor, which gave the region a push towards greater unity and revival of sense of regionalism. The concept and practice show that a new formal regionalism remains absent, although ASEAN+3 has been institutionalized. In fact, trade is not an end in itself, and market mechanism is a key tool to manage cooperation and ensure a win-win situation. Therefore, the success of the ASEAN+3 to form a new regionalism depends on a feasible and practical approach that we pursue.

The findings show that since there is a general consensus that building block approach is the way forward to attain an EAFTA, the increased bilateral/sub-regional FTAs among ASEAN members and the Plus Three countries serve as an option to enable dialogue and as an alternative path toward an EAFTA and eventually a new formal East Asian regionalism. In this context, to make building block approach more likely, each Plus Three country should deal with ASEAN as a group in their free trade arrangements and vice versa. In so doing, sub-regional FTAs between ASEAN and the respective Plus Three countries could implement at full speed at the same time and will work as synergy for an EAFTA. Eventually, East Asian regionalism will be materialized through the synergy of sub-regional FTAs in East Asia namely, ASEAN-China FTA, ASEAN-Japan CEP, ASEAN-ROK FTA.

References

1. Cai, Kevin G., "The Political Economy of Economic Regionalism in Northeast Asia: A Unique and Dynamic Pattern",

An International Quarterly, Vol. 17, No. 2, Summer, 1999.

2. Gilpin, Robert, *Global Political Economy: Understanding the International Economic Order* (New Jersey: Princeton University Press, 2001).

3. Moon, Chung-in, "Political Economy of East Asia Development and Pacific Economic Cooperation", *The Pacific Review*, Vol. 12, No. 2, 1999.

4. Pempel, T. J., *International Finance and Asian Regionalism*.

5. Peng, Dajin, "The Changing Nature of East Asia as an Economic Region", *Pacific Affairs*, Vancouver, Summer 2000.

6. Plummer, Michael G., "ASEAN and Institutional Nesting in the Asia-Pacific: Leading from Behind in APEC", in Vinod K. Aggarwal and Charles E. Morrison (eds.), *Asia-Pacific Crossroads: Regime Creation and the Future of APEC*, Macmillan Press Ltd, London, 1998.

7. Ryu, Geun Woo, "A View of Regionalism and Sub-regionalism in the APEC Context", in John Ingleson (ed.), *Regionalism, Sub-regionalism and APEC*, Monash Asia Institute, Clayton, Vic., 1997.

8. Scollay, Robert & Gilbert, John P., *New Regional Trading Arrangements in the Asia Pacific*, May 2001.

9. Villinger, Roland, "Perspectives on National and Regional Competitiveness", Paper presented to the Seminar on "ASEAN-Japan: Partners in Regional Integration", McKinsey and Company, Bangkok, 29 May 2003.

10. Walter, Andrew Wyatt, "Regionalism in Theoretical Perspective", in Louise Fawcett and Andrew Hurrell (eds.), *Regionalism in World Politics: Regional Organization and International Order*, Oxford University Press, New York, 1995.

11. Key Note Address by Samdech Hun Sen, Prime Minister of the Royal Government of Cambodia, "Cambodia: Fully Engaged in the ASEAN Community", 36th AMM, 16 June

2003, Phnom Penh.

12. Press Statement by the Chairman of the 8th ASEAN Summit, the 6th ASEAN+3 Summit, 4 Nov. 2002.

13. Press Statement by the Chairman of the ASEAN-Japan Summit, 5 Nov. 2002.

14. Joint Media Statement, 35th ASEAN Economic Ministers Meeting, 2 September 2003, Phnom Penh, Cambodia.

15. Final Report of the East Asia Study Group.

A Road Map to the East Asia Community

Daisuke Hiratsuka[①]

Introduction

As of May 5, 2003, 184 regional trade agreements (RTAs) have notified the World Trade Agreement (WTO). Especially in the latter half of 1990s, the world witnessed a wave of RTA. Since 1995 to present, 119 additional RTAs have been notified. Except the North East Asia of China, Japan and ROK, all the major economies in the world had been committed to some FTAs. Responding to the globalization, China, Japan and ROK necessitate promoting a regional cooperation by formation of a free trade area (FTA) as well as facilitation measures to reduce business barriers.

In January 2002, Japan and Singapore agreed the Japan Singapore Economic Partnership Agreement (JSEPA). In November 2002, China reached an agreement of the Framework Agreement on ASEAN-China Economic Cooperation. In the same year, Japan also proposed the ASEAN-Japan Comprehensive

---

[①] Daisuke Hiratsuka, Senior Research Fellow, the Institute of Developing Economies, JETRO. I would like to thank our colleagues, Hirokazu Okumura, Toshihiro Kudo, and Tomoko Kobota for making comments on the draft version of this paper. I am also indebted to Takayuki Takeuchi, who helped some data compilation of trade matrix. However, I am solely responsible for all opinions expressed and for any errors that remain.

Economic Partnership (AJCEP), which is expected to agree the framework of AJCEP in October 2003. Japan and ROK, in June 2003, promised to make effort for a start of negotiation relating to the CEP that includes an FTA and facilitation measures, as early as possible. These new movements of FTAs in East Asia show a great potential for East Asia integration. In this context, this study aims to see potential cooperation in East Asia, to assess the recent development of the ASEAN+3 framework, and to present a possible road map to the formation of East Asia Community.

I. Potentiality of East Asia Integration

The ASEAN+3 is of high potentiality to evolve into an East Asia Community in future. Firstly, the economy of ASEAN+3 that includes 10 ASEAN countries, China, Japan and ROK is considerably large. The combined GDP of these economies amounts to US $ 6,305 billion in 2001, which accounts for 20.1% of the world economy. This is the third largest economic pole in the world that follows the NAFTA, US $ 11,405 billion, 36.3%; and the EU, US $ 7,886 billion, 25.1% in the same year (see Table 1). This envisages that East Asia would form a free trade area that would be equivalent to the North America Free Trade Area (NAFTA) and the EU (European Union).

Secondly, the position of ASEAN+3, in terms of population, has overwhelmed other regions. Total population of ASEAN+3 almost reaches to 2 billion, which represents 32.3% of the world population, while the NAFTA and EU share only 6.8 % and 6.2 % respectively (see Table 1). This large population means a huge potential market of East Asia.

Thirdly, more importantly, there have been complementary trade relationship in East Asia. Japan and ROK are complementary to ASEAN countries and China. ① Also Japan and ROK are partly competing with each other and partly complementary. But, ASEAN countries, by and large, are competing against within region and with China.

Table 1 Economic Position of East Asia in the World

	GDP in 2001 US $ Billion	%share of the world	Population in 2001 Million	%share of the world
Brunei	4	0.01	0	0.01
Cambodia	3	0.01	13	0.21
Indonesia	142	0.45	205	3.35
Laos	2	0.01	5	0.09
Malaysia	88	0.28	24	0.39
Myanmar	8	0.02	50	0.81
The Philippines	71	0.23	78	1.27
Singapore	85	0.27	4	0.07
Thailand	115	0.37	63	1.03
Vietnam	33	0.10	79	1.29
ASEAN10	551	1.76	521	8.50
China	1.167	3.72	1.285	20.96
Japan	4.165	13.26	127	2.08
ROK	422	1.34	47	0.77
ASEAN+3	6.305	20.08	1.981	32.31
U.S.	10.082	32.11	285	4.65
Canada	705	2.25	31	0.51
Mexico	618	1.97	102	1.66
NAFTA	11.405	36.32	418	6.81
EU	7.886	25.11	377	6.15
World	31.400	100.00	6.130	100.00

Source: ASEAN Surveillance Coordinating Unit (ASCU) database for ASEAN 10 and Consensus Economics Inc for the other economies, and the World Bank, the World Development Indicators, 2003 for the World.

---

① Hiratsuka (2003a) measures competitiveness of the ASEAN Six (Indonesia, Malaysia, the Philippines, Singapore, Thailand, and Vietnam) in the 1990s. It obtained the findings that the ASEAN Six and China are strongly competitive in almost same industries and also weak in almost same industries, while Japan is very competitive in industries where the ASEAN Six and China are weak. ROK has been catching up with Japan in several industries.

These competing and complementary trade relationships can be observed by the facts that ASEAN countries, China, Japan and ROK are in different position of competitiveness (see Figure 1, 2, 3 and 4). For instance, in apparel industry, ASEAN and China are in the *export stage* where domestic supply exceeds domestic demands and their competitiveness is increasing or maintains at a high level, while Japan is in the *reverse import stage*, whose domestic supply is less than domestic demands and its competitiveness index is decreasing or quite low. On the contrary, in industrial machinery, Japan is in the *export stage* while ASEAN countries, China and ROK are in the *import substitution stage*, whose domestic supply is less than domestic demands and the competitiveness index is in the rising trend. Japan is very competitive in industries such as automobile, heavy machinery industries, mold and part industry in which high technologies and capitals are required. On the contrary, China is strong in apparel, assembling of electrical family appliances and ASEAN in personal computer and peripheral equipment where large plenty of human resources are required. ROK is in the mid position, that is, increased competitiveness in parts industry and automobile industry. These facts show that factor endowment and location advantages are quite different among the region, and thus, if these economies were integrated by complete reduction of barriers to trade, service and investment, the integrated East Asia would be a *producing area* that is competitive in various industries.

Fourth, procurement system has drastically changed in East Asia[1]. For example, traditionally, Japanese firms operating in East Asia had imported most of parts from Japan. However, at present, they have procured them within the region except for the key ones which are still supplied from Japan. For instance,

---

[1] See Hiratsuka (2003b).

in automobile industry, operating firms in ASEAN countries apply a complementary procurement system, which have procured parts from other affiliated firms operating in the other ASEAN countries. In electrical family appliances, office & telecommunication equipment, personal computer and these parts industries, Japanese firms have procured parts at the lowest prices in East Asia. They have employed many local purchasers to examine parts carefully to make sure they are usable. The dissemination of optimum procurement system has developed a production network in East Asia, which demands a free business area in the region. The dissemination of optimum procurement and development of production network would contribute to increasing effects of the East Asia FTA.

Figure 1

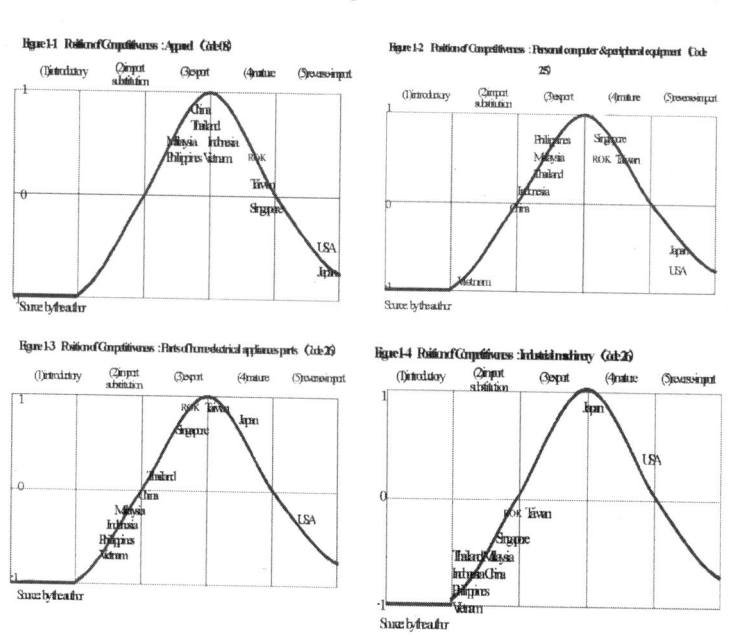

Figure 2 From Traditional Procurement
to Complementary Procurement

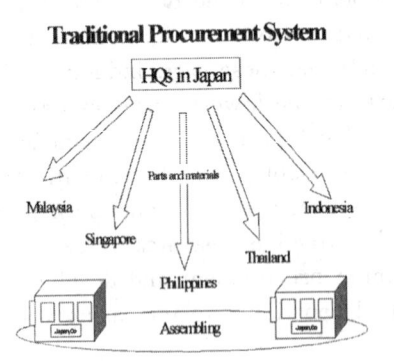

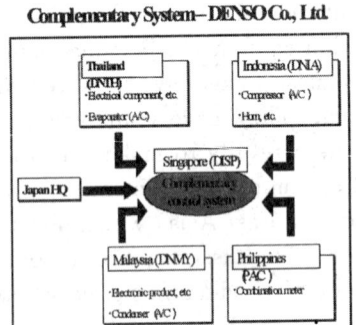

Traditional Procurement System

(diagram: HQs in Japan sending Parts and materials to Malaysia, Singapore, Philippines, Indonesia, Thailand for Assembling)

Complementary System—DENSO Co., Ltd.

(diagram: Japan HQ linked to Complementary control system with Thailand (DNTH) ·Electrical component, etc. ·Evaporator (AC); Indonesia (DNIA) ·Compressor (AC) ·Horn, etc.; Singapore (DISP); Malaysia (DNMY) ·Electronic product, etc. ·Condenser (AC); Philippines (PAC) ·Combination meter)

    The intra-regional trade of ASEAN+3, however, has not developed successfully. The share of intra-regional export of ASEAN+3 is only 33.9 % of its total exports. This figure is relatively small compared to those of other regions such as the NAFTA, 55.5% and the EU, 62.9% (see Table 2). It should be stressed that the ASEAN+3's intra-regional export share increased slightly from 33.5% in 1995 to 33.9% in 2001 while NAFTA's intra-regional exports increased from 42.7% to 55.5% in the same year. The intra-regional export share in 2001 is 43.9% for ASEAN 10, 28.5% for China, 27.4% for Japan, and 34.1% for ROK. This is because exports between ASEAN-China, ASEAN-ROK, China-ASEAN, China-ROK, Japan-China, and Japan-ROK have not expanded enough (see Table 3).
    Strengthening economic relationship policies would expand the intra-regional trade, and that will contribute to expansions of trade and investments. The main pillars of such policies would be a formation of the East Asia Free Trade Area (EAFTA) and facilitation measures that harmonize and streamline the trade and

investment rules such as custom procedure, products standard, transportation and communication regulations and so on.

Table 2 Regional Export and World Export Share in 1995 and 2001

	Regional Exports				Total Export			
	US$ Million		% of Total Export		US$ Million		% of the World Trade	
	1995	2001	1995	2001	1995	2001	1995	2001
ASEAN+3	350,657	411,466	33.5	33.9			20.6	19.7
NAFTA	394,472	639,138	42.7	55.5	924,291		18.2	18.7
EU			62.4	62.4			39.7	36.7
World					5077900		100.0	100.0

Source: IMF, Direction of Trade Statistics Year Book 2002.

Table 3 Export Share of East Asia in 2001(%)

from/to	ASEAN 10	China	Japan	ROK	ASEAN+3	NAFTA	USA	EU
Brunei	16.5	4.1	46.5	12.4	79.4	11.7	11.6	1.5
Cambodia	5.9	1.3	1.0	0.1	8.3	65.0	64.2	24.8
Indonesia	17.8	5.4	20.9	6.3	50.4	16.9	15.3	13.8
Laos	44.5	1.7	1.4	0.0	47.6	1.4	0.9	25.6
Malaysia	25.1	4.3	13.3	3.4	46.1	21.6	20.2	13.6
Myanmar	33.7	4.4	3.3	1.7	43.1	17.9	16.4	14.4
Philippines	15.5	2.5	15.7	3.2	37.0	29.4	28.0	19.3
Singapore	27.0	4.4	7.7	3.9	42.9	16.3	15.4	13.4
Thailand	19.3	4.4	15.3	1.9	40.9	22.2	20.3	16.1
Vietnam	15.0	6.8	17.4	2.6	41.8	8.8	7.6	26.8
ASEAN 10	22.3	4.5	13.6	3.8	44.2	19.5	18.2	14.9
China	6.9		16.9	4.7	28.5	22.4	20.4	15.4
Japan	13.5	7.7		6.3	27.4	33.1	30.4	16.0
ROK	11.0	12.1	11.0		34.1	23.7	20.9	13.1
ASEAN+3	14.6	5.5	9.5	4.3	33.9	25.2	23.1	15.1

Source: IMF, Direction of Trade Statistics Year Book 2002.

II. East Asia Integration

FTA tends to produce positive effects on FTA member economies, while negative effects on non-member economies.

The recent study[1] finds that FTAs would increase export and foreign direct investment but also foreign indirect investment, and that these export-and-investment-increasing effects would be large and long-lasting. Details are discussed as follows:

FTA has *direct effects*. One is a *trade diversion effect*, the static effect, which increases exports within the FTA region, as a result of optimum resource allocation through correction of market distortions, while it decreases exports of the non-member: Prices of imports from FTA member economies decrease and then increase imports from them, but decrease import from non-member economies due to the relative rise of import prices of non-members to members. The magnitude of *trade diversion effect* depends primarily on (1) degree of interdependence and complementarities of trade, (2) the size of the member economies, and (3) reduction of existing barriers.

The other is an *investment diversion effect* that increases investments including foreign direct investment in member country as a result of optimum resource allocation as well. This effect depends upon investment environment.

FTA also has an *indirect effect*, which increases international capital inflows (indirect investment). The *indirect effect* through international capital flight depends on the expected profits. By reduction of barriers, expected rates of return on investment relatively rise to other region and as a result, inflows of international capital increase. This effect is considered to be strong. For instance, Japan will increase international capital inflows when barriers in ASEAN and China are reduced. It is because Japanese firms have a large capital stock in these countries and also import from them for production. That is, Japanese firms can improve their consolidated accounts through the rise of expected profits of their affiliated firms in ASEAN and Japan,

---

[1] See Kazuhiko Oyamada (2003).

when barriers are reduced.

ASEAN Integration

The economic integration process in East Asia still remains in the ASEAN integration stage. The original six ASEAN member states (Brunei, Indonesia, Malaysia, the Philippines, Singapore and Thailand) are expected to achieve the first step towards the formation of the ASEAN Free Trade Area (AFTA), by introducing the Common Effective Preferential Tariff (CEPT), by which tariffs on goods traded within the region, which meet a 40% ASEAN content requirement, are reduced to less than 5 % in 2003. The same will apply for Vietnam by 2006, for Laos and Myanmar by 2008, and for Cambodia by 2010[1].

What effects are expected from the ASEAN integration? ASEAN would gain from the reduction of barriers that increase intra-regional trade. Japan also would benefit from the ASEAN integration, firstly because Japanese firms would expand exports to their affiliated firms in ASEAN, and secondly because Japanese affiliated firms in ASEAN would increase profits and eventually Japanese firms would improve their consolidated accounts. In fact, as March 2003, stock of foreign direct investment by Japan in the ASEAN six amounts to US $ 79 billion, which is larger than that in China, US $ 24 billion.

ASEAN plans to liberalize investment and services, and to facilitate the transnational mobility of goods in the region by various supplementary measures such as improving custom procedures, standards and conformance, and so on. These facilitation measures will improve business environment and Japan will bene-

---

[1] Each member state has the option of excluding products from the CEPT scheme: temporary exclusions covering products to protect temporally but to be included in the scheme by 2005.

fit from it.

Table 4 Outward Foreign Direct Investment Stock of Japan
(FY1951—FY2002, Accumulated. US $ Million)

	Manufacturing	Non-manufacturing	Total
Indonesia	11,869	14,875	26,859
Malaysia	7,379	2,500	9,910
The Philippines	4,863	2,307	7,252
Singapore	7,375	10,123	17,650
Thailand	11,173	4,087	16,216
Vietnam	1,090	215	1,376
ASEAN6	43,748	34,107	79,263
China	16,526	6,570	23,757
ROK	5,056	4,099	9,861
ASEAN+3 Region	65,330	44,775	112,882
Hong Kong, China	2,737	16,982	20,250
Taipei, China	4,916	1,849	7,142
East Asia	72,983	63,606	140,273
USA	112,234	204,973	319,206
Europe	60,093	143,844	207,072
World Total	282,473	547,821	841,784

Source: Ministry of Finance of Japan, Foreign Direct Investment, compiled by JETRO. Notes: Total includes manufacturing, non-manufacturing and branches.

Integration of ASEAN+1

ASEAN can benefit more from the ASEAN + 1 FTA. ASEAN and China agreed the framework of an ASEAN-China Free Trade Area, in November 2002, according to which the original six ASEAN members and China will start tariff reduction for agricultural products in June 2004 and for manufactured goods in 2005, and accomplish them in 2010. The newer ASEAN member countries of Cambodia, Laos, Myanmar and Vietnam (CLMV) and China will start it for agricultural product in 2006 and manufactured goods in 2010, and finish in 2015. In advance to the agreement between ASEAN and China, they agreed to liberalize some of agricultural products, which started in October 2003.

Japan has proposed the Comprehensive Economic Partnership (AJCEP), which aims to strengthen economic partnership between the whole ASEAN and Japan. The 10th Consultation between the ASEAN Economic Ministers (AEM) and Ministry of Economy, Trade and Industry (METI) of Japan, held in Phnom Penh, Cambodia on September 3, 2003, agreed to recommend to the leaders that ASEAN and Japan should implement the elements of the AJCEP as soon as possible by 2012, allowing additional five years for the newer ASEAN member countries. For this purpose, the Ministers agreed that consultations of the start from the beginning of 2004, and that both ASEAN and Japan shall exert maximum efforts to commence their negotiations from the beginning of 2005. [1] Bilateral talks between ASEAN countries and Japan will be launched. Indeed, Japan started the working level committee with Thailand in September 2002, the Philippines in October 2002, and Malaysia in May 2003. Also Japan and Indonesia reached an agreement to start the working level committee in June 2003. These bilateral talks will proceed in parallel with the AJCEP.

From these ASEAN+1 FTAs, ASEAN would get quite a large benefit. Especially, from the ASEAN-Japan FTA, ASEAN would sustain high economic growth driven by a large and long-lasting increase of exports and investments[2]. This is because ASEAN has a closer and complementary trade relationship with Japan, whose economic size is very large, nearly eight times of the ASEAN 10 economy. In fact, ASEAN exports 13.7% of total exports directed to Japan. From these ASEAN+1 FTAs, ASEAN would get quite a large benefit. Especially,

---

[1] The AEM-METI (2003).
[2] See ASEAN-Japan Research Institute Meeting (2003).

from the ASEAN-Japan FTA, ASEAN would sustain high economic growth driven by a large and long-lasting increase of exports and investments[①]. This is because ASEAN has a closer and complementary trade relationship with Japan, whose economic size is very large, nearly eight times of the ASEAN 10 economy. In fact, ASEAN exports 13.7% of total exports directed to Japan. On the other hand, from the FTA with ASEAN, Japan would also benefit substantially, because exports of Japan directed to ASEAN amounts to 13.4 % of total exports of Japan.

Table 5 ASEAN-Japan Relationship in the Last Three Decades

1977	Japanese Prime Minister Takeo Fukuda has met with ASEAN leaders at the Second ASEAN Summit Meeting.
1992	The AEM-METI between ASEAN and Japan has been held every year.
2000 Sep.	The Japan-Singapore Joint Study Group Report
2001 Oct.	The Japan-Singapore Economic Partnership Agreement (JSEPA) has completed negotiation.
2002 Jan.	JSEPA is concluded. The ASEAN-Japan Comprehensive Economic Partnership (AJCEP) has prop.
Sep.	The AEM-METI recommended the Leaders to commence consideration of a framework.
Nov.	The leaders have signed a joint declaration of AJCEP.
2003 Mar	The AJCEP Committee has set up.
Oct.	The framework of AJCEP is expeceted to be agreed.
2004	Completion of the AJCEP between the original ASEAN six members and Japan
2005	Negotiation of the AJCEP
2012	Completion of the AJCEP between the original six ASEAN members and Japan
2015	Completion of the AJCEP between the newer ASEAN members and Japan

Source: Compiled from the Ministry of Foreign Affairs of Japan.

Similarly, ASEAN will get benefit from the ASEAN-China

---

① See ASEAN-Japan Research Institute Meeting (2003).

FTA, but its gain would be smaller than that of ASEAN-Japan FTA. It is because the Chinese economy is more than two times of that of the ASEAN 10 economy, but just 28% of that of Japan. The export of ASEAN directed to China occupies only 4.5% of total exports of ASEAN. On the other hand, China will also benefit from the ASEAN-China FTA, because the size of ASEAN 10 economy is as large as nearly half of that of China.

In reality, the ASEAN-China FTA goes ahead before the ASEAN-Japan FTA. What impact can be expected if ASEAN and Japan were to agree on an ASEAN-Japan FTA after an ASEAN-China FTA? In this case, ASEAN economies would enjoy combined benefits from the two FTAs because ASEAN would be a hub connecting Japan and China. At the same time, Japan would also gain from the ASEAN-Japan FTA. The magnitude of the effects would be considerable for a Japanese economy that has stagnated for a long period of time.

From the ASEAN-ROK FTA, ROK will benefit more than ASEAN, because the combined GDP of the ASEAN 10 economy is larger than that of ROK, and the exports to ASEAN accounts for 11.0 % of total exports of ROK. In addition, ROK firms have not a small foreign direct investment in ASEAN.

Integration of ASEAN+3

The combined GDP of ASEAN countries, China, Japan and ROK amounts to US $ 6,305 billion in 2001, accounting for 20.1% of the world economy. If these economies are integrated, they will benefit greatly to all the members, and thus, East Asia would invite a large plenty of international capital flows from the rest of the world, that is, the NAFTA and the EU (see Figure 3).

Figure 3

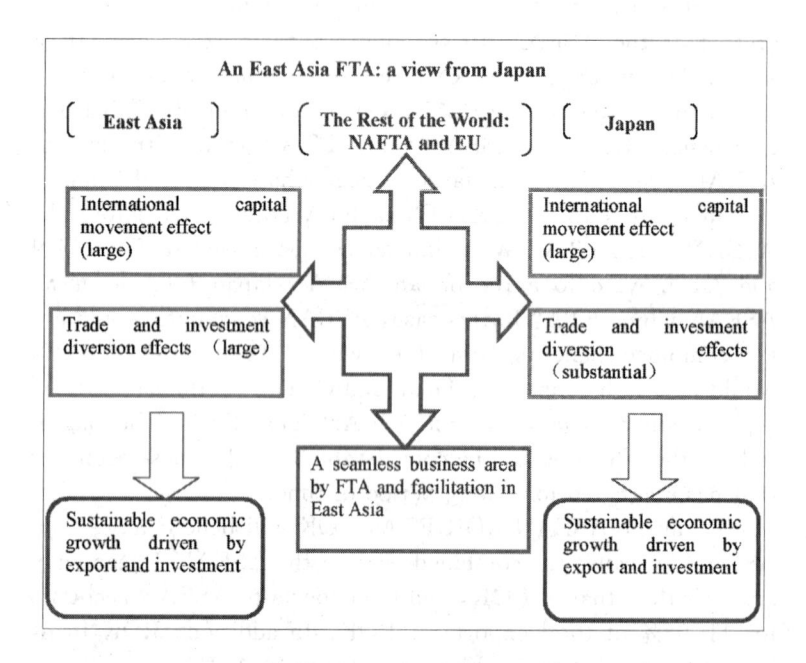

```
An East Asia FTA: a view from Japan
[ East Asia ]   [ The Rest of the World:   [ Japan ]
                  NAFTA and EU ]
```

International capital movement effect (large)		International capital movement effect (large)
Trade and investment diversion effects (large)	A seamless business area by FTA and facilitation in East Asia	Trade and investment diversion effects (substantial)
Sustainable economic growth driven by export and investment		Sustainable economic growth driven by export and investment

For Japan, the combined GDP of ASEAN 10, China and ROK accounts for nearly half of that of Japan, and the export of Japan directed to the region amounts to 27.4 % of total Japanese export, which is larger than the export share to EU, 16.0%, and almost equivalent to the export share to the US, 34.1%. In addition, Japan has a very large capital stock in the region, approximately US $ 130 billion.

The effect from the East Asia FTA seems to be large, but the actual effect depends on business environment. In this regard, each country has to improve trade and investment environment. The policy environments that facilitate business activities in the region such as custom procedure, standards and conformance, and intellectual rights have to be jointly improved by countries in the region. Such joint collaborations that improve policy environments would build mutual trust and solidarity of the region, and foster an international consensus of formation of East Asia FTA as well as institutionalization of East Asia Cooperation.

III. An Assessment of Institutionalized Cooperation in East Asia

The existing ASEAN+3 dialogue relations have been built and strengthened since 1997. The Asian financial crisis that erupted in July 1997 has given rise to the recognition that East Asia urgently needs to institutionalize its cooperation and strengthen economic relation. Since then, the ASEAN+3 processes have developed. The 2nd ASEAN Informal Summit meeting, held in Kuala Lumpur in December 1997, invited the leaders of China, Japan and ROK. The ASEAN+3 leaders discussed the appropriate policy as a response to the crisis, and endorsed the early implementation of the Manila Framework proposed by the Finance and Central Bank Deputies Meeting, in November 1997, to enhance regional surveillance, strengthen economic and technical cooperation, support measures to strengthen the IMS' capacity to respond to financial crises and the proposed financing arrangement.

The regional cooperation has been strengthened by the 2nd ASEAN+3 Summit in December 1998 and 3rd ASEAN+3 Summit in November 1999. The leaders, who met in 1998, recognized a regular meeting and agreed to establish the East Asia Vision Group (EAVG), which was proposed by ROK President Kim Dae-jung. In 1999 the leaders issued a Joint Statement on East Asia Cooperation, which agreed to enhance dialogue process and strengthen cooperation with a view to advance East Asia collaboration in priority areas of shared interest.

The EAVG has contributed to strengthen the dialogue process and regional cooperation. The EAVG, an academic group, chaired by the former Foreign Minister, Han Sung Joo, had a meeting in Seoul in 1999 attended by two academic representatives from each of the ASEAN + 3 countries, and subsequent meetings in Shanghai, Tokyo, Bali and Seoul. The final report of EAVG, which was submitted in November 2001,[1] contains key proposals and concrete measures; They are (1) an East Asia Free Trade Area (EAFTA) liberalizing trade ahead of APEC's goal, (2) an expansion of the framework agreement on an ASEAN Investment Area to all of East Asia, (3) promotion of development and technical cooperation among regional countries, (4) realization of a knowledge-based economy and the establishment of a future-oriented economic structure, (5) establishment of a self-help regional facility for financial cooperation, (6) adoption of a better exchange rate coordination mechanism consistent with financial stability, (7) strengthening of the regional monitoring and surveillance process within East Asia to supplement IMF global surveillance, (8) institutionalizing bilateral and multilateral environment cooperation within the region, (9) establishment of poverty alleviation programs, (10) implementation of a comprehensive human resource program, (11) evolution of the annual summit meeting of ASEAN + 3 process into the East Asian Summit, (12) establishment of an East Asia Forum, and so on.

At the 4th ASEAN + 3 Summit meeting held in November 2000, the leaders discussed the issue of how to promote ASEAN + 3 cooperation[2]. The ASEAN leaders remarked that they should consider the possibility of holding an "East Asia Summit" (EAS) to promote cooperation in East Asia. The leaders agreed

---

[1] The Report of the East Asia Vision Group was submitted to the 5th ASEAN+3 Summit in November 2001. See East Asia Vision Group (2001).

[2] See the Ministry of Foreign Affairs of Japan (2000).

to establish the East Asia Study Group (EASG), which would consider the possibility of the EAS as well as the EAFTA.

The EASG, consisting of thirteen Senior Officials of Meeting (SOM) leaders of ASEAN countries, China, Japan and ROK, and the Secretary-General of ASEAN, was mandated to assess the recommendation by the EAVG. In July 2001, a Working Group at the level of Director-General was set up to assist the work of the EASG. The EASG held six meetings from March 2001 to October 2002, and its Working Group also held six meetings from July 2001 to August 2002. ROK and the Chair of the ASEAN Standing Committee served as the Co-chairs of the EASG and its Working Group. The final report was submitted to the 6th ASEAN+3 Summit in Phnom Penh, Cambodia, in November 2002.

The EASG recommends 26 concrete measures,[1] 17 short-term measures and 9 medium-term and long-term measures. The EASG recommends that the government of East Asia countries consider the establishment of an EAFTA, as a long-term goal. The EASG also come to a conclusion that the East Asia Summit will serve to strengthen regional cooperation and recommends pursuing the evolution of the ASEAN+3 Summit into an East Asian Summit as a way to institutionalize cooperation in East Asia.

---

[1] See the East Asia Study Group (2002).

Table 6 26 Measures Recommended by the East Asia Study Group

Short-term measures
(1) form and East Asian Business Council
(2) establish GSP status and preferential treatment for the least developed countries
(3) foster an attractive investment environment
(4) establish an East Asia Investment Information Network
(5) develop resources and infrastructure jointly
(6) provide assistance and cooperation in infrastructure, information
(7) cooperate through technology transfer and joint technology development
(8) develop information technology jointly
(9) build a network of East Asian think-tanks
(10) establish an East Asia Forum
(11) implement a comprehensive human resource development program
(12) establish poverty alleviation program
(13) take concreted steps to provide access to primary health care for the people
(14) strengthen mechanism for cooperation on non-traditional security issues
(15) work together with cultural and educational institutions to promote a strong sense of identity and an East Asia Consciousness
(16) promote networking and exchange of experts in the conservation of arts
(17) promote East Asian studies in the region
Medium-term and long-term measures
(1) form an EAFTA
(2) promote investment by SMEs
(3) establish an East Asia Investment Area
(4) establish a regional financing facility, and coordination
(5) pursue a more closely coordinated regional exchange rate mechanism
(6) pursue the evolution of the ASEAN+3 Summit into an East Asia Summit
(7) promote closer regional marine environmental cooperation
(8) build a framework for energy policies and strategies
(9) work closely with NGO in policy consultation

Source: East Asia Study Group, *Final Report of the East Asia Study Group.*

Table 7 The ASEAN+3 Process

1997 Dec. 14—16	The 1st ASEAN+3 Summit (the 2nd ASEAN Informal Summit) in Kuala Lumpur	The leaders of China, Japan and ROK were invited. The first ASEAN + 3 summit was followed by separate ASEAN+1 summits.
1998 Dec. 15—16	The 2nd ASEAN+3 Summit (The 6th ASEAN Summit) in Hanoi	An East Asia Vision Group was proposed by ROK. The Leaders recognized the importance of holding a regular meeting among them.
1999 Nov. 28	The 3rd ASEAN+3 Summit (the 3rd ASEAN Informal Summit) in Manila	The ASEAN+3 leaders issued a Joint Statement on East Asia Cooperation that they agreed to enhance dialogue process and strengthen cooperation.
2000 May 6	ASEAN+3 Finance Minister Meeting in Chiang Mai	The ASEAN+3 agreed the Chiang Mai Initiative to strengthen East Asia Finance Cooperation.
Jul.	ASEAN+3 Foreign Minister Meeting	
Nov. 24	The 4th ASEAN+3 Summit (the 4th ASEAN Informal Summit) in Singapore	The summit concluded the East Asia Study Group would consider the possibility of an East Asian Summit as well as the possibility of a free trade and investment in East Asia.
2001 Jul. 24	ASEAN+3 Foreign Minister's Meeting	
Nov. 5	The 5th ASEAN+3 Summit (the 7th ASEAN Summit) in Bandar Seri Begawan	The East Asia Vision Group submitted the Report of the East Asia Vision to the ASEAN+3 Summit.
2002 Jul. 30	ASEAN+3 Foreign Minister	The need for regular ASEAN+3 Director General Meeting was endorsed in order to promote the institutionalization.
	Trilateral Meeting of the Foreign Minister of China, Japan and ROK	
Aug. 30	ASEAN+3 Director General in Seoul	

Nov. 4	The 6th ASEAN+3 Summit (the 8th ASEAN Summit) in Phnom Penh	The leaders expressed willingness to support the phased evolution of the ASEAN+3 summit into an East Asian summit.
		The Final Report of the East Asia Study Group. Many ASEAN leaders stated that cooperation for the Initiative for ASEAN Integration from China, Japan and ROK is important.
2003 May 6—7	The First ASEAN +3 Study Group	The Group on Facilitation and Promotion of Exchange of People and Human Resource Development
Jun. 17	ASEAN+3 Foreign Minister Meeting	
Jul. 3—4	The Second ASEAN +3 Study Group	The Group on Facilitation and Promotion of Exchange of People and Human Resource Development
Oct.	The Seventh ASEAN+3 Summit	

Source: Compiled by the author.

IV. A Road Map to the East Asia Community

At the ASEAN + 3 Summit meeting in November 2002, with regard to the report by the EASG, many leaders emphasized the significance of forming an East Asia free trade area,[①] and that the leaders of ASEAN+3 task the AEM+3 to conduct a feasibility study on the benefits, challenges, and implications of an EAFTA. They also expressed willingness to support the phased evolution of the ASEAN + 3 Summit into an East Asia Summit. Why we need an East Asia Summit and an organization of body of East Asia Community? Business society in East Asia needs a free business area, where all the rules of trade and investment are harmonized within the region. In accelerating such

---

[①] See the Ministry of Foreign Affairs of Japan (2003).

an economic integration, a regional institution is necessary.

Figure 4

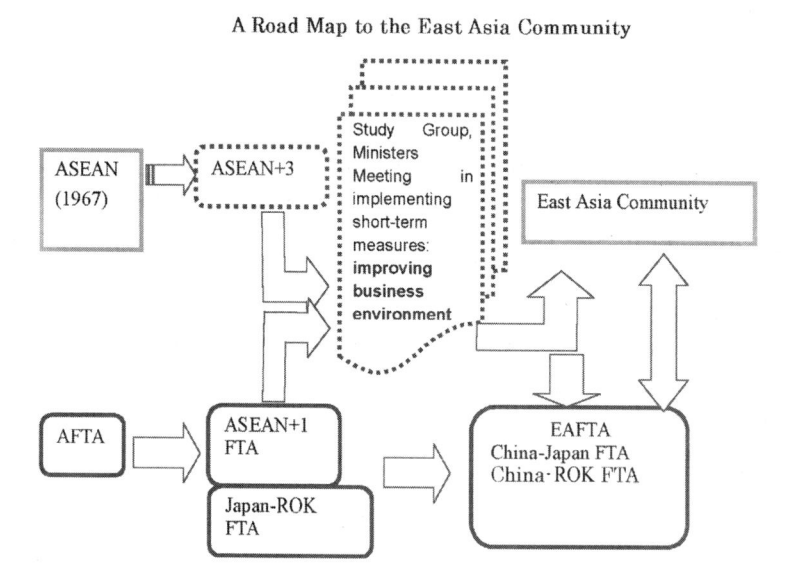

A Road Map to the East Asia Community

```
┌──────────┐     ┌──────────┐   ┌─────────────────┐   ┌──────────────────┐
│  ASEAN   │ ──▶ │ ASEAN+3  │   │ Study Group,    │   │ East Asia        │
│  (1967)  │     │          │   │ Ministers       │   │ Community        │
└──────────┘     └──────────┘   │ Meeting in      │   └──────────────────┘
                                │ implementing    │
                                │ short-term      │
                                │ measures:       │
                                │ improving       │
                                │ business        │
                                │ environment     │
                                └─────────────────┘

┌──────┐      ┌──────────┐        ┌──────────────────┐
│ AFTA │ ──▶  │ ASEAN+1  │  ───▶  │ EAFTA            │
└──────┘      │ FTA      │        │ China-Japan FTA  │
              │          │        │ China-ROK FTA    │
              │ Japan-ROK│        │                  │
              │ FTA      │        └──────────────────┘
              └──────────┘
```

By the way, what kind of road map to the East Asia Community can we describe? How the ASEAN + 3 framework can evolve into the East Asia community? First, implementation of the short-term measures would build a step to the East Asia Community. The measures recommended by the EASG contain significant tasks ahead for East Asia to meet the challenge of development; fostering an attractive investment environment, developing resource and infrastructure jointly, providing assistance and cooperation in infrastructure, information technology, human resources development and ASEAN regional economic integration, cooperation through technology transfer and joint technology development, developing information technology jointly to build telecommunications infrastructure and provide greater access to the Internet, implementation of a comprehensive human resources development program for Asia, establishment of poverty alleviation programs. In order to implement these tasks and to be well coordinated, institutionalizing cooperation is inevitable.

In implementing the short-term measures recommended by the EASG, study groups and ministerial level meetings would be formed. These meetings would gradually shape the East Asia Community and foster mutual trust and build consensus to establish the East Asia Community.

The step has already started. The first meeting for the ASEAN+3 Study Group on facilitation and promotion of labor exchanging and human resources development was held in Tokyo in May 2003, in Jakarta in July 2003, and in Bangkok in August. Some ASEAN members are interested in an increase of cross-border labor mobility. Facilitation of labor mobility would be one of the elements of the East Asia Community. The first ASEAN+3 Energy Policy Governing Group Meeting was held in Bangkok in August.

Academic circles can play a significant role in promoting institutionalization by studying why institutionalization of East Asia cooperation is necessary from various aspects.

References

AEM-METI, The Tenth Consultation between the Economic Ministers and the Ministers of Economy, Trade and Industry of Japan, *Joint Media Statement*, 3 September 2003, Phnom Penh, Cambodia.

ASEAN-Japan Research Institute Meeting (2003), *ASEAN-Japan Comprehensive Economic Partnership: Vision and Tasks Ahead*, July 22, 2003, the Institute of Developing

Economies, JETRO.

The East Asia Study Group, *Final Report of the East Asia Study Group*, 4 November 2002, Phnom Penh, Cambodia.

The East Asia Vision Group, *Towards An East Asian Community: Region of Peace, Prosperity and Progress*, 2001.

Hiratsuka, Daisuke (2003a), "Competitiveness of ASEAN, China and Japan", in Chapter 9, Yamazawa and Hiratsuka (eds.), *ASEAN-Japan Competitive Strategy*, the Institute of Developing Economies (forthcoming).

—— (2003b), "Competitive Strategy in the ASEAN Six Countries: Summary Finding from Individual Papers" in Chapter 1, Yamazawa and Hiratsuka (eds.), *ASEAN-Japan Competitive Strategy*, the Institute of Developing Economies (forthcoming).

Kazuhiko Oyamada (2003), "Forward-looking Impacts of Trade Relation Liberalization Between Japan and ASEAN Members", in Chapter 2, Yamazawa and Hiratsuka (eds.), *Towards ASEAN-Japan Comprehensive Economic Partnership*, the Institute of Developing Economies (forthcoming).

The Ministry of Foreign Affairs of Japan, "Summary of ASEAN + 3 Summit Meeting", 24 November 2000, http://www.mofa.go.jp/region/asia-paci/conference/asean3/summary0011.htm.

The Ministry of Foreign Affairs of Japan, "Summary of ASEAN + 3 Summit Meeting", 4 November, 2003, http://www.mofa.go.jp/region/asia-paci/conference/asean3/summary0211.htm.

An East Asian FTA: Recent Progress and Policy Implications

Inkyo Cheong[1]

Introduction

　　This paper examines the background of the recent embrace of trade agreements by China, Japan, and ROK. Discussions of a Japan-ASEAN FTA are under way, after talks of an FTA between ASEAN and China blossomed in late 2000. China and Japan are competitively promoting bilateral FTAs with ASEAN. As discussions of an FTA with ASEAN heat up in China and Japan, ROK has also begun reviewing the economic feasibility of an FTA with ASEAN. If China, Japan, and ROK competitively pursue bilateral FTAs with ASEAN, this may result in several important problems, including spaghetti bowl effects, a hub-and-spoke dilemma, or struggles for regional leadership. This report tries to show that an East Asian FTA covering the whole region is economically desirable, and stresses that East Asian countries should introduce a region-wide FTA rather than multiple bilateral or sub-regional FTAs. An East Asian FTA can be realized only in the long term because of economic, political, and social obstacles. East Asia, which already lags behind other regions in terms of regionalism, should not passively wait for the

---

[1] Inkyo Cheong, Senior Fellow, Korean Institute of International Policy.

East Asian FTA, which is likely to take some time to be established.

Recently East Asian countries have begun to scrutinize new vision of an East Asian economic cooperation and to consider various ways to execute such a vision. Despite the fact that the world economy is focusing on strengthening economic links through the formation of FTAs, there have been few discussions on similar cooperative efforts in East Asia. However, with a combined market of US $ 6. 2 trillion, a population of almost 2 billion, and a trade volume of US $ 2. 6 trillion in 2001, the region enjoys high industrial output, deposits of natural resources and further advances in economic development, which sets the stage for the possibility of an economic cooperation as well as greater economic benefits from regional economic integration such as an East Asian free trade agreement. Recent efforts by China, Japan, and the U. S. to forge closer economic relations with East Asian countries also hint at East Asia's economic potential.

Discussions on an East Asian FTA (EAFTA) were first officially initiated at the ASEAN+3 meeting in Brunei in November 2001. Discussions of an ASEAN-Japan FTA have progressed rapidly since talks of an FTA between ASEAN and China blossomed in late 2000. Japan is especially hastening discussions on an FTA with ASEAN for fear of losing its leadership position to China in the area of regional economic cooperation. On his January 2002 visit to Southeast Asia, Japan's Prime Minister Koizumi Junichiro proposed the establishment of the ASEAN-Japan FTA Study Group. Meanwhile, as discussions of an FTA with ASEAN heat up in China and Japan, ROK has also begun reviewing the rationality of an FTA with ASEAN.

If China, Japan, and ROK competitively pursue bilateral FTAs with ASEAN, this may result in several important problems such as the spaghetti bowl effects, a hub-and-spoke dilemma, regional leadership struggle, political instability, etc. Therefore, this paper tries to show that an East Asian FTA covering the whole region is economically desirable, and stresses that East Asian countries should introduce a region-wide FTA, rather than multiple bilateral or sub-regional FTAs. An East Asian FTA can be realized in the long term because of economic, political, and social obstacles. East Asian countries, which already lag behind countries in other regions in terms of regionalism, should not passively wait for the East Asian FTA, which is likely to take some time to be established. Rather, the current momentum of increasing discussions and interest in FTAs should be progressively promoted in order to realize the East Asian FTA. That is, a strategic approach is needed to develop the bilateral and sub-regional FTAs, currently under discussion, into an East Asian FTA.

I. Recent Developments Towards an East Asian FTA

Recently, there has been growing interest in FTAs in East Asia that could be attributed to the proliferation of regionalism, the East Asian financial crisis, and East Asia's awareness to boost its economic cooperation, China's WTO accession and the expansion of East Asian personal networks through various forms of meetings.

The main regional trade agreement in East Asia is the ASEAN Free Trade Area (AFTA). Initially composed of six member countries including Malaysia, Indonesia, Thailand, the Philippines, Singapore and Brunei, AFTA was formed as a result of the fourth ASEAN Summit meeting in 1992. With Vietnam joining in 1995, Myanmar and Laos in 1997 and Cambodia in 1999, AFTA developed into a regional trade agreement overseeing the entire Southeast Asian region. Recently, these countries have been discussing bilateral FTAs with China, Japan,

India and CER (the FTA between Australia and New Zealand), and it is known that the U. S. is considering establishing an FTA with ASEAN countries. ①

Until recently, the Northeast Asian countries — China, Japan, and ROK — have not participated in any regional trade agreements. After the financial crisis, however, these countries began to show a great interest in establishing FTAs. In 1998, ROK announced its plan to proceed with an FTA with Chile and also began a joint study with Japan. The ROK-Chile FTA negotiations were launched in December 1999 and in October 2002 the FTA was concluded. In addition to the FTA with Chile, ROK has been participating in joint research on the economic effects of bilateral FTAs with Japan, New Zealand and Thailand. The results of the joint research on the FTA with Japan, which started in 1999, were announced at international symposiums in Seoul and Tokyo respectively held in May and September 2000. Thereafter, by forming the Japan-ROK FTA Business Forum, the private sector of the two countries discussed the promotion direction for the FTA. Leaders at the Japan-ROK summit held in March 2002 agreed to form a government-led joint study group to give impetus to the discussions on the FTA. It is reported that the ROK government will establish its ground plan for the FTA with Japan based on the group's study results.

An occasion that showed the most dramatic change in the FTA policies of Northeast Asian countries was at the Singapore ASEAN-China summit in November 2000, when Chinese Premier Zhu Rongji proposed the possibility of an FTA with ASEAN. ②China proposed tariff reductions on 600 agricultural

---

① The U. S. announced a new trade initiative with ASEAN, implying the possibility of bilateral FTAs with some ASEAN countries. See "Fact Sheet: Enterprise for ASEAN Initiative" at www. whitehouse. gov.

② During the ASEAN+3 Summits, each country of Northeast Asia holds a bilateral summit with ASEAN.

items for ASEAN countries, and announced its wish to conclude an FTA with ASEAN by 2004 at the Phnom Penh ASEAN-China summit. Meanwhile, Japan also made it clear that it planned to promote an FTA with ASEAN within the next ten years. On November 6, 2002, the New Strait Times, the most acknowledged English newspaper in Southeast Asia, published an editorial stating "Japan, playing catch up with China, seeks a piece of the Free Trade Area Pie." In other words, instead of playing a leading role in promoting East Asian Regionalism, Japan was reacting passively to China's FTA policy.

Table 1 Progress of Regionalism in East Asia

FTAs	Progress				
	Discussion	Joint Study	Negotiation	Conclusion	Implementation
AFTA					V
AFTA-China			V		
AFTA-Japan		V			
AFTA-ROK	V				
AFTA-India	V				
AFTA-US	V				
China-Japan-ROK	V				
East Asian FTA	V				
Japan-Chile		V			
Japan-Canada	V				
Japan-Mexico			V		
Japan-Taiwan	V				
Japan-Singapore					V
ROK-Chile				V	
ROK-Japan		V			
ROK-Mexico	V				
ROK-New Zealand		V			
ROK-Singapore	V				
ROK-Thailand		V			

Source: Cheong (2002b).

Suggestions for a China-Japan-ROK FTA are mostly raised by private industries. For example, during the 15th ROK-Japan business conference held in Tokyo on October 29, 1998, ROK presenters proposed that the government of ROK examine the possibility of concluding a free trade agreement encompassing China, Japan, and ROK. Later, ROK business circles and economic organizations requested that the government promote a CJK FTA. At the China-ROK Economic Symposium (March 2002), held by the Chosun Daily of ROK and People Daily of China, in Beijing, ROK businessmen emphasized the promotion of a China-ROK FTA and a CJK FTA[①].

One of the most important developments towards an East Asian FTA is China's entry into the WTO and China's progressive approach to regionalism. According to Cao (2002), the goal of an FTA might differ country by country, however, common backgrounds can be a policy response against the expansion of regionalism and the complements of the shortcomings of the multilateral trading system. He also points out that a country could secure benefits in terms of trade and investment by concluding an FTA, and raise the ability to cope with shock from any possible economic crisis.

It is highly possible that China will be more progressive in considering bilateral and sub-regional FTAs in Northeast Asia after 2005. China announced plans to establish an FTA with ASEAN within 10 years; however the date could be advanced. China might launch an earlier FTA with the original six member countries (ASEAN-6) with a mid-to-long-term goal of launching an FTA with all ten ASEAN countries. The biggest advantage for China regarding the FTA policy is that once China's leaders promote an FTA within a certain region, the government can make rapid progress under its socialistic system of centralized de-

---

① In a survey conducted by the Federation of Korean Industries (FKI, 2001) targeting its member companies, ROK companies answered that the U. S. (36.8%) and China (29.3%) would be the two most desirable partners for bilateral FTAs.

cision-making. This contrasts with Japan and ROK where members in vulnerable industries and diverse interest groups could obstruct FTA negotiations. When China realizes the economic necessity of an FTA and decides that the internal and external conditions are ready, China will promote FTAs with its neighboring countries, in addition to ASEAN. The proposal for a study on an FTA of China, Japan and ROK can be an important momentum for China's FTA policy.

Japan did not pay serious attention to the formation of preferential trading blocs until 1998, emphasizing its consistent and endless efforts to maintain free trade under the multilateral trading system. The Ministry of Foreign Affairs (MOFA) also held a negative position toward regionalism in 1998. MOFA (1998) emphasized the problems of regional trading blocs and underlined the importance of strengthening the multilateral trading system. However, as ROK and Chile announced their plan to proceed with an FTA, Japan began to show an interest in entering an FTA with ROK. Japan established its first FTA with Singapore in January 2002, and is under negotiation with Mexico.

As East Asian countries have experienced disadvantages from the effects of regionalism in other regions, countries in East Asia have begun to consider establishing its own regional trade bloc recently. The 1997 financial crisis led the East Asian countries to realize the need to strengthen economic cooperation. A relationship between East Asia's financial crisis and regionalism can be found in studies by Bergsten (2000), Eichengreen (2002), Yamazawa (2001) and Yip (2001). Yamazawa (2001) asserts that the turning point in East Asian regionalism was the Asian financial crisis. "Through the experience of that awful time, policy makers in this region acknowledged that they were not equipped to prevent and manage such a crisis. They were irked by their helplessness and undue dependence on the international financial institutions in Washington, and they began to toy with the idea of resolving their problems for themselves within Asia."[1] Yip (2001) states that "on the monetary side, the single greatest push for East Asian regionalism was the financial crisis of 1997—1999."

Bergsten (2000) suggests that "another motivation for Asian regional initiatives is the failure of the existing international economic institutions to provide East Asia with a role consistent with its economic progress." In other words, East Asian countries have been neglected by international organizations like the IMF and IBRD. For example, although Japan's scale of economy is half the scale of the U. S. and Europe, its quota in these organizations is only 1/3 and 1/5 the quota of the U. S. and Europe, respectively. ROK, which ranks 11th in terms of scale of economy, has a very small quota, while China, ranked 2nd in purchasing power, was relegated to 11th place in the size of its quota. Disturbed by their small quotas, countries in East Asia began considering East Asian regionalism as a means of elevating their status in the international community.

The development of personal networks has been an important factor in accelerating recent talks on East Asian regionalism. While discussing economic cooperation between East Asia and Europe through ASEM, East Asian countries began to consider the need to reposition themselves at the regional level against the single entity of Europe. The ASEAN + 3 Summit first took place in 1997 when Malaysia's Prime Minister Mahathir unofficially invited the political leaders of China, Japan and ROK to ASEAN's 30th anniversary. This event sparked an acceleration of discussions on intra-regional economic cooperation and consolidation in East Asia. From the first to fourth Summit

---

[1] Bustelo (2002) denies that East Asia's financial crisis provided an opportunity to establish East Asia's regionalism by stating, "the short-and medium-term effects of the financial crisis might involve a backlash against regional and trans-Pacific economic integration".

meetings, the main agenda was on overcoming the financial crisis and strengthening intra-regional economic cooperation. At the third ASEAN+3 Summit in the Philippines in 1999, the "Joint Agreement on East Asian Cooperation" was announced as the basic principle of a long-term cooperation plan. The areas for cooperation were diverse, including trade, investment, technology transfers, e-commerce, agriculture, small and medium-sized businesses, tourism, and the development of the Mekong river basin.

After the financial crisis, East Asian countries realized the limit of export-oriented developmental policy, which mainly targeted the U.S. market. Being heavily dependent on a major export market like the U.S. made East Asia vulnerable to the negative effects stemming from a stagnating world economy. In order to prevent exposure to such risks, East Asian countries should strive to restructure and create their own demand by curbing dependence on non-Asian regions for exports, creating domestic demand or making intra-regional demand the driving force for stable economic growth. Besides the domestic efforts like improving the economic system, intra-regional trade liberalization through an FTA can be an effective scheme. Regarding this aspect, Munakata (2001a) points out that the East Asian regional market should be integrated to stimulate regional demand. While East Asian countries are concerned about the "hollowing out" of industries triggered by China's industrialization, they hope to make the most of China's economic growth. Moreover, as the stagnation of the world economy triggered a drop in East Asia's exports to other regions, the incentive for East Asian countries to expand exports to China is growing.

The possibility of an East Asian FTA has been actively discussed at ASEAN+3 meetings. An East Asian FTA was proposed by the East Asian Vision Group (EAVG)[1] in a report to the ASEAN+3 Summit in 2001, and the issue is expected to be at the top of the agenda at future ASEAN+3 Summit meetings. The East Asian Study Group (EASG), which was assigned to follow up the proposals by the EAVG, also proposed mid-to-long-term cooperative measures and additional subjects for study in its final report at the ASEAN+3 Summit at Phnom Penh in 2002. Some of the measures proposed in the report are the transformation of the ASEAN+3 Summit to the East Asia Summit, the establishment of an East Asia Investment Area, and an East Asian FTA. Through the official studies by EAVG and EASG, the members of ASEAN+3 began to realize the need for an FTA as a means of promoting economic integration in the region in the long-term, to cope with the economic integration in North America and Europe, and to promote the introduction of institutional measures for trade and investment liberalization in the region. This report recommends that the ASEAN+3 Economic Ministers undertake a feasibility study to examine the impacts, problems, and implications of an East Asian FTA.

While promoting an East Asian FTA may be difficult since there are tricky issues at hand, such as the economic gap between member countries and the struggle for leadership over the region, it may be feasible that East Asian countries promote an East Asian FTA while resolving these issues in the long term. However, there is a slight chance that rapid progress may be made in East Asian regionalism as East Asia feels the need to

---

[1] East Asian Vision Group was composed of twenty-six representatives from thirteen member countries (two representatives per country), and was assigned to produce a report for East Asian economic cooperation. The Vision Report was reported to the ASEAN+3 Summit held in Brunei Darussalam in November 2001. The report recommends that East Asia should pursue economic integration through the liberalization of trade and investment, developmental and technological cooperation, and information technology (IT) development.

strengthen economic cooperation in the face of the continuous global expansion of regionalism and the integration of the world economy concentrated in North America and Europe. This point has already been discussed at the ASEAN+3 Summit, and based on enough progress, leaders may discuss the possibility of an East Asian FTA in the future ASEAN+3 meeting. In November 2001, at the fifth Summit in Brunei, the participants examined the establishment of an East Asian FTA as suggested in the EAVG report. This was regarded to be especially meaningful to the three Northeast Asian countries, since it will initiate economic cooperation among them.

Since China's proposal to pursue an FTA with ASEAN during the Singapore ASEAN + 3 Summit meeting in November 2000, interest is mounting over whether China can become a leader in economic integration. Regarding FTAs, China and Japan show different approaches. As seen in its FTA with Singapore, Japan emphasizes the concept of the "New Age Agreement" or "Economic Partnership Agreement" which promotes financial cooperation, IT cooperation, and limited human resource mobilization while excluding the agricultural sector from the liberalization package. Meanwhile, the current ASEAN-China FTA under discussion shows China's intent to include even agricultural sector, under the "Early Harvest" package for ASEAN countries, so that they can benefit economically even before the conclusion of an agreement. These examples show the difference in the approaches of China and Japan. One country excluded the agricultural sector due to the weakness of its own agricultural sector, implying that the form it pursues will likely be used in future FTAs.

In contrast, the other country decided to promote FTAs while supporting the struggling regional countries. As long as Japan maintains its current position, it seems to be difficult for Japan to become a leader in economic integration. Recently the

Japanese government has been reflecting about FTAs, since ASEAN stresses the liberalization of its agricultural sector during the discussion of the ASEAN-Japan FTA, it will be difficult for Japan to exclude agriculture from the liberalization, as it was able to do for the FTA with Singapore.

The three Northeast Asian countries of China, Japan and ROK are now showing a more aggressive attitude toward establishing an East Asian FTA. China has already completed a joint study with ASEAN for a bilateral FTA, and is now discussing the FTA at the government level. Japan has also formed a joint study group with ASEAN. [1] At the Phnom Penh ASEAN-China Summit, ASEAN and China signed the Framework Agreement on ASEAN-China Economic Cooperation, which will serve as the fulcrum for establishing the free-trade area by 2010 for the older ASEAN members and 2015 for the newer members with flexibility on sensitive commodities. As China and Japan strengthen economic cooperation with ASEAN, ROK will inevitably re-evaluate an FTA with ASEAN. [2] ROK concluded an internal examination on the feasibility of an FTA with ASEAN, and it is known that it would propose official discussion on an ASEAN-ROK FTA in 2003 based on the result of this study.

II. Why East Asian Regionalism Lags Behind Europe and America

The world is tri-polar in terms of economics, but only bipolar in terms of regional institutions/initiatives. Along with North

---

[1] Munakata (2002) analyzes that "the November 2001 agreement between China and ASEAN to negotiate a free trade agreement sent a shock wave throughout Japan. Some speculated that Japan might try to block this initiative, which could deal a blow to Japan's regional leadership."

[2] During the ASEAN-ROK Summit in November 2001, Singaporean Prime Minister Goh Chok Tong suggested an FTA between ASEAN and ROK.

America and the EU, East Asia has developed into one of the world's three economic pillars; the Asian development model was greatly praised and the East Asian development was referred to as a "miracle" before the financial crisis. [1] However, struggles over hegemony and the lack of a leading country have hindered the development of an economic bloc in East Asia.

East Asia is the only remaining region without a regional economic bloc like the EU or NAFTA. Although regarded as one of the three major economic pillars, East Asia has the lowest level of economic cooperation compared to the EU and North America. Therefore, countries in East Asia need to strengthen regional economic cooperation.

Table 2 Status of East Asia's Economy (2001)   (unit: %)

	Population	GDP	Trade	FDI(2000)
Northeast Asia	24.1	20.1	12.7	7.7
ASEAN	8.7	1.9	5.7	1.8
East Asia	32.8	22.0	18.4	9.5
EU	6.2	23.7	17.0	43.9
NAFTA	6.9	40.0	22.0	24.0

Source: IMF (2002), *Direction of Trade Statistics: Yearbook.*
DRI (2002), *The World Economic Outlook*, 1st Quarter.
UNCTAD (2002), *World Investment Report.*

In the meantime, there have been some unsuccessful attempts to establish regionalism in East Asia. Some cases in point are when Malaysian Prime Minister Mahathir proposed the establishment of an EAEG and when Japan attempted to create an Asian Monetary Fund in 1997, with both ending in failure. Yip (2001) shows that East Asia's regional economic integration will be difficult to achieve due to the different economic stance of each

---

[1] According to the World Bank (1993), East Asian countries grew at an annual rate of 7.4%, Africa 1.8% and Latin American countries 1.7% in the 1980s. East Asian economies kept a sustained and high economic growth at the beginning of the 1990s.

country and the opposition of non-Asian countries. Malaysia's proposal to create an EAEG including ASEAN member countries, China, Japan and ROK was perceived as an alliance of East Asian countries to confront North American and European economic integration amidst delays in the conclusion of the Uruguay Round. However, the proposal broke down due to a lukewarm response from East Asian countries and opposition from the U.S.. Although Malaysia modified its proposal to merely holding periodic conferences to discuss regional economic issues and coordinating economic policies, it ultimately collapsed under the strong objection of non-Asian countries. Japan suggested establishing an Asian Monetary Fund with US $100 billion, which East Asian countries could finance and manage without dependence on the IMF. But again, the plan was not realized owing to the wariness of several Southeast Asian countries toward Japan and the objections of Western countries.

There are currently two FTAs among East Asian countries: an AFTA of Southeast Asia and a Japan-Singapore FTA. Japan and ROK have been conducting a feasibility study on the economic impact of a bilateral FTA since 1999. China and Japan are in the process of negotiating bilateral FTAs with ASEAN. An East Asian FTA, which is an FTA including both regions in East Asia, is under discussion. During the ASEAN+3 Summit in 1999, the Philippines proposed unifying East Asia into one market by concluding an FTA.

According to Bustelo (2002), economic integration or regionalism has been occurring informally in East Asia for decades; however, except ASEAN, East Asia still seems far from establishing a formal regionalism like that of Western Europe. The major characteristic of such an informal regional agreement is that there are no spillover effects from economic issues to other technical dimensions. Bustelo believes that such a dimensional limit can even be applied to ASEAN regionalism. However, his opinion is based on East Asian regionalism prior to the financial crisis so it may no longer be relevant to the ongoing debate on the official development of an East Asian FTA.

Possible reasons for the stagnation of East Asian regionalism include the high dependence on trade with the U.S., different political systems, certain aspects of the industrial structure, high economic growth before the crisis, historical factors and the lack of an initiating country.

A trade structure that is heavily dependent on the U.S. has led to greater East Asian interest in economic cooperation with the superpower and less interest in promoting similar cooperation within the region. ① More than 20% of the total exports of most East Asian countries are to the U.S., while Japan and Malaysia's export dependence rates on the U.S. are about 30%. As a result, East Asian countries have not felt a serious need to establish an East Asian regional trade bloc.

Under the Cold War ideology of the 1970s and 1980s when the East Asian economy began to develop full-scale, the U.S. refrained from provoking trade frictions and absorbed exports from developing East Asian countries despite its severe trade deficit. Consequently, East Asian countries looked towards the U.S., which provided large open markets with relatively fewer trade barriers. The U.S., for its part, did not want the formation of a separate trade bloc in East Asia, emphasizing the fact that the U.S. was the biggest importer of East Asian goods.

Despite the great global interest in FTAs in the 1980s, developing countries in East Asia did not feel the need for such agreements since their economies were growing rapidly and they were being praised as the 'miracle of East Asia'. The East Asian region could record higher economic growth rates, and "thus did

---

① This fact is reflected in trade flows. Eichengreen (2002) shows that East Asia's intra-regional trade ratios are low by the standard of the EU.

not feel any need to secure markets through discriminatory economic integration agreements". (Munakata 2001b, p. 2) Developing countries in East Asia achieved an increase in exports and economic growth from a favorable loose international trade environment with the Generalized System of Preferences (GSP) provided by advanced countries.

Except Japan, developing countries in East Asia had similar export structures. It was thought that the East Asian market was not large and thus it was unlikely to expand intra-regional trade. Therefore, expanding exports to lucrative non-Asian third markets like the U.S. was considered as a shortcut to economic growth.

Moreover, problems in industrial structures also hindered the development of East Asian regionalism. Even with the establishment of an FTA, if the benefits of regional trade liberalization are limited because countries in the region have similar industrial structure, regionalism is not likely to develop into deep integration in the short run. Unlike Northeast Asia, Southeast Asia got a head start in developing regionalism, to be exactly, launching AFTA in January 2002. Nevertheless, Southeast Asia has not shown much interest in extending AFTA to Northeast Asia to form an East Asian FTA. There are several possible explanations for this, and the fact that the industrial structure of Southeast Asian countries is not conducive to economically benefit from an FTA is one of the reasons. With AFTA, industries in member countries did not stand to gain much from the agreement and thus did not exert pressure to accelerate economic integration.

A considerable part of the manufacturing sector was established through foreign direct investment and major components were brought in from parent companies located overseas. These characteristics made it difficult to satisfy the preferential rules of origin under AFTA. Currently, the volume of intra-regional trade is around 25% of AFTA's total exports, and 60% to 70% of that is composed of transactions between Singapore, Malaysia, and Indonesia. If trans-shipments from Singapore's free port are excluded, the volume of regional trade is only 5%. The only industries that benefited from AFTA were probably the oil and mining sectors. Even in Malaysia, where the volume of regional trade with other ASEAN countries amounts to 20% to 25%, only 3% of the goods exported to ASEAN are subject to AFTA's Common Effective Preferential Tariffs (CEPT). Thus, AFTA has failed to attract the interest and support of the private sectors and its expansion to other regions such as Northeast Asia has been limited.

Political factors also negatively affected the development of an East Asian FTA. East Asia has experienced wars and ideological conflicts. Still holding memories of Japan's hostile invasions, China, ROK, and several Southeast Asian countries tend to distrust Japan on political issues. *The Economist* (2002) describes Chinese-Japanese relations as "less than cordial", stating that China and Japan mistrust each other.

China experienced ideological conflicts with other East Asian countries because of its socialist system, and ROK, Vietnam and Cambodia were internally divided by ideological differences. Southeast Asian countries created ASEAN to confront the fall of Indochina to communism, with the political purpose of strengthening ties and voicing positions. Faced with potential competition over regional leadership in East Asia, neither Japan nor China could initiate regional cooperation through regionalism during the Cold War as any active gesture to establish a trading bloc by either country could provoke the other country. In addition, Japan's history of military aggression makes East Asian regionalism even harder to develop. Eichengreen (2002) says that "Asian governments are suspicious of strong supranational institutions", and "regional integration tends to be organized on the basis of 'soft institutionalism'".

In contrast, in the case of Europe, economic integration was promoted to dissipate the remaining hostilities of war and as a result, went beyond "Fortress Europe" to adopt a unified currency and parliament. However, similar developments did not happen in East Asia. Differences between Europe and East Asia arise from the fact that East Asian countries share few economic and political similarities compared to the countries in Europe. East Asia also lacks a leader or leading country to initiate economic integration. In the case of European unification, Jean Monnet and Robert Schuman laid the foundation by insisting that strengthened economic cooperation would help maintain peace. [1] However, such figures have yet to appear in East Asia. In Europe, the main disputing players, Germany and France, took the leading role to influence economic integration and induce the participation of neighboring countries whereas no East Asian country has emerged to play a similar role for East Asian integration. Japan is the most promising country in terms of economic power, but it has not yet taken a leadership role to an extent befitting its stature.

At the same time, Yip (2001) believes that East Asian regionalism has been delayed owing to political factors rather than economic reasons. He points out that many East Asian countries were under a system of regional security established by the U.S., thus were not able to construct an independent regionalism. After World War II, the U.S., in order to protect its own interests in East Asia, tried to hinder foreign nations from expanding their power and continued to cooperate economically with East Asia while facilitating regional order and security. As a result, the U.S. gained hegemony in East Asia and may react

---

[1] Refer to Fontaine (1992) for the roles of Jean Monnet and Robert Schuman in the early stage of European integration.

sensitively to East Asia's economic integration efforts that exclude the U.S. in light of the following three concerns: 1) East Asian countries might build up military power through economic growth, and as a result, threaten order and security in the region. 2) Conflicts between East Asia and the West might intensify and East Asia might attain regional leadership through the economic integration, 3) The smaller countries of East Asia might unite with a regional power like China and Japan and challenge U.S. hegemony.

On the other hand, there is opposition to economic integration in East Asia within the region. Historically, China has been known to avoid formal economic/political cooperation initiatives that can influence its internal policy decisions. Also there still remains antagonism and competition among East Asian countries stemming from Japan's past imperialism. Japan's refusal to make an official apology impedes East Asia's regional integration.

Recently, the politically antagonistic relationships in Northeast Asia seem to have been mitigated to some extent. Munakata (2001a) observes that "trilateral relations among the U.S., Japan and China are improving simultaneously, an unusual situation, since the terrorist attacks," and "Tokyo-Beijing tensions have substantially eased." Munakata (2002) describes this phenomenon by stating, "it is remarkable that the competitive tension among China, Japan and ROK created enhanced momentum for regional cooperation." She also suggests "East Asian leaders should not let this historic opportunity slip away".

III. How to Achieve an East Asian FTA

This chapter discussed regionalism within East Asia, which is now in progress, and reasons for its slow development in East Asia. Cheong (2002b) assumed eight hypothetical FTAs in East Asia and estimated their economic effects. The findings show that member countries would benefit from both bilateral FTAs and regional FTAs, like a China-Japan-ROK (CJK) FTA and an East Asian FTA. However, the analysis shows that greater economic benefits would be derived under a regional FTA like a CJK FTA rather than under a bilateral FTA. Although the simulation used in the study estimated that a CJK FTA and East Asian FTA would bring a similar level of economic benefits, the chapter argues that greater benefits would be gained under an East Asian FTA than a CJK FTA, which could be verified with a more sophisticated economic model and analytical method. Here, a question we need to answer is how to achieve the East Asian FTA.

There are several possible ways to promote an East Asian FTA. Under current conditions, it may be difficult to promote an FTA covering the whole East Asian region in the short term, due to various reasons, although it is the most economically desirable approach for the region. Therefore as the second best alternative, an East Asian FTA should be phased in starting with the FTAs currently under discussion. Each country in Northeast Asia may form a bilateral FTA with ASEAN, and gradually develop and expand the bilateral FTAs to an East Asian FTA. A similar scenario is to establish an East Asian FTA based on bilateral FTAs currently under active negotiation. Japan has already concluded an FTA (EPA) with Singapore; Japan and ROK are in the process of reviewing a bilateral FTA; and China and Japan are pursuing bilateral FTAs with ASEAN. Sooner or later, ROK will pursue an ASEAN-ROK FTA. Then, East Asia will observe a web of bilateral FTAs in the region. These FTAs would contribute to regional trade liberalization, and increase the need for an East Asian FTA while fostering a foundation for it.

However, consolidating different FTAs could be tremendously difficult since the different trade regulations under various bilateral FTAs will have to be standardized into one agreement.

Young (2002) states that "it is highly unlikely that an East Asian FTA will evolve by itself as a result of amalgamation of bilateral FTAs". Also, there is a possibility that the competition between China and Japan, countries currently vying for regional leadership, may be intensified through bilateral FTAs with ASEAN, making an East Asian FTA more difficult.

The third option is to create a CJK FTA in Northeast Asia, rather than multiple bilateral FTAs, and then to move in the direction of consolidating it with AFTA. Wanandi (2000) supports this approach to the East Asian FTA, asserting that a region-wide FTA can be established in the mid-to-long-term through bilateral negotiations and activation of sub-regionalism in East Asia. He emphasizes that the AFTA together with the Japan-ROK FTA will play the most important role in forming an East Asian FTA.

Although Japan and ROK are officially discussing a bilateral FTA, it will be difficult for the two countries to ignore China's position, considering the political and economic relations of countries in Northeast Asia. With its entry to WTO and negotiation of an FTA with ASEAN countries, China expects to build a stable market economy and to be ready to promote FTAs in the near future. China's recent proposal of examining a CJK FTA has complicated the FTA issue in Northeast Asia. ROK supported the Chinese proposal, which was presented at the China-Japan-ROK Summit at Phnom Penh, while Japan proposed that the Japan-ROK FTA currently under discussion be concluded first before pursuing a China-Japan FTA.

As the examination of a CJK FTA starts next year, Japan may wish for an early start on its FTA negotiations with ROK; however, it may not be easy for ROK to accept Japan's request. ROK has no assurance of benefiting from an FTA with Japan.

Japan absolutely needs an FTA with ROK[①], and it has a relatively advantageous position in negotiations, but has not been progressive in discussing a balanced agreement that would be acceptable to ROK. Since 1999, Japan has held the position that in an FTA with ROK, agricultural sectors be excluded. Japan has also tried to include the additional FTA plus measures that were included in the Japan-Singapore FTA. Related with this point, it is worth noting Tanaka (2002)'s views on Japan's FTA policy. He criticizes Japan's policy of promoting FTAs with neighboring countries in order to solve its domestic problems; rather, he argues, Japan should reinforce its industrial restructuring and boost domestic demand through economic stimulation prior to promoting an FTA with ROK.

Discussions on a CJK FTA and a Japan-ROK FTA will be carried out simultaneously starting from 2003, but considering the current situation, the Japan-ROK FTA is likely to progress more quickly. This presumption is based on the fact that the two countries have discussed their bilateral FTA since 1999. Furthermore, in addition to discussing their bilateral FTA, Japan and ROK should examine a scheme to invite China to participate in the two countries' FTA. In other words, Japan and ROK should utilize their FTA as a strategic framework for a CJK FTA in the mid term and an East Asian FTA in the long term. Thus when Japan and ROK form an FTA, it should be designed with China in mind as a potential member.

It would be ideal to have China as an initial member, but China is not ready to join. Because of this, China seems to propose a joint study on a CJK FTA. If Japan and ROK complete their FTA, then move to establish another FTA with ASEAN to

---

[①] Japan wants to conclude an FTA with ROK to escape from the difficulties from its economic recession and industrial structural adjustment, and to cope with China's aggressive FTA policy, etc. Japan's MOFA (2002) indicates that ROK is its most important FTA partner.

gradually initiate an East Asian FTA, China will inevitably feel conflicted about whether to participate in the East Asian FTA discussions or to construct its own independent regionalism. From an economic perspective, it is desirable for China to participate in an East Asian FTA. Rather than participating in an FTA of Japan-ROK-AFTA led by Japan, China could cope with a Japan-led East Asian regionalism by concluding an FTA with ASEAN early on and extending it to ROK.

In addition to the technical difficulties involved in consolidating multiple FTAs into a single FTA, the sequencing of FTAs in East Asia can raise other issues such as a hub-and-spoke problem, a struggle over regional leadership, political instability, etc. Also, without a clear understanding of the problems these issues could lead to, it will be difficult to construct a policy direction for East Asian economic cooperation. Countries aspire to become the regional FTA hub country in order to attain the benefits of trade expansion and FDI inflows. For instance, increased competitiveness by importing the most suitable raw materials from multiple spokes customs-free and expanding foreign direct investment inflow are some of the advantages. Also a hub country has many advantages in negotiating new FTAs and is in a better position to persuade its prospective partners to accept the conditions of its existing FTAs or other conditions favorable to itself. In a specific region, a hub country could also display its political and economic leadership. This is one of the reasons that China is promoting an FTA with ASEAN and Japan is promoting bilateral FTAs with ROK and ASEAN.

On the other hand, Wonnacott (1996) theoretically shows that constructing an FTA covering the whole region is more advantageous than a hub-and-spoke system. Investment is made in the most efficient industries only in a hub region, and spill over effects will be limited in the latter approach. In addition, a hub-and-spoke structure is relatively inefficient compared to a regional FTA due to the increase of trade-related costs. Since a hub constructs a complex trade network with multiple spokes, traders' compliance costs increase. Also businesses of the hub will pursue rent-seeking behavior. That is, firms in a hub try to maintain monopolistic positions in the hub-and-spoke structure, hindering a competitor from one spoke from branching out to another spoke. Finally, under a hub-and-spoke system, firms in a hub country are more likely to enforce a managed trade system, resulting in lower gains from specialization and trade. This is because, a spoke may have to accept worse provisions in a one-on-one bilateral negotiation with a hub than it would if it were to join an FTA instead which included that hub. Snape (1996) illustrates that multilateral trade liberalization can be impeded as a hub-and-spoke system develops in a specific region. Since individual spokes have preferential access to a hub, they will resist multilateral tariff reduction for sensitive items. Findlay (2000) concludes that the hub-and-spoke structure contains many dangers. There are strong incentives for economies to try to become the hub in an attempt to dominate economies in their region, leading to a structure of layers of discrimination and potential conflicts.

If ASEAN concludes bilateral FTAs with each of the Northeast Asian countries, it is possible that AFTA will become the hub and the three countries in Northeast Asia will remain as spokes. Scholars of Southeast Asia, including Chia Siow Yue and Hadi Soesastro hold the position that Southeast Asia can be a hub in an East Asian FTA.[①] According to these scholars, the

---

[①] Chia Siow Yue strongly advocated the hub role for ASEAN in East Asian regionalism at the Asian Economic Panel Meeting, Keio University, Tokyo, Japan, May 14−15, 2002. A similar point is made by Soesastro (2001, pp. 235-6), who states that "ASEAN may become some kind of a hub in East Asia, in which separate relations are developed between ASEAN (AFTA) and each of the three Northeast Asian countries."

Southeast Asian region could be a hub through bilateral FTAs with China, Japan and ROK, and the FTA with Australia and New Zealand since Southeast Asia has already launched AFTA and has the longest history of regionalism in East Asia.

However, it is questionable whether concluding multiple bilateral FTAs directly translates into becoming a hub. If the Southeast Asian region concludes bilateral FTAs with Northeast Asian countries, it will formally become a hub region. However, if Japan signs an FTA with ASEAN and further concludes bilateral FTAs with other countries, it is highly possible that Japan will become a *de facto* hub. A country can be a hub when it is equipped with economic power to lead other regions, advanced trading systems, and possesses political and diplomatic capabilities. Examples from Europe and North America show that either complete economic integration is formed or a country with strong political and diplomatic capabilities or strong economic power becomes a hub. [1] The EU, achieving complete integration, became a hub in FTAs with other regions and the U.S. became a hub in NAFTA due to its economic power and advanced trade system.

In addition to this, the characteristics of the Southeast Asian region can be a problem. Regarding this, Eichengreen (2002), quoting Katsenstein (1996), wrote that the decision-making system of member countries in AFTA interrupts the development of regionalism. "In comparison to Europe, [Southeast] Asian regionalism is not well institutionalized. Operating by consensus in regional organizations, Asian states exercise effective voting powers over collective actions." Not only has the consensus-based decision-making process hindered AFTA from achieving economic cooperation effectively, it will also render AFTA

---

[1] For example, although Mexico, a member of NAFTA, has established free trade with 32 countries through 10 FTAs, it is hardly recognized as a hub. In contrast, although the U.S. has fewer FTAs, it is considered the hub for NAFTA.

an example of "soft institutionalism" or "weak formal institutions" in the future. Under such circumstances, it is unrealistic for AFTA to lead the East Asian economic integration.

Regarding the hub role of ASEAN, Soesastro (2002) states that ASEAN needs to decide in the near future whether it will promote an East Asian FTA or bilateral FTAs with China, Japan and ROK. According to Soesastro, bilateral FTAs with individual Northeast Asian countries might be more beneficial for ASEAN; however, in that case, the content of AFTA, which ASEAN countries are forming, must be made more substantial.

Of course, China can be a hub like Japan. China and Japan's competitive pursuit over concluding bilateral FTAs with Southeast Asia, a situation that is happening in Northeast Asia, seems to be in line with their plan to secure a superior position in East Asia by emerging as a hub in East Asian regionalism. China's conclusion of an FTA with ASEAN will substantially improve its position for regional leadership. However, achieving an East Asian FTA will be even more complicated. A policy proposal made by Japanese Prime Minister Koizumi in Singapore in January 2002 on an East Asian FTA reveals Japan's competition with China over the regional leadership. ① Cao (2002) presents China's position on an FTA with ASEAN. According to him, an ASEAN-China FTA and a Japan-ROK FTA will coexist in East Asia for a while in the future with an East Asian FTA being established through the integration of both FTAs. Yet, he does not hide his opinion that establishing an East Asian FTA is most realistic with ROK and Japan individually joining the ASEAN-China FTA. Here, we see that China and Japan are competing

---

① During a speech entitled "Japan and ASEAN in East Asia—A Sincere and Open Partnership" in Singapore on January 14, 2002, Japanese Prime Minister Koizumi states "our goal should be the creation of a 'community that acts together and advances together.' And we should achieve this through expanding East Asia Cooperation founded upon the Japan-ASEAN relationship."

for the regional leadership through FTAs. If China and Japan are successful at concluding bilateral FTAs with ASEAN, it will be very difficult to build an East Asian FTA by integrating those two bilateral FTAs, because of the leadership struggle between China and Japan.

Conclusion

With an overview of the progress of worldwide regionalism, this paper discussed regionalism within East Asia, which is in process, and reasons for its slow development in East Asia. In many cases, the negative effects are emphasized more than the positive ones despite the fact that the positive effects exceed the negative ones. Since a social system to make a reasonable decision through a comprehensive evaluation does not always work, an FTA process is inevitably delayed. Winning public support at home is the foremost issue in concluding an FTA smoothly. Governments should endeavor to enhance people's understanding of the economic effects and the strategic importance of FTAs. While minority groups that will suffer from an FTA have voiced their opposition to the agreement, the majority who stand to benefit from it, have been passive in their reaction.

Regardless of how important a China-Japan-ROK FTA is, in terms of economic gains and strategic goals, such an agreement will not be easy to negotiate because the three countries have very different political, social, and historical perspectives. Unfortunately, mutual distrust among these countries is the greatest impediment to a political decision regarding the FTA. Ohnishi and Yin (2002, 70) point out that "building trust among the people of the three countries, rather than presenting the economical calculation of benefits, is the necessary step to realize the Japan-ROK FTA or China-Japan-ROK FTA." Border conflicts, distorted Japanese history textbooks, and the apparent pursuit of regional leadership by China and Japan damage the prospects for mutual trust among the three countries.

The governments must make an effort to resolve such political and social conflicts. It should be recognized, however, that sometimes these conflicts serve to emphasize the urgent need for concluding an agreement. For instance, one purpose for initiating European economic integration in the 1950s was to strengthen economic cooperation in order to prevent a war between Germany and France.

Since Japan and ROK are in the process of officially reviewing the possibility of an FTA, it is highly possible that the Japan-ROK FTA would be the first FTA in the Northeast Asia region. As previously mentioned, a Japan-ROK FTA is meaningful by itself, however, the two countries should adhere to an open policy to establish a Northeast Asian FTA by allowing China's participation with certain conditions. Improving the relationship between China and Japan could also be a decisive factor in establishing an East Asia FTA. Cheow (2001) asserts, "as long as relations between Asia's two powers (China and Japan) are not clearly ironed out, it is almost impossible to envisage greater and further pan-Asian economic co-operation." However, these political and social conflicts do not always act as obstacles to the development of FTAs. For example, it is well known that the EU was initiated with the purpose of preventing a war between Germany and France by strengthening economic cooperation. Unfortunately, East Asia did not have momentum to convert hostile relationship into more cooperative one.

References

Bergsten, C. Fred. 2000. "The New Asian Challenge", *Institute for International Economics (IIE) Working Paper 00-4*, IIE, Washington D. C..

Bustelo, Pablo. 2002. "The Impact of the Financial Crises on East Asian Regionalism", forthcoming in Liu, Fu-Kuo and Philippe Regnier (eds.), *Regionalism in East Asia: Paradigm Shifting?* Curzon Press, London.

Cao, Shi Gong. 2002. "Progress of China-ASEAN FTA and China's Position." Presented at 2002 International Forum on Northeast Asia Trade Policy Cooperation, Nanjing, China.

Cheong, Inkyo. 2002a. "Korea's FTA Policy: Focusing on Bilateral FTAs with Chile and Japan", KIEP, Seoul.

——. 2002b. "East Asian Economic Integration: Recent Development of FTAs and Policy Implications", KIEP, Seoul.

Cheow, Eric Teo Chu. 2001. "How to Define a Region of Closer Economic Co-operation in Asia?" Presented at the International Conference on Regional Economic Co-operation in Asia: Challenges for Europe. Organized by the Vienna Institute for International Economic Studies, Vienna, October.

Economist, "A Survey of Japan." April 20th—26th, 2002.

Eichengreen, Barry. 2002. "What to Do with the Chiang Mai Initiative." Presented at the Asian Economic Panel in Tokyo. Organized by KIEP, Center for International Development of Harvard University, and Keio University. May.

Federation of Korean Industries (FKI). 2001. "Korea Industries' Perception of an FTA", FKI, Seoul. *In Korean.*

Findley, Christopher. 2000. "Old Issues in New Regionalism." Presented at the 2000 APEC Economic Outlook Symposium. Manila, Philippines, July.

Fontaine, Pascal. 1992. "A New Idea for Europe: The Schuman Declaration—1950 — 2000", European Communities, Brussel.

Katsenstein, Peter J. 1996. "Regionalism in Comparative Perspective", *Cooperation and Conflict* 31: 123-59.

MOFA (Ministry of Foreign Affairs, Japan). 1998—2000. *Blue Book on Diplomacy* 1998, Volume 1. Tokyo. December. *In*

Japanese.

———. 2002. "Japan's FTA Strategy." Tokyo. October. *In Japanese.*

Munakata, Naoko. 2001a. " Focus on the Benefits Not Threats of Regional Economic Integration", *PacNet Newsletter*, CSIS, Jakarta. November 16.

——— 2001b. "Evolution of Japan's Policy toward Economic Integration", *CNAPS Working Paper*, the Brookings Institution, December.

——— 2002. "Seize the Moment for East Asian Economic Integration", *PacNet Newsletter*. CSIS, Jakarta. February 1.

Ohnishi, Hiroshi and Yin, Qing Zhu. 2002. "Effects of the Japan-Korea and Japan-Korea-China FTA Estimated by an Northeast Asian Model", presented at the Northeast Asian Economics Association Annual Meeting. Sejong Center for the Performing Art, Seoul, February 15.

Snape, Richard. 1996. " Which Regional Trade Agreement." In Bora, Bijit and Christopher Findley (eds.), *Regional Integration and the Asia Pacific*, Oxford University Press, Melbourne.

Soesastro, Hadi. 2001. "Towards an East Asian Regional Trading Arrangement", in Tay, Simon S. C., Jesus P. Estanislao, and Hadi Soesastro (eds.), *Reinvesting ASEAN*, ISEAS, Singapore.

Tanaka, Naoki. 2002. "Choice of Japan in the 21st Century and FTA Issues", the 23rd Symposium on FTA in East Asia. Tokyo. October 7.

UNCTAD. 2002. *World Investment Report.*

Wanandi, Jusof. 2000. "East Asian Institution Building". Remarks made at the 2000 annual meeting of the Trilateral Commission in Tokyo. (www.trilateral.org).

Wonnacott, Ronald. 1996. " Trade and Investment in a Hub-and-spoke System Versus a Free Trade Area." *World*

Economy 19: 237-52.

World Bank. 1993. *The East Asian Miracle—Economic Growth and Public Policy*. Oxford University Press, London.

Yamazawa, Kataro. 2001. "Approaches to Regional Economic Co-operation in Asia and Future Prospects." Presented at Regional Economic Co-operation in Asia: Challenges for Europe. Organized by the Vienna Institute for International Economic Studies. Vienna. October.

Yip, Wei Kiat. 2001. "Prospects for Closer Economic Integration in East Asia." *Stanford Journal of East Asian Affairs*, Vol. 1: 106-11.

Young, Soogil. 2002. "Challenges of Free Trade Agreements in the Asia-Pacific Region." Korea National Committee for Pacific Economic Cooperation (KOPEC), Seoul. August. *Unpublished Paper*.

Thai Perception on East Asian Cooperation

Nattapong Thongpakde[①]
Duangrudee Sirisatien
Wanasin Sattayanuwat
Pawanee Bumrungsri

I. Economic Structure of East Asia

This section investigates economic structure of ASEAN and the East Asian (EA) countries. It will also compare these data to those of other major economic groupings in order to observe EA's position in the world economy. In this paper, the East Asian economy consists of Southeast Asian, i. e. ASEAN 10 and Northeast Asian (NEA) economy including economies of Japan, China, Hong Kong and ROK.

ASEAN is small compared to other economic groups with regards to size of GDP and population. However, the size of the economy increases significantly if ASEAN integrates with NEA. EA establishes remarkable economic power. In 2001, it combined population of 2 billion persons and gross domestic product

---

[①] Nattapong Thongpakde, Dean, School of Development Administration, National Institute of Development Administration (NIDA) and Senior Consultant, Thailand Development Research Institute (TDRI). Duangrudee Sirisatien, Wanasin Sattayanuwat and Pawanee Bumrungsri are researchers, Thailand Development Research Institute (TDRI).

of US $ 6,427 billion. China is the biggest with respect to population (the highest in the world) while the Japanese economy is the largest (the second highest in the world). In the same year, the population of EU was 378 and that of NAFTA and FTAA was 416 and 825 million persons respectively (Table 1).

Whereas EA is notable in size compared to those of other groupings. However, left out China the size of population would be 703 million persons and the economy would be US $ 4,725 billion while the share of export in the world reduced to 21.3 percent and import to 20.7 percent. This suggests essential position of China in the region.

Compared to EU and NAFTA, EA is more diversifying. Japan is an industrial and fully developed country. ROK, Hong Kong and Singapore are NICs. ASEAN 6 and China are developing countries and CLMV are less developed countries. In 2001, the income per capita of Japan was US $ 32.6 thousand, 117 times that of Cambodia (US $ 277). Shares of manufacturing sector ranged from 7 percent for Myanmar to 35 percent for China. For higher income countries service sector is a dominant sector as presented in share of GDP.

ASEAN is even more diverse. The structure of production in ASEAN is mixed; some countries are still dominated by agricultural sector. Income highly varies among members as can be seen in coefficient of variation of GDP per capita. The coefficient of variation of GDP per capita of ASEAN was 1.94 in 2001; EA was 1.51 in 2001, compared to 0.34 of EU and 0.68 of NAFTA (Table 2).

ASEAN is open to the world market. Among ASEAN members, only the ratio of trade in GDP of Indonesia and Laos is less than one. NEA is less open with the exception of Hong Kong. This ratio of EA as a group was 0.5 less than that of EU but higher than NAFTA's. However, ASEAN is not the big player in the world; its share of world export was 7.3 percent and import was 6.7 percent. Nonetheless, EA, with its export amounting to US$ 1,588 billion in 2001, its export share in the world was 26.3 percent, while the share of import was 25.4 percent. This figure was still lower than other groups; NAFTA share of export and import were 26.1 and 33.3 % respectively. EU establishes the highest one.

II. Trade and Investment

Trade and investment are fundamentals for economic cooperation. Accordingly, this section explores trade structure of East Asian economies. Intra-and inter-regional trade will be measured up. Trade indices will be calculated to analyze attributes of trade competition and complemetarity among countries in the region. Trend of FDI in the region will also be illustrated.

Intra-Regional Trade

Trend of intra-regional trade within economic groups is continuously increasing. (Table 3). NAFTA's recent trade within its group amounted to 54.8 percent in 2001, a much increase from 33.6 percent in 1980. In the same year trading within upcoming FTAA also arrived at 60.1 percent, increasing from 43.4 percent in 1980. EU trade within its group was about 60 to 65 percent. Trade within ASEAN rose to 22.4 in 2001 from 17.4 in 1990, not so high compared to trade within EU, NAFTA and FTAA.

Since the economic crisis in 1997, Intra-ASEAN export shrunk during 1998—1999, from 24.2 percent to 21.6 percent, and rose again in 2000 to 23.2 percent. In terms of imports, ASEAN depends on each other less since its intra-regional share of import was only 21.8 in year 2000. (Tables 4 and 5)

Intra-regional trade of EA has been increasing but trade with outside is still important especially for ASEAN. Further investigating direction of export indicates that destination within ASEAN is important for ASEAN exports; however, its exports to NEA is higher and its share is increasing; while that to EU is declining and to US is high and stable. NEA export among the countries inside the region is essential especially in the case of China, which exports mainly to Hong Kong and Japan. ASEAN is less influential as destination of export for NEA compared to the US and EU. ROK and Japan export shares to ASEAN are higher than that to China and to Hong Kong, which can be explained by the link between trade and investment.

Exploring import structure, ASEAN depends on outsider for import more than for export. NEA, especially Japan, is the major source of imports for ASEAN. China and Hong Kong import more from NEA than from ASEAN. Hong Kong's, Japan's, and ROK's shares of imports from ASEAN and EU are not that much different while their shares of import from the US are higher. This may illustrate trade and investment linkage between ASEAN and NEA that subsidiary companies import parts and machinery from parent companies. Furthermore with different level of development from ASEAN and China, Japan and ROK need to import capital and technology intensive goods from the US.

Kobsak Putrakul and others (2003) conducted analysis of the contribution of export growth within EA (excluding Japan that is included in G-3). The results indicated that during 1990 – 2002 the major source of increasing of intra-regional trade came from the increasing in the exports among countries in North East Asia remarkably within China, Hong Kong and Taiwan economies, and ROK, contributing to 50 percent of intra-regional export growth. Trade among South East Asia countries accounted to 20 percent. The rest was trade between NEA and

SEA. However, the growth rates of exports between ASEAN and NEA were the highest.

Export and Import Products of East Asia

This paper finds the similarity of their major products through investigating export and import products of ASEAN and NEA countries based on two-digit HS classification. With respect to export, during 1996 — 2000, electrical and electronic equipment (HS 85) and machinery (HS 84) were major export products for ASEAN, ROK and Japan. These two products were also major imports for all three countries. Another principal export of ASEAN was mineral fuels, oils distillation products (HS 27). HS 87 (vehicles apart from railway or tramway) was the third highest export product for ROK and Japan, while the main import products for both countries was HS 27 (mineral fuels, oils distillation products) (Tables 6-8).

Major export products of China in 2000 were HS 85 (electrical and electronic equipment) followed by HS 84 (machinery) and HS 62 (article of apparel, accessories, not knit or crochet). For the import side, top three import products of China in the same year were HS 85 (electrical and electronic equipment), HS 84 (machinery), and HS 27 (mineral fuels, oils distillation products) accounting for 47 percent of total import value of China (Table 9).

Hong Kong's chief merchandise exports were quite different from others in the region. The top-three export products during 1996—2000 were composed of HS 62 (article of apparel, accessories, not knit or crochet) followed by HS 61 (articles of apparel, accessories, knit or crochet) and HS 85 (electrical and electronic equipment). The main import products were HS 85 (electrical and electronic equipment) followed by HS 84 (nuclear reactors, boilers and machinery), and HS 39 (plastics and articles thereof) (Table 10).

Machinery and electronics are dominant export products in the region. Garment is major product for some countries. There are studies suggest that the pattern of EA trade illustrate the product cycle pattern. Export production has been shifted from high-income countries such as Japan to NICs and later to SEA. Countries in the region have been moving up the product ladder, from labor-intensive goods like garment to more technology-skill-intensive goods like electronics and machinery.

Export Similarity Index

The trade pattern reflects competition and complementarities. To investigate further on trade competition, export similarity index has been calculated[①]. The index indicates the similarity of the export commodity structures of selected two countries. ESI value of 100 indicates that two countries' export structures are the same. Vice versa, ESI value of 0 reveals that two countries' export structures are the most different.

Export similarity index of ASEAN and NEA increased marginally from 69 to 69.7 due to the decline of index in the case of ASEAN and Hong Kong. All indexes for China, Japan and ROK rose significantly. ROK and Japan showed closer export structure to ASEAN than to China. (Table 10).

Comparing the export structuring of individual NEA country and NEA as a group showed that Hong Kong established the declining of index compared to the group as well as to individual country. Japan's index increases and exhibits closer ties to ROK

[①] Formula of Trade Similarity Index is $S(ab,c) = (\sum_i \text{Minimum}[X_i(bc)]) * 100$ where $S(ab,c)$ is Trade Similarity Index between country A and country B in market C, $X_i(ab)$ is weight of commodity i in A's trade to C, and is weight of commodity i in B's trade to C.

more than to China.

Within ASEAN, all countries' index increases when comparing individual members to ASEAN export structure. Malaysia's index was the highest, while that of Indonesia was the lowest. Comparing ASEAN members with each other, Singapore and Malaysia illustrated the strongest ties. Indonesian structure was less similar to others although the index was increasing. The Philippine index, matching up with each member, marginally declined with the exception of that of Singapore rising from 63.4 to 70.5. Thailand index was highest when measured up with Malaysia.

Comparing individual ASEAN members and each NEA country or region, the index increased for each case with the exception of Hong Kong whose index values declined compared with every ASEAN country except Indonesia. Another exception was the match up between China and the Philippines. Among ASEAN members, Thailand establishes the highest index comparing with NEA group and with China and ROK. Singapore export structure is more similar to Japan while Malaysia export structure is more similar to ROK. These two countries show lower index values with China.

RCA Rank Correlation

To investigate comparative advantage in trade, Revealed Comparative Advantage (RCA) index is calculated.[1] The Spearman's rank correlation between RCA ranking on various products between two countries is, then, calculated to capture nature of similarity in comparative advantage. The match of the ranking of RCA between two countries can, to some extent, in-

---

[1] $RCA = (X_{ik}/\sum X_k)/(X_{iw}/\sum X_w)$ where X_{ik} is the value of sector i export of country k, and X_{iw} is the total value of world export of product i.

dicate similarity of comparative advantage. RCA Rank Correlation coefficients value of 1 points out that the ranking of RCA between the respective countries is perfect match. Value of RCA Rank Correlation coefficient of 0 implied that export products establishes a totally different pattern of comparative advantage.

Table 11 shows the results of RCA rank Correlation for Thailand and ASEAN compared to EA and selected countries. It is shown that Thailand's comparative advantage was close to the Philippines' and to China's. Comparative advantage of Thailand was quite different from the US and EU and showed minor correlation with Japan's and Singapore's structure. ROK and Malaysia were, to some extent, showing the same pattern of comparative advantage.

ASEAN also showed negative relationship of RCA indexes with EU's and US's and had closer comparable pattern with China, Hong Kong and ROK.

Box 1 International Standard Industrial Classification (ISIC)

ISIC Rev. 2

1-Agriculture, Hunting, Forestry and Fishing

2-Mining and Quarrying

3-Manufacturing

31-Manufacture of Food, Beverages and Tobacco

32-Textile, Wearing Apparel and Leather Industries

33-Manufacture of Wood and Wood Products, Including Furniture

34-Manufacture of Paper and Paper Products, Printing and Publishing

35-Manufacture of Chemicals and Chemical, Petroleum, Coal, Rubber and Plastic Products

36-Manufacture of Non-Metallic Mineral Products, except Products of Petroleum and Coal

37-Basic Metal Industries

38-Manufacture of Fabricated Metal Products, Machinery and Equipment

39-Other Manufacturing Industries

To further investigate this issue, the paper does the same exercise within product group. Products are grouped by ISIC classification (2nd revision). The box above gives details on products classified by ISIC standard.

Table 12 shows RCA rank correlation coefficients of Thailand and selected countries in 2000. For Agricultural products, the correlation between Thailand and Indonesia, the Philippines, Malaysia and ROK were higher than other countries including China. The correlation with EU and US were low. In Food processing Thailand had high correlation with ASEAN and NEA, namely China, Japan, and ROK. Thailand had similar comparative advantage in textile and garment closer to ASEAN than to China. For ISIS 35 Thailand also had similar structure with ASEAN and ROK. Thailand established with China the similar comparative advantage pattern in machinery and equipment (including electronics) and basic metal. For the latter product, the index between Thailand and ROK was high. Thailand comparative advantage is noticeably closer to ASEAN than to NEA.

With respect to results on RCA rank correlation of ASEAN countries against other countries (Table 13), ASEAN showed comparable RCA pattern with NEA in basic metal industries (ISIC37), machinery equipment (ISIC 38), agricultural products (ISIC1), and food processing (ISIC31). The result also denoted ASEAN's comparable trade structure with China's and Hong Kong's in wood and wood product (ISIC 33) and paper and paper products (ISIC 34).

Intra Industry Trade Index

The analysis illustrates the competition structure between ASEAN and NEA. It also indicates that the trade pattern of Thailand is closer to ASEAN than to NEA. However, the networking of MNC also shows structure of complementarity in trade among countries. One major phenomenon explaining international trade is intra-industry trade, which can be realized by the trade of similar products with similar countries (especially border trade) or by a division of labor through which parts of products have been produced in many locations according to the location advantage.

To investigate this issue, intra-industry trade index[1](IIT) is calculated to capture complementary structure. The index captures trading of two countries within same product group; high IIT shows high trade proportion in that particular product group. For countries showing a low IIT index, there are less trading in that product group and a possibility to compete in the third country. The details are shown in Table 14 and Table 15.

Table 14 shows the sector that Thailand established high RCA rank correlation with NEA that also showed high intra-industry trade; there are ISIC 38; Manufacture of Fabricated Metal Products, Machinery and Equipment. Countries that show high IIT matched up with Thailand were NEA, Malaysia and the Philippines.

Table 15 shows that IIT for ASEAN and selected countries. Sectors that experience high IIT were ISIC 38; Manufacture of Fabricated Metal Products, Machinery and Equipment. ASEAN established high IIT with every NEA countries and also with the US and EU. The data in Table 14 and Table 15 indicate that Thailand trade structure and comparative advantage are similar to ASEAN (especially Malaysia), China and ROK. ASEAN and NEA are more similar within its respective group than with different regions. This similarity shows that they can be competitors. However, intra-industry trade also increases. This shows the complementarity structure with the rising networking of production and trade in the region especially in the case of computer and machinery.

---

[1] $IIT = (1-(|X_{ij}-M_{ij}|/(X_{ij}+M_{ij}))) * 100$ where X_{ij} is the value of country i's export of product j to the market under investigation, and M_{ij} is the import value of the country of product j from the market under focus.

Evidence from Khobsak Putrakul and others (2003) also shows that, in recent years, division of labor and product internationalization is a key feature of trade structure in EA. During 1991 and 1998, countries in EA, with the exception of China and Hong Kong, experience higher level of intra-industry trade especially for Thailand and the Philippines. The importance of intra-industry trade can be emphasized by the quote from the 2002 OECD Economic outlook, as cited in Kobsak Putrakul and others (2003), that,

" The growing internationalization of production system, which increasingly involves vertical trading chains spanning a number of countries, each specializing in a particular stage of production, is an important feature behind the changing nature and the increasing scale of world trade. The extent of the intra-industry trade is typically much higher across categories of manufactured goods than it is across trade in non-manufactured goods and highest for the more sophisticated manufactured products such as chemical, machinery, transport equipment, electrical equipment, and electronics. This is because sophisticated manufacturing products are more likely to benefit from economies of scale in production and are easier to differentiate to the final consumers, and so facilitate trade in similar products. More complex manufactured products that rely on many components and/or processes many also benefit more readily from splitting up production across countries. ... Furthermore of particular interest when considering intra-industry trade and the internationalization of production are those countries where exports and imports account for a very high proportion of GDP ... although there is far from a perfect correspondence, these countries all tend to have a relatively high intra-industry trade. "

Foreign Direct Investment

With internationalization of production, direct investment from abroad is a crucial mechanism pushing economic growth. The important investors are US, EU and Japan. Table 16 shows the distribution of net foreign direct investment. FDI still concentrated in industrial countries, like the US and EU. However, China shares of FDI rose significantly in 1995 to 11.03 percent although it declined to 5.92 percent in 2001. ASEAN share of FDI declined sharply since 1995 from 7.3 percent to 1.76 percent in 2001.

III. Asian Trade Agreements

Never before that bilateral FTAs and regional economic cooperation in Asian countries have been more flourished. The basic form is free trade Area; however, many are Closer Economic Cooperation that are comprehensive and involve more than tariff reduction. Many agreements are in the process so we expected the completion in a few years.

This trend indicates that countries in the region focus on export-led growth and are uncertain on the completion of WTO agreements. These countries are afraid of being left out of the group as outsiders. The case of Japan is a good example, as it changes the position in cooperation with ASEAN when China launches the establishment of ASEAN-China FTA. The joint Declaration of the Leaders of ASEAN and Japan on the Comprehensive Economic partnership was announced one day after the signing of the China-ASEAN economic cooperation.

Singapore is the most active in the region. Japan and Singapore concluded the Japan-Singapore Economic Partnership Agreement in January 2002, which, coming into effect in

November 2002, covers tariff cuts and a broad agreement on movement of people, investment rules and technical cooperation between two countries. However, the scope is still partial and too limited to be employed as a framework for ASEAN trade negotiation.

Thailand direction in regional agreement is quite clear under the leadership of the present government. Bilateral trade is pushed regardless of the size and location of the trading partners. At the same time AFTA and RTA with ASEAN and others are also pursued. WTO is not the main issue at the policy level although government officials still work hard on WTO negotiation. The main objective of Thai government is to open up market for exports. It is arguable whether bilateral trade creates equal trade negotiating power between small and big countries. The negotiation always avoids sensitive issues and focuses on issues of big countries' interest. Western countries concern more on trade in services, investment and IPP, ignoring agriculture issues. However, bilateral is good in discussing NTB and technical assistance which is not the focus and not easy to implement at multilateral level.

IV. Rationales of EA Economic Cooperation: Shortcomings and Advantages

The above discussion illustrates that bilateral and regional FTA agreements are fashionable. This part of the paper evaluates the limitation and advantages of East Asia economic cooperation, from ASEAN perspective with special reference to Thailand.

While expanding ASEAN seems reasonable, EA cooperation has marked shortcomings. One major shortcoming is that intraregional trade in EA is smaller compared to other large grouping like EU and NAFTA. Thus, final demand in EU and USA is still important for exports. Inter-regional trade is also imperative with respect to imports.

The importance of the US and EU demand is more apparent if one considers the linkage of the industry. Some export products within EA are not for the final demand in the region but for reprocessing to export to the US and EU. Thus, the growth rates of these two regions are still notable for intra-regional trade growth. Monetary Authority of Singapore published a study in 2003, as cited in Kobsak Pultrakul and others (2003), that about 36 percent of total export in the region (Japan excluded) is intra-regional exports, of which 22 percent were demanded in the region as final products and intermediate products for regional demand. The rest about 14 percent were reprocessed and sent to the US, EU and Japan and the rest of the world. This signifies importance of G-3 economic growth.

The implication is that EA must not establish a closed regionalism. Multilateral trade agreements are nonetheless important for trade expansion. Furthermore, it is inevitable that slow down in the US and EU economy will affect EA exports.

The formation of FTA requires public support. However, China is emerging as a major competitor with some countries. The analysis of export structure indicates that Thailand and China are competing in many sectors. Apichat Pongsirirushakun et. al. (2002) investigated exports products in major markets. The finding is that there were many products of which Thai share of export experienced declining while Chinese shares of export were rising. This makes it harder to ask for public support for EA Free trade Area. It also reveals the necessity of adjustment in each country in order to be competitive.

Furthermore, while ASEAN has notable experience in cooperation and close relationship among its members, which has been developed for some time, political situation in NEA is not as smooth as in the case of ASEAN due to historical background. The close cooperation in NEA is still in the stage of development. It is expected that negotiation to reach regional FTA agreement will not be an easy task. Likewise, one who favors bilateral trade negotiations will argue that cooperation among many countries may create more trouble than negotiation within small group, like between two countries or ASEAN. Bigger groups have various interests, more diverse economic structure, larger difference in political system and culture, wider range of issues to be settled.

Moreover, regionalism can undermine multilateral trade negotiations. Bilateral and regional cooperation require resources and time to accomplish. When these resources are committed, less resource and concentration will be devoted to multilateral trade negotiation. There are not enough qualified people in developing countries to go around for meetings, no resources to do research, no time for consensus buildings. Consequently, multilateral negotiation will get lower priority when bilateral and regionalism is the focal strategy. Policy makers will feel content as if they perform enough freer trade when they sign some bilateral FTAs and do not feel the need to pursue multilateral negotiations.

While the limitations of EA cooperation cannot be ignored, there are many advantage points for EA cooperation.

While one can view China as a competitor in export markets, the evidence shows that China has been emerged as a major market for ASEAN and EA as well. Even as it is true that since 1998 China became number one exporter of EA (next to Japan) and other countries' export growth were declining or showing down trend. On the other hand, the strong increase of China exports occurs along with the noticeable increase of EA export to China. It increased from $ 2.6 billion in 1998 to $ 50.5 billion in 2002. Thailand export to China in the first five months of 2003 increased to 6.8 percent in total export.

Thus there is an obvious advantage for the region when

China comes out as a new market for ASEAN and NEA with large number of population whose income is increasing. High growth rate of FDI to China also induced intra-regional trade form production chain in the region. China also provides location advantage based on its lower cost and abundant resources for production.

To avoid the confusing overlapped trade agreements, as one can see in Figure 1 for the case of Thailand, EA cooperation can avoid spaghetti-bowl tariff system. With many trade agreements, many tariff rates can be imposed on one product depending on the origin of import. Even imports from the same origin, tariff rate on specific product can be different due to different local content. If each ASEAN member forms FTA with NEA respectively, there will be 40 agreements instead of one agreement when EAFTA is created. Also if the trend of bilateral continues, the region will face abundant amount of free trade agreements.

EA cooperation can improve regional competitiveness. Internationalization of production brings about FDI as MNC searching for the most efficient location to produce parts or components. The EA cooperation can make the region a strategic one for production network, especially as China becomes visible. The free flow of trade and investment in the region, thus, strengthens regional competitiveness as well as national competitiveness.

Though there are some trade agreements across continents and involving distant countries, it is easier to cooperate for countries with geographical proximity. FTAs always start among neighboring countries. EA has closer historical and cultural relations with each other than with the west. It should be easier to buildup based on existing familiar institutions and market environment.

With respect to existing institution, EA cooperation does not start from zero. Framework on ASEAN+3 is built and can be expanded to establish the framework for EA cooperation or EAFTA. Those measures that are timely and appropriate recommended in the Final Report of the East Asia Study Group can be scrutinized and carried out.

Furthermore, when an economic group includes lower income economies, it is imperative to assist them to develop. CLMV are ASEAN members with much lower income than others. However, ASEAN has limited resources, especially after the crisis, to perform this duty effectively. EA, which include industrial high-income countries, can set up adjustment fund to facilitate trade liberalization. Furthermore, CLMV can get support from EA cooperation in the form of Special and Differential Treatment (S&DT), technical assistance for capacity building, and infrastructure development. This will make the adjustment to FTA easier and more acceptable.

Lastly, advantage of EA grouping is to strengthen position on multilateral negotiation. EA grouping can also enhance trade negotiation position better than bilateral or individual country in multilateral negotiation. Its size will be compatible to EU and NAFTA. However, the influence on multilateral negotiation will also depend on the consensus building in the group.

Conclusion

The above information on economic and trade structure leads to the suggestion that ASEAN is too small to engage only in its own grouping. Crisis also showed that cooperation in ASEAN was not enough to prevent the adversity. Thailand, a small country, and ASEAN, a small economic group, cannot wait for the conclusion of multilateral agreements for freer trade. Under the situation that there will be large trade blocs, Thailand and ASEAN are too small to stand-alone. Thus, deeper integration with NEA is logical; some even say it is necessary.

The previous section points out the shortcomings of EA cooperation, nevertheless the advantages are quite substantiating. Thus, we should be aware of the limitations and get the best results out of the integration.

The analysis also shows that economic structure of Thailand is similar to that of ASEAN members, so trade expansion with NEA will complement Thailand economic structure. A gravity model employed in Kobsak Putrakul and others (2003) confirmed that there are potential for bilateral trade expansion between Thailand and Japan, China, Taiwan and India. Therefore, EA cooperation is good for Thailand trade. The paper also concludes that

"... With the rise of East Asia in the world economy, intra-regional trade will play an increasingly more important role for each country within the region. For the case of Thailand, not only we are likely to gain in the short-run driven by export growth to country such as China, but in the medium and longer term, as long as the regional cooperation keeps expanding faster than the G3 countries, prosperity within the region will help propel momentum for the intra-regional exports which will be instrumental in providing additional engine of growth to the Thailand for the medium-term."

Larger group offers more benefits to countries involved. The simulation by Scollay R. and J. Gilbert (2001) indicated that ASEAN + 3 would increase welfare more than ASEAN +1 and for only NEAFTA. Including Agriculture in FTA is also important since it will increase welfare significantly (Table 17).

With the importance of production networking to enhance export, EA cooperation must be designed to enhance competition position of the region compared to other regions of the world. It is important that the regional cooperation is set to attract FDI and linkage into production and trade networking under the trend of global production. Regionalism must not intend to protect producers. With closer economic integration in East Asia, each country in the region will need to develop its own niches based on its realistic comparative advantage.

To attract FDI and improve competitiveness, ASEAN also needs to integrate more. As stated in Chalongphob Sussangkarn (2003) "ASEAN needs to become much more serious in fully implementing AFTA to make the region more attractive as an investment destination. This also requires the harmonization of the rules, procedures and regulation that will lower the cost of producing, transporting and generally doing business in ASEAN."

Every country in the region still needs to streamline trade and industrial policy. Although Thailand AFTA tariff rates are lower than their MFN rates. Tariff rates are still high even for agricultural products. Since trade with non-ASEAN economies is still important for Thailand in terms of MFN. Tariff rates should not be much higher than AFTA rates. Otherwise, it will induce trade diversion and inefficiency. Furthermore, domestic producers who use imported parts from outside ASEAN will face the difficulty in completing with AFTA products. Under the globalization pressure, it is vital to upgrade the industry by improving technological capability. It will significantly enhance competitiveness. Thailand needs to restructure its economy more than other ASEAN members, since the above analysis reveals that China's export competition is more prevailing to Thailand than to other ASEAN countries.

Role of China and Japan will be crucial for the success of economic group. Countries in the region cannot deny that China, to some extent, is a competitor but it also generates opportunity to enhance respective country's competitiveness and market access. China will be important in market source and low cost production, as is mentioned above. Roles of Japan will be noteworthy in assisting industrial upgrading. Japanese firms can create production networking in the region and transfer technology via subcontracting and training. This will increase individual country's competitiveness as well as company's efficiency.

To avoid waste of resources, the cooperation should be built on existing institutions. East Asia Free Trade Area (EAFTA) should be established as a medium term target. Framework on ASEAN+3 should be built on and expanded to be the framework for EAFTA. It is possible that ASEAN can bring the respective arrangements with China, Japan, ROK and the Closer Economic Partnership (CEP) with Australia and New Zealand under an overall CEP framework. This will greatly reduce the problems and complication for ASEAN to manage its future external economic relations and cooperation in East Asia.

To get benefit from the integration EA should be comprehensive and broad. It is important to include sensitive sectors in the liberalization although there is limitation of the timeframe for adjustment. Elek (2003) stated that it is hard to deal with sensitive sectors in small group. Sensitive issues can be dealt in bigger groups because of the possibility of cross-sector negotiation. Thus, bilateral is not working in this issue and it is possible to accomplish it in the RTA or through a multilateral approach. Issues on agriculture and service sectors cannot be avoided. The agreement should at least set the timeframe for inclusion of sensitive sectors in the FTA.

Nipon Poupongsakorn (2003) emphasized the importance of agriculture in the ASEAN-Japan Closer Economic Partnership. "…since agriculture is still the most important sector in many ASEAN economies especially CLMV. It is not only providing bread and butter and safety net for the majority of their population, but it is also the sector that they have comparative advantage. Trade in agriculture will, therefore, significantly contribute to their economic growth and improve the living standards of millions of ASEAN farmers." In other word, opening the agricultural market may be better than financial assistance to developing countries.

He also suggests the adjustment measures required for ASEAN and Japan to cope with the agricultural issue. ASEAN should set up program to enable farmers to shift away from inefficient non-competitiveness of agricultural production, set up social protection program to protect vulnerable farmers and build up capacity of farmers and food processors to export products that meet SPS standard. For Japan, it needs to find a more innovative means of food security that is less market distorted and needs to bring down price support. To cope with multi-functionality of agriculture issue, Japan should provide direct and cost-effective mechanism to support agriculture production as a public good. This will lower social cost and reduce international trade barriers.

EA cooperation is beneficial to Thailand and ASEAN. It should be formed with the clear vision of what we want to achieve, and to accomplish by the most efficient way to reach its full potential. East Asian countries must adapt the economies and institutions to cope with the process of globalization and dynamism of international trade and investment. EA cooperation will be a critical means for the adjustment.

Table 1 Economic Indicators, 2001

	Population Million	GDP (current BIL.US $)	GDP per capita current US $)	%ofGDP Agriculture	Manufacturing	Service and others	Exports of goods and services BIL US $	%of GDP	%of world export	Imports of goods and services BIL US $	%of GDP	%of world import	degree of Openness
Brunei	0.3	..	..	..	..	..	..	..	..	..	..	..	..
Cambodia	12.3	3.4	277.5	36.9	..	..	1.8	53.2	0.0	2.1	61.3	0.0	1.1
Indonesia	209.0	145.3	695.3	16.4	26.1	57.5	59.7	41.1	1.0	47.3	32.6	0.8	0.7
Laos	5.4	1.8	325.9	5..9	17.7	31.4	0.5	36.3	0.0	0.6	47.6	0.0	0.6
Malaysia	23.8	88.0	3,698.8	8.5	30.6	60.9	102.4	116.3	1.7	86.2	98.0	1.5	2.1
Myanmar	48.3	..	..	57.2	7.2	35.6	..	0.5	..	..	1.1	..	..
Philippines	78.3	71.4	912.2	15.2	22.4	62.3	35.2	49.3	0.6	33.9	47.4	0.6	1.0
Singapore	4.1	85.6	20,733.0	0.1	23.4	76.4	148.6	173.6	2.5	130.0	151.8	2.3	3.3
Thailand	61.2	114.7	1,874.4	10.3	32.0	57.7	76.0	66.3	1.3	69.0	60.2	1.2	1.3
Vietnam	79.5	32.7	411.7	23.6	19.6	56.8	17.9	54.7	0.3	18.6	56.8	0.3	1.1
ASEAN-10	522.3	543.0	1,146.5	11.8	26.6	61.6	442.1	81.4	7.3	387.8	71.4	6.7	1.5
China	1,271.9	1,159.0	911.3	15.2	35.4	49.4	299.4	25.8	50.0	271.3	23.4	4.7	0.5
Hong Kong	6.7	161.9	24,073.7	0.1	5.9	94.0	233.0	143.9	3.9	224.4	138.6	3.9	2.8
Japan	127.0	4,141.4	32,600.7	1.4	21.6	77.1	432.5	10.4	7.2	406.4	9.8	7.1	0.2
ROK	47.3	422.2	8,917.2	4.4	30.0	65.6	181.1	42.9	3.0	171.2	40.6	3.0	0.8
NEA	1,453.0	5,884.5	4,050.0	4.3	24.5	71.2	1,146.1	19.5	19.0	1,073.3	18.2	18.6	0.4
EA	1,975.2	6,427.5	3,336.3	4.9	24.7	70.4	1,588.2	24.7	26.3	1,461.2	22.7	25.4	0.5
EU-15	378.2	7,889.9	20,862.6	2.2	19.9	77.9	2,829.4	35.9	46.3	2,735.3	34.7	47.5	0.7
Canada	31.1	694.5	22,343.4	2.6	18.7	78.7	304.3	43.8	5.0	268.4	38.6	4.7	0.8
Mexico	99.4	617.8	6,214.3	4.4	19.4	76.3	170.6	27.6	2.8	185.2	30.0	3.2	0.6
USA	285.3	10,065.3	35,277.4	1.6	17.2	81.1	1,103.1	11.2	18.3	1,466.9	15.0	25.5	0.3
NAFTA	415.8	11,377.6	27.3618	1.8	17.4	80.7	1,578.0	13.9	26.1	1,920.4	16.9	33.3	0.3

Source: World Development Indicators, World Bank, 2003.

Thai Perception on East Asian Cooperation 161

Table 2 Coefficient of Variation of GDP per capita, 1960-2001.

	1960	1970	1980	1990	1995	2000	2001
EU-15	0.48	0.43	0.37	0.34	0.37	0.35	0.34
NAFTA	1.10	0.70	0.58	0.70	0.74	0.68	0.68
NEA	0.67	1.02	0.98	0.96	0.94	0.89	0.86
EA	0.80	1.26	1.52	1.33	1.33	1.54	1.51
ASEAN-9 *	0.53	1.01	1.73	1.54	1.52	1.98	1.94
ASEAN-6	0.46	0.94	1.73	1.17	1.15	1.56	1.53

* exclude Myanmar.
Source: Calculated from World Development Indicators, World Bank. 2003.

Table 3 Percent of Intra-regional Trade

	1980	1985	1990	1995	1999	2000	2001
NAFTA	33.6	43.9	41.4	46.2	54.6	55.7	54.8
FTAA	43.4	49.7	46.6	52.5	60.0	60.8	60.1
EU	60.8	59.2	65.9	62.4	63.3	62.1	61.2
ASEAN	17.4	18.6	19.0	24.6	21.7	23.0	22.4
APEC	57.9	67.7	68.3	71.8	71.8	73.1	72.5

Source : UNCTAD Handbook of Statistics On line, www.unctad.org.

Table 4 Share of Export by Selected Countries, 1996-2000 Unit: Percent

Country	YEAR	ASEAN-10	China	Hong Kong	Japan	ROK	NEA	EU	USA	The Rest of the world
ASEAN-5	1996	24.8	2.9	6.5	14.2	3.3	26.9	14.4	18.6	15.4
	1997	24.2	3.0	6.7	13.0	3.3	26.1	15.1	19.3	15.3
	1998	21.3	3.2	5.9	11.3	2.5	22.9	16.8	21.3	17.7
	1999	21.6	3.1	5.5	12.2	3.3	24.2	15.9	20.7	17.6
	2000	23.2	3.6	5.5	13.2	3.7	26.0	14.3	19.4	17.0
China	1996	6.8	0.0	21.8	20.4	5.0	47.2	13.1	17.7	15.1
	1997	7.0	0.0	24.0	17.4	5.0	46.4	13.1	17.9	15.7
	1998	6.1	0.0	21.1	16.1	3.4	40.6	15.3	20.7	17.3
	1999	6.3	0.0	18.9	16.6	4.0	39.5	15.5	21.5	17.1
	2000	7.0	0.0	17.9	16.7	4.5	39.1	15.3	20.9	17.7
HongKong	1996	9.5	29.0	0.0	5.3	1.2	35.6	17.5	25.5	12.0
	1997	8.6	30.2	0.0	5.0	1.1	36.3	17.4	26.1	11.6
	1998	6.4	29.4	0.0	3.4	0.8	33.7	18.8	28.8	12.3
	1999	6.2	29.1	0.0	3.1	0.9	33.2	19.3	29.6	11.8

		2000	7.1	29.7	0.0	2.8	1.0	33.4	18.0	29.7	11.8
Japan		1996	17.9	5.3	6.2	0.0	7.1	18.6	15.4	27.5	20.6
		1997	16.6	5.2	6.5	0.0	6.2	17.8	15.6	28.1	21.8
		1998	12.0	5.2	5.8	0.0	4.0	15.0	18.5	30.9	23.7
		1999	13.0	5.6	5.3	0.0	5.5	16.3	17.8	31.1	21.8
		2000	14.3	6.3	5.7	0.0	6.4	18.4	16.3	30.0	20.9
ROK		1996	15.7	8.8	8.6	12.2	0.0	29.5	11.9	16.9	26.1
		1997	15.0	10.0	8.6	10.8	0.0	29.4	12.4	16.0	27.1
		1998	11.6	9.0	7.0	9.2	0.0	25.3	13.8	17.4	32.0
		1999	12.3	9.5	6.3	11.0	0.0	26.9	14.1	20.6	26.1
		2000	11.7	10.7	6.2	11.9	0.0	28.8	13.6	21.9	23.9
EU		1996	2.5	0.9	1.1	2.1	0.9	4.9	61.6	6.9	24.1
		1997	2.5	0.9	1.1	1.9	0.8	4.6	60.2	7.5	25.2
		1998	1.5	0.9	0.9	1.6	0.4	3.8	61.4	8.1	25.1
		1999	1.5	0.9	0.8	1.7	0.5	3.9	62.1	8.8	23.8
		2000	1.6	1.0	0.8	1.8	0.7	4.4	60.4	9.4	24.2
USA		1996	6.9	2.0	2.1	10.9	4.4	19.4	20.6	0.0	53.0
		1997	7.0	1.9	2.1	9.7	3.8	17.5	20.6	0.0	54.9
		1998	5.8	2.2	1.8	8.6	2.5	15.2	22.1	0.0	56.9
		1999	5.8	2.0	1.7	8.5	3.4	15.6	22.0	0.0	56.6
		2000	6.2	2.2	1.7	8.5	3.7	16.1	21.4	0.0	56.3

Source: Calculated form PC-TAS, UN.

Table 5 Share of Import by Selected Countries, 1996-2000 Unit: Percent

Country	YEAR	ASEAN-10	China	Hong Kong	Japan	ROK	NEA	EU	USA	The Rest of the world
ASEAN-5	1996	17.7	3.0	2.4	22.2	4.3	31.8	15.1	15.2	20.1
	1997	18.1	3.6	2.4	20.6	4.3	30.9	14.5	16.3	20.3
	1998	20.2	4.1	2.6	18.9	4.5	30.1	13.5	17.9	18.2
	1999	20.9	4.5	2.5	19.0	4.8	30.8	12.1	16.4	19.7
	2000	21.8	4.8	2.4	19.6	4.4	31.2	10.9	14.6	21.4
China	1996	7.8	0.0	5.6	21.0	9.0	35.6	14.3	11.6	30.6
	1997	8.7	0.0	4.9	20.4	10.5	35.8	13.5	11.5	30.6
	1998	9.0	0.0	4.7	20.2	10.7	35.6	14.8	12.0	28.5
	1999	9.0	0.0	4.2	20.4	10.4	34.9	15.3	11.8	29.0
	2000	9.9	0.0	4.2	18.4	10.3	32.9	13.7	9.9	33.6
HongKong	1996	10.4	36.7	0.0	13.4	5.4	55.4	11.2	7.8	15.2

	Year									
	1997	10.3	36.8	0.0	13.5	5.1	55.4	11.2	7.7	15.3
	1998	10.1	40.1	0.0	12.5	5.1	57.7	10.7	7.4	14.1
	1999	10.0	43.3	0.0	11.6	4.9	59.8	9.3	7.0	13.9
	2000	10.4	42.9	0.0	12.0	5.0	59.8	8.8	6.8	14.2
Japan	1996	15.0	11.6	0.7	0.0	4.6	16.9	14.1	22.8	31.1
	1997	14.8	12.4	0.7	0.0	4.3	17.3	13.3	22.4	32.1
	1998	14.2	13.2	0.6	0.0	4.3	18.1	13.9	24.0	29.7
	1999	14.9	13.8	0.6	0.0	5.2	19.6	13.8	21.8	29.9
	2000	15.7	14.5	0.4	0.0	5.4	20.3	12.3	19.1	32.6
ROK	1996	8.0	5.7	0.8	20.9	0.0	27.4	14.1	22.2	28.3
	1997	8.7	7.0	0.6	19.3	0.0	26.9	13.1	20.8	30.4
	1998	9.7	6.8	0.5	17.8	0.0	25.1	11.6	21.7	31.8
	1999	10.2	7.4	0.7	20.2	0.0	28.3	10.5	20.8	30.1
	2000	11.3	8.0	0.8	19.8	0.0	28.6	9.8	18.2	32.0
EU	1996	2.7	1.8	0.7	3.7	0.7	6.9	61.3	7.7	21.4
	1997	2.9	2.0	0.8	3.7	0.8	7.3	59.8	8.3	21.7
	1998	2.8	2.1	0.8	3.9	0.9	7.6	60.1	8.4	21.1
	1999	2.8	2.4	0.8	4.0	1.0	8.1	59.2	8.3	21.6
	2000	2.9	2.8	0.8	3.9	1.0	8.5	56.0	8.5	24.1
USA	1996	8.4	6.7	1.3	14.4	2.8	25.2	18.0	0.0	48.4
	1997	8.2	7.3	1.2	13.8	2.7	25.0	18.1	0.0	48.7
	1998	8.0	8.0	1.2	13.2	2.6	25.0	19.3	0.0	47.7
	1999	7.6	8.3	1.0	12.7	3.1	25.1	19.0	0.0	48.3
	2000	7.3	8.6	1.0	12.0	3.3	24.8	18.0	0.0	49.9

Source: Calculated form PC-TAS, UN.

Table 6 Share of ASEAN'S Trade of Top 10 Products 1996-2000

		Export					
Rank	Code	Product	1996	1997	1998	1999	2000
1	85	Electrical, electronic equipment	28.26	28.54	29.98	31.54	33.31
2	84	Nuclear reactors, boilers, machinery, etc	19.84	20.86	21.53	21.68	20.82
3	27	Mineral fuels, oils, distillationproducts, etc	9.26	9.06	7.53	8.04	10.19
4	39	Plastics and articles thereof	1.63	1.80	1.91	2.00	2.27
5	44	Wood and articles of wood, wood charcoal	3.36	3.06	2.16	2.38	2.04
6	62	Articles of apparel, accessories, not knit or crochet	2.00	1.78	1.83	1.84	1.81
7	90	Optical, photo, technical, medical, etc apparatus	1.49	1.61	1.65	1.56	1.64

8	15	Animal,vegetable fats and oils ,cleavage products,etc	2.33	2.60	2.81	2.34	1.63
9	40	Rubber and articles thereof	2.87	2.36	2.13	1.76	1.62
10	29	Organic chemicals	1.15	1.34	1.36	1.78	1.59
sum top 10 Export products			72.18	73.01	72.90	74.93	76.91
unit:Million US $			236.193	242.220	224.198	254.917	311.519
Total export			100	100	100	100	100
unit:Million US $			327.233	331.761	307.539	340.216	405.020

Import							
Rank	Code	Product	1996	1997	1998	1999	2000
1	85	Electrical,electronic equipment	26.84	27.72	32.01	32.54	33.46
2	84	Nuclear reactors,boilers,machinery,etc	19.99	20.01	18.92	16.86	17.13
3	27	Mineral fuels,oils,distillation products,etc	7.67	7.91	7.03	8.20	10.99
4	39	Plastics and articles thereof	2.55	2.61	2.67	2.82	2.88
5	87	Vehicles other than railway,tramway	4.32	3.48	1.73	2.15	2.75
6	90	Optical,photo,technical,medical,etc apparatus	2.22	2.42	2.45	2.52	2.64
7	29	Organic chemicals	2.22	2.24	2.31	2.36	2.42
8	72	Iron and steel	3.53	3.32	2.35	2.56	2.40
9	73	Articles of iron or steel	1.83	1.81	2.15	1.87	1.39
10	71	Pearls,precious stones,metals,coins,etc	1.73	1.64	1.11	1.36	1.34
sum top 10 Import products			72.89	73.17	72.72	73.24	77.40
unit:Million US $			261.819	258.703	189.579	207.182	266.711
Total import			100	100	100	100	100
unit:Million US $			359.187	353.569	260.691	282.864	344.601

Source:PC-TAS,UN.

Table 7 Share of ROK's Trade of Top 10 Products,1996-2000

Export							
Rank	Code	Product	1996	1997	1998	1999	2000
1	85	Electrical,electronic equipment	27.05	25.01	24.05	26.71	26.92
2	84	Nuclear reactors,boilers,machinery,etc	10.36	10.69	9.74	12.93	17.26
3	87	Vehicles other than railway,tramway	9.04	9.05	8.64	9.15	8.86
4	27	Mineral fuels,oils,distillationproducts,etc	2.98	3.93	3.47	4.04	5.44
5	89	Ships,boats and other floating structures	5.49	4.79	6.06	5.21	4.78
6	39	Plastics and articles there of	3.88	4.23	4.26	4.16	4.23
7	72	Iron and steel	3.52	3.65	4.85	3.66	3.46
8	29	Organic chemicals	2.17	2.62	2.51	2.45	2.88
9	54	Manmade filaments	4.80	4.61	3.80	3.21	2.79

10	60	Knitted or crocheted fabric	1.12	1.47	1.45	1.51	1.46
sum top 10 Export products			70.41	70.05	68.83	73.03	78.08
unit:Million US$			91.328	95.374	91.070	104.939	134.499
Total export			100	100	100	100	100
unit:Million US$			129.715	136.151	132.302	143.685	172.267

Import

Rank	Code	Products	1996	1997	1998	1999	2000
1	27	Mineral fuels,oils,distillation products,etc	16.15	18.93	19.51	19.10	23.73
2	85	Electrical,electronic equipment	14.55	16.82	20.82	22.82	22.13
3	84	Nuclear reactors,boilers,machinery,etc	17.10	14.03	10.52	11.69	13.01
4	90	Optical,photo,technical,medical,etc apparatus	4.20	4.07	3.70	3.95	4.21
5	72	Iron and steel	4.51	4.31	3.52	3.72	3.73
6	29	Organic chemicals	3.36	3.49	3.64	3.32	3.09
7	71	Pearls,precious stones,metals,coins,etc	4.02	4.86	5.05	3.11	1.82
8	39	Plastics and articles thereof	1.68	1.70	1.78	1.87	1.69
9	76	Aluminium and articles thereof	1.31	1.44	1.50	1.53	1.33
10	26	Ores,slag and ash	1.04	1.21	1.84	1.57	1.31
sum top 10 Import products			67.91	70.85	71.87	72.68	76.04
unit:Million US$			102.099	102.463	67.037	87.034	122.031
Total import			100	100	100	100	100
unit:Million US$			150.334	144.614	93.281	119.751	160.479

Source:PC-TAS,UN.

Table 8 Share of Japan's Trade of Top 10 Products,1996—2000

Export

Rank	Code	Product	1996	1997	1998	1999	2000
1	85	Electrical,electronic equipment	23.16	22.47	22.18	23.26	25.09
2	84	Nuclear reactors,boilers,machinery,etc	24.56	23.66	22.33	21.16	21.30
3	87	Vehicles other than railway,tramway	18.02	19.01	20.32	20.02	18.64
4	90	Optical,photo,technical,medical,etc appartus	6.05	6.18	5.95	6.45	7.02
5	99	Commodities not elsewhere specified	2.41	2.65	3.02	3.17	3.51
6	72	Iron and steel	3.00	3.05	3.07	2.72	2.70
7	29	Organic chemicals	2.70	2.61	2.66	2.59	2.48
8	39	Plastics and articles thereof	2.21	2.24	2.17	2.32	2.34
9	89	Ships,boats and other floating structures	2.34	2.34	2.61	2.38	2.14
10	40	Rubber and articles thereof	1.49	1.41	1.48	1.45	1.28
sum top 10 Export products			85.94	85.62	85.81	85.53	86.50

unit: Million US $			353.171	360.517	333.058	357.167	414.572
Total export			100	100	100	100	100
unit: Million US $			410.947	421.053	388.136	417.610	479.248
		Import					
Rank	Code	Products	1996	1997	1998	1999	2000
1	27	Mineral fuels, oils, distillation products, etc	17.43	18.56	15.43	16.10	20.40
2	85	Electrical, electronic equipment	10.43	10.51	11.22	11.95	13.23
3	84	Nuclear reactors, boilers, machinery, etc	9.40	9.79	10.57	10.69	11.09
4	90	Optical, photo, technical, medical, etc apparatus	3.10	3.31	3.73	3.76	3.63
5	03	Fish, crustaceans, molluscs, aquatic invertebrates nes	4.08	3.78	3.80	3.99	3.37
6	44	Wood and articles of wood, wood charcoal	4.57	4.45	3.27	3.49	2.97
7	62	Articles of apparel, accessories, not knit or crochet	3.12	2.69	2.72	2.82	2.74
8	87	Vehicles other than railway, tramway	3.79	3.20	2.91	2.91	2.73
9	61	Articles of apparel, accessories, knit or crochet	2.21	2.03	2.30	2.22	2.16
10	29	Organic chemicals	2.12	2.20	3.26	2.36	2.13
sum top 10 Import products			60.25	60.51	58.22	60.29	64.45
unit: Million US $			210.400	205.043	163.382	186.903	244.710
Total import			100	100	100	100	100
unit: Million US $			349.186	338.842	280.634	309.995	379.663

Source: PC-TAS, UN.

Table 9 Share of China's Trade of Top 10 Products, 1996—2000

		Export					
Rank	Code	Product	1996	1997	1998	1999	2000
1	85	Electrical, electronic equipment	13.35	13.43	14.66	16.90	18.49
2	84	Nuclear reactors, boilers, machinery, etc	7.21	7.50	9.07	9.82	10.76
3	62	Articles of apparel, accessories, not knit or crochet	9.65	9.26	8.47	7.99	7.57
4	61	Articles of apparel, accessories, knit or crochet	5.05	6.41	6.28	6.03	5.39
5	64	Footwear, gaiters and the like, parts thereof	4.70	4.67	4.56	4.45	3.95
6	95	Toys, games, sports requisites	3.96	4.11	4.22	3.95	3.69
7	27	Mineral fuels, oils, distillation products, etc	3.93	3.82	2.82	2.39	3.15
8	94	Furniture, lighting, signs, prefabricated buildings	2.02	2.08	2.35	2.77	2.82
9	42	Articles of leather, animal gut, harness, travel goods	3.13	3.05	2.86	2.69	2.64
10	39	Plastics and articles thereof	2.38	2.65	2.81	2.63	2.56
sum top 10 Export products			55.37	57.00	58.10	59.62	61.01
unit: Million US $			83.636	104.192	106.797	116.216	152.051
Total export			100	100	100	100	100

Rank	Code	Products	1996	1997	1998	1999	2000
	unit:Million US $		151.048	182.792	183.809	194.931	249.203
		Import					
1	85	Electrical, electronic equipment	13.65	15.45	18.80	21.27	22.54
2	84	Nuclear reactors, boilers, machinery, etc	21.66	17.40	17.56	16.80	15.30
3	27	Mineral fuels, oils, distillation products, etc	4.96	7.27	4.84	5.39	9.19
4	39	Plastics and articles thereof	6.35	7.16	7.46	7.01	6.42
5	72	Iron and steel	4.90	4.26	4.17	4.32	4.25
6	29	Organic chemicals	2.25	2.14	2.48	3.32	3.69
7	90	Optical, photo, technical, medical, etc apparatus	2.55	2.56	2.84	3.03	3.23
8	74	Copper and articles thereof	1.50	1.52	1.59	1.86	2.07
9	48	Paper & paperboard, articles of pulp, paper and board	2.14	2.43	2.57	2.40	1.76
10	44	Wood and articles of wood, wood charcoal	1.12	1.39	1.40	1.76	1.65
	sum top 10 Import products		61.08	61.57	63.70	67.16	70.10
	unit:Million US $		84.805	87.663	89.335	111.277	157.802
	Total import		100	100	100	100	100
	unit:Million US $		138.833	142.370	140.237	165.699	225.094

Source:PC-TAS,UN.

Table 10 Export Similarity Index

	NEA		Japan		HongKong		China		ROK		ASEAN-6		Indonesia		Malaysia		Philippines		Singapore		Thailand	
	1996	2000	1996	2000	1996	2000	1996	2000	1996	2000	1996	2000	1996	2000	1996	2000	1996	2000	1996	2000	1996	2000
NEA	100.0	100.0	81.4	81.9	53.7	47.4	59.9	69.1	76.1	81.0	69.7	36.3	45.5	58.1	61.3	60.8	59.6	63.5	62.7	68.1	75.7
Japan	81.4	81.9	100.0	100.0	44.3	41.4	43.3	52.0	65.6	72.9	61.5	64.7	22.7	32.4	54.3	61.7	49.6	54.4	66.5	64.2	53.8	62.6
HongKong	53.7	47.4	44.3	41.4	100.0	100.0	56.4	52.8	49.3	41.3	47.1	41.6	29.9	35.1	41.0	36.6	50.3	38.0	44.4	38.4	50.3	45.2
China	59.9	69.1	43.3	52.0	56.4	52.8	100.0	100.0	54.5	59.6	54.6	60.8	46.9	53.9	45.0	51.5	55.5	51.5	46.2	50.9	60.4	67.9
ROK	76.1	81.0	65.6	72.9	49.3	41.3	54.5	59.6	100.0	100.0	65.1	72.2	35.4	45.3	57.9	65.4	57.4	58.7	59.0	66.0	58.5	70.9
ASEAN-6	69.0	69.7	61.5	64.7	47.1	41.6	54.6	60.8	65.1	72.2	100.0	100.0	51.6	56.1	79.4	87.1	70.7	72.8	77.8	82.3	69.7	72.7
Indonesia	36.3	45.5	22.7	32.4	29.9	35.1	46.9	53.9	35.4	45.3	51.6	56.1	100.0	100.0	46.4	50.8	38.5	38.0	32.3	40.6	44.8	50.6
Malaysia	58.1	61.3	54.3	61.7	41.0	36.6	45.0	51.5	57.9	65.4	79.4	87.1	46.4	50.8	100.0	100.0	73.7	72.1	72.3	86.6	58.5	63.1
Philippines	60.8	59.6	49.6	54.4	50.3	38.0	55.5	51.5	57.4	58.7	70.7	72.8	38.5	38.0	73.7	72.1	100.0	100.0	63.4	70.5	62.3	60.0
Singapore	63.5	62.7	66.5	64.2	44.4	38.4	46.2	50.9	59.0	66.0	77.8	82.3	32.3	40.6	72.3	86.6	63.4	70.5	100.0	100.0	55.8	59.3
Thailand	68.1	75.7	53.8	62.6	50.3	45.2	60.4	67.9	58.5	70.9	69.7	72.7	44.8	50.6	58.5	63.1	62.3	60.0	55.8	59.3	100.0	100.0

Source: Calculated from PC-TAS, UN.

Table 11 RCA Rank Correlation Coefficient 2000

	EU	India (1999)	China	Hong Kong	Japan	ROK	USA	Singapore	Indonesia	Malaysia	Philippines
Thailand	-0.23	**0.37**	**0.43**	**0.26**	0.05	**0.30**	-0.09	0.04	**0.36**	**0.25**	**0.48**
ASEAN-6	**-0.47**	0.20	**0.28**	**0.28**	0.04	0.19	-0.17	-	-	-	-

Bold : Correlation is significant at the .01 level (2-tailed)
Italic : Correlation is significant at the .05 level (2-tailed)
Source : Calculated from PC-TAS, UN. 1996-2000.

Table 12 RCA Rank Correlation Coefficient of Thailand and Selected Countries, 2000

	ISIC1	ISIC2	ISIC31	ISIC32	ISIC33	ISIC34	ISIC35	ISIC36	ISIC37	ISIC38	ISIC39
EU-15	-0.11	0.18	-0.11	**-0.36**	-0.10	0.08	0.01	-0.10	**0.22**	**-0.19**	-0.05
Philippines	**0.49**	0.17	**0.45**	**0.36**	**0.46**	**0.38**	**0.38**	**0.34**	**0.23**	**0.30**	**0.29**
Indonesia	**0.52**	0.09	**0.43**	**0.41**	**0.40**	**0.34**	**0.42**	**0.29**	**0.38**	**0.35**	0.14
Malaysia	**0.44**	**0.34**	**0.42**	**0.39**	*0.29*	**0.45**	**0.42**	**0.49**	**0.49**	**0.39**	*0.19*
Singapore	**0.41**	**0.26**	**0.40**	**0.36**	*0.24*	**0.30**	**0.20**	**0.24**	**0.47**	**0.32**	0.10
USA	-0.04	0.05	0.03	0.04	-0.13	-0.00	-0.01	-0.03	**0.27**	*-0.06*	-0.08
China	**0.31**	0.02	**0.43**	**0.18**	**0.66**	**0.37**	-0.06	0.13	**0.31**	**0.34**	**0.20**
Hong Kong	**0.31**	0.16	**0.30**	**0.22**	**0.56**	**0.23**	**0.39**	**0.26**	**0.37**	**0.30**	**0.28**
Japan	**0.37**	*0.22*	**0.38**	-0.13	0.05	0.11	0.04	0.10	**0.28**	**0.09**	*-0.16*
ROK	**0.41**	**0.25**	**0.36**	**0.14**	**0.60**	**0.48**	**0.39**	**0.25**	**0.45**	**0.30**	0.11
India(1999)	0.04	0.11	0.06	-0.01	-0.08	0.07	0.01	-0.13	*0.12*	*0.11*	-0.02
Number of products	376	115	385	864	70	153	1,005	154	396	1324	169
% export of Thailand to world 2000	6.75	1.45	10.56	10.48	2.02	1.26	10.51	1.74	2.19	46.91	3.71

Bold: Correlation is significant at the .01 level (2-tailed)
Italic: Correlation is significant at the .05 level (2-tailed)
Source: Calculated from PC-TAS, UN. 1996−2000.

Table 13 RCA Rank Correlation Coefficient of ASEAN-6 and Selected Countries, 2000

	ISIC1	ISIC2	ISIC31	ISIC32	ISIC33	ISIC34	ISIC35	ISIC36	ISIC37	ISIC38	ISIC39
EU-15	**-0.27**	-0.02	**-0.15**	**-0.43**	**-0.47**	-0.12	-0.06	**-0.32**	**0.15**	**-0.36**	**-0.24**
USA	-0.12	0.04	-0.05	0.05	*-0.32*	0.06	0.03	0.12	0.37	0.01	-0.05
China	**0.24**	*-0.19*	**0.31**	**0.16**	**0.32**	**0.41**	-0.06	0.14	**0.34**	**0.36**	**0.22**
Hong Kong	**0.28**	0.17	**0.30**	**0.22**	**0.32**	**0.30**	**0.25**	0.15	**0.39**	**0.33**	*0.17*
Japan	**0.32**	0.04	**0.35**	**-0.15**	0.00	0.14	*0.08*	0.11	**0.29**	**0.11**	0.06

ROK	**0.25**	*0.21*	**0.28**	**0.13**	0.13	**0.41**	**0.34**	**0.22**	**0.40**	**0.24**	**0.22**
India(1999)	**0.38**	0.07	*0.24*	*0.25*	0.14	**0.28**	0.05	0.15	*0.23*	*0.24*	0.07
Number of products	376	115	385	864	70	153	1,005	154	396	1324	169
% export of Thailand to world 2000	3.19	6.16	4.43	6.63	2.81	1.44	11.43	0.81	2.03	58.07	2.08

Bold: Correlation is significant at the .01 level (2-tailed).
Italic: Correlation is significant at the .05 level (2-tailed).
Source: Calculated from PC-TAS, UN. 1996—2000.

Table 14 Intra Industry Trade Index of Thailand, average 1996—2000, weight by export plus import.

	ISIC1	ISIC2	ISIC31	ISIC32	ISIC33	ISIC34	ISIC35	ISIC36	ISIC37	ISIC38	ISIC39
China	0.26	0.60	0.15	0.87	0.04	0.11	0.93	0.07	0.18	18.94	0.06
ROK	0.05	0.00	0.10	0.32	0.01	0.06	1.48	0.09	0.17	11.49	0.06
Hong Kong	0.11	0.02	0.04	1.65	0.02	0.10	1.16	0.05	0.19	12.86	2.45
Japan	0.04	0.01	0.14	0.24	0.04	0.06	1.63	0.27	0.38	15.87	0.49
USA	0.18	0.00	0.22	0.18	0.05	0.07	0.68	0.05	0.02	13.77	0.61
Indonesia	0.12	1.69	0.15	0.60	0.04	0.49	3.90	0.13	0.10	4.80	0.03
Malaysia	0.09	0.02	0.34	0.28	0.09	0.13	2.14	0.11	0.35	27.46	0.14
Philippines	0.04	0.00	0.23	0.14	0.01	0.10	1.79	0.05	0.06	28.68	0.01

Source: Calculated from PC-TAS, UN. 1996—2000.

Table 15 Intra Industry Trade Index of ASEAN (6), average 1996—2000.

	ISIC1	ISIC2	ISIC31	ISIC32	ISIC33	ISIC34	ISIC35	ISIC36	ISIC37	ISIC38	ISIC39
China	0.08	2.15	1.70	0.84	0.32	0.24	2.10	0.22	0.73	22.41	0.21
ROK	0.02	0.11	0.17	0.59	0.05	0.13	2.59	0.13	0.53	21.99	0.18
India	0.14	0.04	0.25	0.47	0.03	0.14	2.90	0.08	1.00	7.61	0.74
Hong Kong	0.11	0.02	0.72	2.16	0.21	0.42	2.19	0.16	0.62	28.55	2.45
Japan	0.05	0.03	0.21	0.22	0.10	0.21	1.87	0.25	0.53	23.29	0.61
USA	0.07	0.18	0.30	0.27	0.11	1.43	1.31	0.08	0.18	23.37	0.58
EU	0.10	0.05	0.26	0.76	0.30	0.46	2.06	0.19	0.35	17.60	1.00

Source: Calculated from PC-TAS, UN. 1996-2000.

Table 16 Distribution of Net Foreign Direct Investment (%)

	1975	1980	1985	1990	1995	1998	1999	2000	2001
USA	10.98	29.54	36.10	24.15	17.78	26.13	26.70	21.00	17.50
NAFTA	28.10	43.33	42.13	29.20	23.58	31.19	30.11	26.48	24.49
EU-15	42.25	37.10	28.57	48.39	35.91	37.90	46.19	54.49	47.61
ASEAN-10	5.58	4.25	4.01	6.05	7.30	2.91	1.99	0.75	1.76
China	..	..	2.99	1.74	11.03	6.39	3.58	2.62	5.92
Hong Kong	..	..	..	..	..	2.16	2.27	4.23	3.06
India	0.36	0.14	0.19	0.12	0.66	0.38	0.20	0.16	0.46
Japan	..	0.49	1.15	0.89	0.01	0.48	1.14	0.56	0.83
ROK	..	0.01	0.42	0.39	0.55	0.79	0.86	0.63	0.43
World	100	100	100	100	100	100	100	100	100

Source : World Development Indicators 2003, World Bank.

Table 17 Effect on Economic Welfare of Various Regional Trade Agreements
% of annual GDP (% of GDP excluding agricultural liberalization)

Agreement	ASEAN	China	ROK	Japan	USA
China+ROK+Japan	-0.26 (-0.16)	+0.1 (-0.2)	+1.0 (+0.6)	+0.1 (+0.2)	+0.0 (+0.0)
ASEAN-China	+0.9 (+0.5)	+0.0 (+0.1)	-0.1 (-0.1)	+0.0 (+0.0)	+0.0 (+0.0)
ASEAN-Japan	+1.1 (+0.2)	-0.1 (-0.1)	-0.2 (-0.1)	+0.0 (+0.1)	+0.0(+0.0)
ASEAN+3	+1.5 (+0.6)	+0.1 (-0.2)	+1.1 (+0.8)	+0.2 (+0.2)	-0.1 (+0.0)
ASEAN+3+CER	+1.3 (+0.6)	+0.0 (-0.1)	+1.1 (+0.9)	+0.2 (+0.2)	-0.1 (+0.0)

Source ;R. Scollay and J. Gilbert (2001).

References

Apichat Pongsirirushakun, et. al. (2002), "Thailand's International Trade, Investment and Competitiveness", paper presented at the 2002 Year-end Conference on Meeting the Challenges from Globalization, Thailand Development Research Institute, December 14—15.

Chalongphob Sussangkarn (2003). " Thailand and the China-ASEAN FTA", *TDRI Quarterly Review*, Vol. 18, No. 1 , March 2003 pp. 13-20.

Elek Andrew (2003). "East Asian Economic Integration;

Critical Policy Choices", paper presented at APEC Study Center Consortium Conference 2003, Phuket, Thailand.

 Kobsak Putrakul and Others (2003). "Can We Count on Intra-Regional Trade as a Sauce of Growth?" Paper presented at Bank of Thailand's Symposium on Managing the Recovery: Challenge Ahead,20—21 August, Bangkok, Thailand.

 Nipon Poupongsakorn (2003). " Agriculture: Viewpoint from ASEAN", paper presented at the ASEAN-Japan Research Institute Meeting (AJRIM), Tokyo,July 22—23.

 Scollay R. and J. Gilbert (2001). *New Subregional Trade Arrangement in the Asia Pacific*, Institute of International Economic,Washington D.C..

The East Asia Free Trade Agreement: An ASEAN Perspective

Mohd Haflah Piei[1]

Introduction

It has been slightly more than a decade since the concept of the East Asia Economic Group (EAEG) was first mooted by Malaysia's Prime Minister. It was originally conceived of as an informal regional organisation to serve as a loose consultative forum where East Asian economies consult each other on issues of common concern as and when the need arises. It also meant to serve as a defensive strategy to counter the creation of a single Europe and the North America Free Trade Area (NAFTA), as well as to lobby for ASEAN interests in the then ongoing Uruguay Round of the GATT negotiation.

At the time, the East Asian economies were growing at a very rapid rate of 8.1 per cent per annum on the average (between 1987—1991), such that the region had eventually assumed a new role as the regional grouping consisting of some of the most dynamic economies in the world. This growth performance even surpassed those of the developed economies and other parts of the developing world. The NIEs of the East Asian economies

---

[1] Mohd Haflah Piei, Deputy Director, Malaysian Institute of Economic Research.

had achieved an average annual growth of 8.3 per cent, roughly three times the growth rate of the world economy at 2.9 per cent while ASEAN's growth rate, excluding the Philippines, was 6.9 per cent, more than twice the growth of the world economy. This phenomenal growth performance continued until the Asian economic crisis struck the region in mid-1997.

Rapid growth in the region's economies had been matched and reinforced by their strong trade performance, which is characterised by its increasing contribution to world trade, as well as intra-regional trade. Intra-East Asian trade, for example, had grown rapidly from US $196.4 billion in 1987 (a year after the 1985 — 1986 recession) to US $405.4 billion in 1991, thus registering a growth of 106 per cent. Meanwhile, exports from the NIEs as a whole, grew 73 per cent, while their exports to the ASEAN countries grew by 125 per cent. Total trade between ASEAN and NIEs increased by 156 per cent, while Japan trade with ASEAN increased by 85 per cent. In the absence of AFTA, which was launched later in 1993, intra-ASEAN trade, expanded by 114 per cent over the same years. This phenomenal growth, much higher than the world average of 46.9 per cent was testimony to the increasing economic linkages between the East Asian economies.

The degree of East Asian economic interdependence was further enhanced by the increasing flow of foreign direct investment (FDI), technology and labour into, and among, countries in the region. All these processes evolved without being based on any co-operation framework of any kind, regional or bilateral, and was completely market driven.

These developments have led to the rapid emergence of regional production networks. The enhanced trade integration that had already been achieved by the region's economies created further pressures for regional policy co-ordination, especially in those areas that would facilitate even further trade integration in the region. These policies that would enable the regional process to develop further, extend well beyond trade liberalisation. In short, regionalization in East Asia had created the need for a regional policy framework that would maintain the momentum of regionalization, and hence Malaysia's EAEG proposal.

However, the proposal was met with intense objection and criticism, and was a source of extreme controversy. Critics of the initiative[1] argued that the EAEG proposal threatened to "divide the Pacific region in half," and that politically and economically, it was not feasible. Supporters of the proposal, which included former Japanese foreign minister, on the other hand, argued that EAEG would "counter balance emerging organisations in Europe and North America and improve the bargaining positions of Asian countries". Many Japanese business leaders also criticised the sharp repudiation of the EAEG idea, especially that advocated by the US, by pointing out that "the United States was in fact drawing a line down the Pacific by signing the NAFTA". It was only after a lengthy debate and intense exchanges between the opposing sides that the proposal was later accepted, albeit after being substantially reshaped, diluted and renamed as the East Asian Economic Caucus (EAEC). The EAEC, later accepted as a caucus within APEC, had in effect been kept in the doldrums since then by the latter.

The re-emergence of the idea of creating some form of regional economic co-operation among East Asian economies arguably came about in the aftermath of the Asian crisis. It was only after this that the EAEC idea began to be taken more seri-

---

[1] See Harry Harding, "International Order and Organisation in the Asia-Pacific Region," Robert S. Ross (ed.), *East Asia in Transition: Towards a New Regional Order*, Institute of South East Asian Studies (ISEAS), Singapore, 1995.

ously. First, there was the Chiang-Mai Initiative of ASEAN+ 3[1], which mainly involved regional financial co-operation between and among members of ASEAN, China, Japan and ROK. As a result, to date, six bilateral swap arrangements (BSAs) between Japan-ROK, Japan-Thailand, Japan-the Philippines, Japan-Malaysia, China-Thailand, and China-Japan with a combined size of US $17 billion have been concluded and signed. Following this, there was an offer from China's Premier Zhu Rongji of a Free Trade Agreement between China and ASEAN (ASEAN-China FTA) to be effective in 10 years' time. This offer is of great historical significance and importance, as well as an unprecedented political move by China to signal its desire for a long-term friendship and economic co-operation with ASEAN[2].

China's offer has sparked a round of similar offers by other major East Asian economies. For example, the ASEAN-China FTA has sparked intense discussion in Japan on ways to strengthen its own links with ASEAN, and not to be left behind, it proposed an initiative for an ASEAN-Japan Comprehensive Economic Partnership (Japan-ASEAN CEP)[3]. ROK has

---

[1] This initiative was the result of a meeting between the ASEAN Finance Minister and Finance Ministers of China, Japan and ROK in Chiang Mai, Thailand, 6 May 2000.

[2] The agreement to form ASEAN-China FTA was signed by ASEAN member countries and China at the ASEAN Summit at Phnom Penh, Cambodia, 2002. "The Agreement shall commence in early 2003 and be concluded by 30 June 2004 in order to establish the ASEAN-China FTA covering trade in goods by 2010 for Brunei, China, Indonesia, Malaysia, the Philippines, Singapore and Thailand, and by 2015 for the newer ASEAN Member States". See *Framework Agreement on Comprehensive Economic Cooperation between the Association of Southeast Asian Nations and the People's Republic of China.*

[3] The objective is "... that the implementation of measures for the realization of the partnership, including elements of a possible free trade area, should be completed as soon as possible within 10 years..." See *Joint Declaration of the Leaders of ASEAN and Japan on the Comprehensive Economic Partnership*, ASEAN-Japan Summit, 5 November 2002.

also signalled an interest in establishing closer links with ASEAN. At the ASEAN Summit in Brunei, President Kim Dae-Jung agreed to set up a study group to review a possible ASEAN-ROK FTA. The Report of the East Asian Vision Group, an initiative launched by President Kim recommended several "key proposals and concrete measures to broaden East Asia co-operation. These include the proposal for the establishment of the East Asia Free Trade Area, and the liberalisation of trade well ahead of the APEC goals"[①]. In order to promote this initiative further, a proposal was made at the 5th ASEAN + 3 Summit to establish an ASEAN + 3 secretariat. To signal its support, there was an offer by Malaysia to host the secretariat in Kuala Lumpur, and to meet its expenses for the first three years of its operation.

At the same time, a number of individual ASEAN economies are pursuing bilateral trade agreements with the Northeast Asian countries, Japan, China and ROK. Singapore, for example, had signed a Closer Economic Partnership Agreement with Japan in January 2002. Thailand has conducted a joint study with ROK looking into the feasibility of forming an FTA between the two economies and it has also agreed to set up a joint task force to study how to promote closer economic cooperation with Japan. Even Malaysia, which was strongly critical of the trend towards bilateral FTA, is now in negotiations with

---

[①] Subsequently, the East Asian Study Group (EASG) was established to assess the recommendation of the EAVG. In its final report, the EASG strongly supported the EAVG proposal "to form an EAFTA well-ahead of the Bogor Goal of trade liberalization set by APEC". See *Final Report of the East Asian Study Group*, ASEAN Secretariat, Jakarta, 2002.

A more recent initiative is the creation of the East Asia Community of Cooperative Peace and Prosperity proposed by Malaysia's Prime Minister, Mahathir Mohamed, at the First East Asian Congress in Kuala Lumpur on August 2003.

Japan to form an Economic Partnership Agreement.[1]

Against this background, some questions immediately come to mind. First, what exactly triggered off this new interest in East Asia economic co-operation, something that was deemed not feasible in 1990, but that suddenly became a matter of significant concern to countries in the region? Second, what are the new circumstances and challenges that caused this turn-around in policy stance and direction? Third, what would be the most appropriate architecture, principles and modalities of the proposed EAFTA? These are some of the crucial questions that this paper attempts to address mainly from the perspectives of the ASEAN member countries.

This paper is organized as follow. The next section will highlight some of the major features of the ASEAN economies with special emphasis on its economic relationship with the East Asian countries, China, Japan and ROK. Given the current and potential challenges and circumstances facing the ASEAN member countries, it is argued that it will make good economic sense for ASEAN countries to establish a framework agreement to strengthen its economic co-operation with the three East Asian economies. The next section will discuss the possible architecture of the proposed regional economic co-operation framework, which focuses, among others, on the modalities, principles and scope of the proposed initiative. This is to be followed by a discussion on the merits and demerits of the proposed initiatives. The last section will summarise some of the major policy implications of this paper.

---

[1] See Christopher Findley, Mohd Haflah Piei and Mari Pangestu, " Trading with Favourites: Risks, Motives and Implications of FTAs in the Asia Pacific". Paper prepared for the workshop on Trade Policy Issues in East Asia, The Center for Strategic and International Studies, Jakarta, March 2003.

I. The ASEAN Economy

The ASEAN region has a population of about 0.5 billion, a total area of 4.5 million square kilometres, a combined gross national product of about US $ 570 billion and a total trade of about US $ 780 billion in the year 2000. In terms of its total GDP, it is about 11.9 per cent and 52.5 per cent of those of Japan and China respectively, and about 25 per cent higher than ROK's GDP in year 2000.

As for its growth rate, the region has definitely done comparatively well, if not better, than those registered by the three East Asian economies. The average annual growth rate for all the ASEAN member countries, with the exception of the Philippines, had been well above 5 per cent during the period just before the financial crisis struck the region. Growth was badly affected by the crisis with most countries in the region, particularly in Indonesia, Thailand and Malaysia, and to a lesser extent the Philippines and Singapore that were registering negative or very low growth during the two years following the crisis, i.e. 1998 and 1999. Since then, most economies have shown sustainable recovery although they are still well below their pre-crisis levels.

With regards to its GNP per capita, it is quite diverse and may be categorized into three groups of economies with Singapore and Brunei in the highest income group. The four new members of ASEAN (Cambodia, Lao PDR, Myanmar and Vietnam) are in the lowest income group with per capita income of less than US $ 300, while the remaining countries (Malaysia, Thailand, the Philippines and Indonesia) constitute the middle income group with per capita income ranging from US $ 680 in the case of Indonesia to about US $ 3,600 in the case of Malaysia (Table 1).

Table 1 Basic Economic Indicators of East Asian Countries

Country	Population (million) 1998	GDP annual growth rate 1990-2000	GNP/capita (US $ 1998)	GDP(US $ billion) (2002)	Inflation (2000, %)	Current account(% of GDP, 2001)	Unemployment (%)
Japan	126.3	1.3	32380.0	4746.0	-0.7	2.2	5.0
ROK	46.4	5.7	7970.0	457.0	3.4	1.0	3.7
China	1238.6	10.3	750.0	1080.0	1.5	2.6	n.a
ASEAN							
Brunei	0.3	n.a	21962.0	n.a	2.1	71.2	4.3
Indonesia	203.7	5.8	680.0	153.0	10.8	3.2	6.1
Malaysia	22.2	7.7	3600.0	90.0	1.3	7.3	3.9
Philippines	75.1	3.3	1050.0	75.0	6.5	6.4	11.2
Singapore	3.2	8.0	30060.0	92.0	1.5	21.0	3.2
Thailand	61.1	7.4	2200.0	122.0	2.5	4.4	3.6
Cambodia	10.7	5.5	280.0	3.1	n.a	n.a	7.4
Laos	5.0	6.7	180.0	1.7	27.1	n.a	7.3
Myanmar	44.4	6.3	n.a	n.a	10.3	n.a	7.1
Vietnam	77.6	8.6	180.0	31.0	4.3	1.3	7.4
ASEAN+3	1914.6	-	-	6868.1			

Source: ASEAN Secretariat.

Most of the ASEAN economies, particularly with regard to the original six member countries of ASEAN (ASEAN 6), are generally open economies that are outward-oriented and trade dependent. This is shown by the high total trade to GDP ratios (Table 2).

Table 2 Trade Dependencies Ratio, 1996-1999

Country	1996	1997	1998	1999
Brunei	1.328	0.985	0.770	0.909
Indonesia	0.442	0.460	0.798	0.514
Malaysia	1.485	1.540	1.903	1.872
Philippines	0.583	0.743	0.903	0.858
Singapore	2.648	2.797	2.572	2.691
Thailand	0.703	0.800	0.788	0.855

ASEAN's trade registered modest increment over the 1995 —2000 period growing at the rate of 4.0 per cent per annum, compared to 17.3 per cent and 15.5 per cent over the 1980—1990 and 1990—1995 periods. The share of total ASEAN trade in world trade had increased to about 6 per cent during the 1995— 1999 period from a level of about 3.5 per cent during the 1980— 1990 period (Table 3). ASEAN as a region is more of an exporter to the world rather than an importer, inasmuch as its trade balance with the world has mostly been positive. This trend has been more distinctive in the years after the crisis due to import suppression and/or export enhancing policies that the crisis-affected economies implemented.

Together with the three East Asian countries, Japan, ROK and China, the East Asian regional shares of world total trade had increased rapidly from 12.8 per cent in 1980 to 17.8 per cent in 1999. This regional trade share is slightly higher than those of the US, but is only half of EEC share of 37.9 per cent in 1999 (Table 3). Another interesting trend has been that the region is fast becoming an important source of world export where the regional export share had increased from 13.0 to 20.0 per cent of world exports (Table 4) and its trade balance had been showing an increasing surplus during the same time period.

Table 3 Total Trade of East Asian Economies, the US and EEC(US $ billion, %)

	1980		1985		1990		1995		1999	
	(US billion)	(%)	(US billion)	(%)	(US billion)	(%)	(US billion)	(%)	(US billion)	(%)
World	3751232	100.0	3850429	100.0	6898949	100.0	10208754	100.0	11473636	100.0
United States	477740	12.7	574767	14.9	910126	13.2	1354423	13.3	1739124	15.2
EEC	1595103	42.5	1432805	37.2	3027329	43.9	3932463	38.5	4352347	37.9
Japan	271719	7.2	307705	8.0	522985	7.6	779074	7.6	729940	6.4
ROK	39502	1.1	61347	1.6	142217	2.1	260940	2.6	263387	2.3
China	37644	1.0	69809	1.8	116569	1.7	281118	2.8	360649	3.1
Singapore	39390	1.1	50806	1.3	120266	1.7	215462	2.1	232191	2.0
ASEAN 9	92686	2.5	89691	2.3	193902	2.8	440163	4.3	452682	3.9
ASEAN+3	480941	12.8	579358	15.0	1095939	15.9	1976750	19.4	2038849	17.8

Note: Figures in percentage represent total share in world trade.

Table 4 Export of the World, East Asia, the US and EEC (US $ billion, %)

	1980		1985		1990		1995		1999	
	(US billion)	(%)	(US billion)	(%)	(US billion)	(%)	(US billion)	(%)	(US billion)	(%)
World	1832508	100.0	1874505	130.8	3381690	111.7	5070827	128.9	5663310	130.1
US	220781	13.8	213146	14.9	393106	13.0	583451	14.8	690680	15.9
EEC	751159	47.1	708197	49.4	1488305	49.2	2018290	51.3	2208491	50.7
Japan	130435	8.2	177189	12.4	287678	9.5	443047	11.3	419207	9.6
Singapore	19377	1.2	22812	1.6	52753	1.7	118187	3.0	114730	2.6
ROK	17439	1.1	30289	2.1	67812	2.2	125588	3.2	143647	3.3
ASEAN 9	52169	3.3	49692	3.5	91612	3.0	204417	5.2	255046	5.9
China	18139	1.1	27329	1.9	62760	2.1	148955	3.8	194931	4.5
ASEAN+3	237559	14.9	307311	21.4	562615	18.6	1040194	26.5	1127561	25.9

Note: Figures in percentage represent total share in world export.

Table 5 Import of the World, East Asia, the US and EEC (US $ billion, %)

	1980		1985		1990		1995		1999	
	(US billion)	(%)	(US billion)	(%)	(US billion)	(%)	(US billion)	(%)	(US billion)	(%)
World	1918724	100.0	1975924	100.0	3517259	100.0	5137927	100.0	5810326	100.0
United States	256959	13.4	361620	18.3	517020	14.7	770972	15.0	1048435	18.0
EEC	843944	44.0	724609	36.7	1518964	43.2	1914173	37.3	2143856	36.9
Japan	141284	7.4	130516	6.6	235307	6.7	336027	6.5	310733	5.3
ROK	22063	1.1	31058	1.6	74405	2.1	135352	2.6	119740	2.1
China	19505	1.0	42480	2.1	53809	1.5	132163	2.6	165718	2.9
Singapore	24013	1.3	26237	1.3	60954	1.7	124394	2.4	111071	1.9
ASEAN 9	40525	2.1	39999	2.0	53809	1.5	235746	4.6	197636	3.4
ASEAN+3	247390	12.9	270290	13.7	478284	13.6	963682	18.8	904898	15.6

Note: Figures in percentage represent total share in world import.

East Asia, United States (US) and European Union remained the major trading partners of ASEAN in 2000. They accounted for almost 60 per cent of the total global trade of ASEAN with East Asia being the largest trading partners of ASEAN contributing about 30.5 per cent well above the US and EU shares of 16.6 and 12.3 per cent respectively. Table 6 indicates the relative position of ASEAN with respect to other selected regional arrangements.

Table 6 Global Trade of ASEAN Countries in 2000(US $ billion)

	East Asia	USA	EU	Taiwan	HongKong	ROW	Total Global
Singapore	55.8	44.0	33.5	14.2	14.4	110.7	272.6
Malaysia	79.1	33.8	22.3	8.4	6.7	30.2	180.5
Thailand	35.4	22.2	17.3	5.4	4.3	47.5	132.1
Indonesia	29.7	11.8	8.5	3.6	1.8	40.2	95.9
Philippines	28.0	16.6	9.8	4.8	3.1	7.2	69.5
Vietnam	9.9	1.1	4.1	2.7	0.9	10.3	29.0
Cambodia	0.4	0.5	0.3	0.3	-	1.5	3.0
Laos	0.1	Neg.	0.1	Neg.	Neg.	0.3	0.4
Total	238.4	130.0	95.9	39.4	31.2	247.9	782.7
Percentage of Global Trade	30.5	16.6	12.3	5.0	4.0	31.7	100.0

II. ASEAN-East Asian Trade Relations

In 2000, ASEAN-East Asian total trade amounted to about US $ 200 billion (approximately 30.5 per cent of ASEAN global trade), growing by about 30 per cent since 1993 when the amount of ASEAN-East Asian trade was about US $ 150 billion. Roughly 56.5 per cent of ASEAN total trade with the East Asian economies was contributed by Japan, another 30 per cent by China, and the remaining 20 per cent by ROK. (Table 7)

On the export side, ASEAN exports to the three East Asian economies had expanded by more than two-fold from about US $ 41.6 billion in 1993 to US $ 99.9 billion in 2000. China has been the fastest growing export market for ASEAN followed by ROK and Japan. In 1993, ASEAN exported only US $ 4.5 billion to China (or equivalent to 1.8 per cent of ASEAN global export), but by year 2000, ASEAN exports to China had increased by about 7.5 times to about US $ 33.8 billion. Similarly, ASEAN's proportion of China's total imports too has been showing rapid increase from 6 per cent in 1991 to 9.9 per cent in 2000 (Table 7).

On the import side, ASEAN imports from the East Asian countries had remained at around US $ 100 billion per year between 1993—2000 except for 1998 and 1999 when it contracted significantly to about US $ 67.1 billion and US $ 75 billion, respectively, during the crisis years.

The balance of trade between ASEAN and the three East Asian countries as a group has always been negative, increasing rapidly in 1997 from -US $ 28 billion in 1993 to a peak of -US $ 37.8 billion in 1997, before it dropped sharply to -US $ 15.4 billion, -US $ 7.6 billion and -US $ 0.9 billion during the three years after the crisis struck the region (Table 7). This has been mainly due to export expansion, as well as import suppression policies implemented by the crisis-hit countries in ASEAN.

The biggest trade deficit registered by ASEAN has been its trade with that of Japan, and to a lesser extent, ROK. Trade balance with China however has been registering positive amounts in the last three year since the crisis. However, with rapid recovery taking place in ASEAN, it is to be expected that the trade balance with the East Asian economies would worsen, particularly trade balance with Japan. This may have some critical bearings on the effort to establish a free trade area in the region in the sense that the initiative must not worsen ASEAN trade balance vis-à-vis the East Asian economies.

III. Structure of ASEAN-East Asia Trade

In the early 1990s, the top five ASEAN export items to East Asian countries were electrical equipment, oil and fuel, computer, machinery, wood, and fish products. Together they form 75.7 per cent, 72.2 per cent and 67.7 per cent of ASEAN exports to China, ROK and Japan. By 2000, the share of the top five products in the export of ASEAN had slightly changed where there had been a slight reduction in the share to about 70 per cent in the case of China and increase to about 77.9 per cent and 71.34 in the case of ROK and Japan respectively. These indicate that ASEAN export had become more diversified whereas the export to ROK and Japan had become more specialised and concentrated.

Another feature observed in the ASEAN export pattern of the three East Asian economies was that the order of importance of its export items had changed quite distinctively, away from commodities and more towards manufactured products. For instance, in the case of ASEAN exports to China, "lubricant and fuel", "wood", as well as "fats and oils" were the top three export items of ASEAN. Together they contributed 63.3 per cent towards ASEAN's exports to China. By 2000, their export shares had sharply contracted to only 17.7 per cent. Their positions were taken over by computers/machinery and electrical equipment, which collectively amounted to 48.4 of all ASEAN exports to China. (Table 8a)

A similar shift in the pattern of ASEAN exports to Japan and ROK can also be observed, with the exception of "lubricants, fuel and oil" which still remains the top ASEAN export item to ROK, and ASEAN's second most important export item to Japan. This situation will remain for a longer time considering that Japan and ROK are lacking in these natural resources.

With the exception of Japan, ASEAN imports from East Asia are more diversified than its exports, based on the share of the top 10 or top 5 of ASEAN's import items from the three economies. In 1993, ASEAN's top 5 import items, together, contributed about 36 per cent and 55.6 per cent toward ASEAN total imports from China and ROK, respectively, compared to 74.3 per cent in the case of Japan. By 2000, ASEAN imports from these countries have become less diversified with the share of the top five import items increasing to 56.8 per cent, 70.2 per cent and 75.54 per cent of ASEAN imports from China, ROK and Japan, respectively.

Table 7 ASEAN Trade with Japan, China and Korea (US $ million)

	1993 Expt	1993 Imp	1993 B of Tr	1994 Expt	1994 Imp	1994 B of Tr	1995 Expt	1995 Imp	1995 B of Tr	1996 Expt	1996 Imp	1996 B of Tr
China	4529	4326	193	5304	5759	-455	6201	7130	-922	7474	9218	-1744
Japan	30952	55703	-27751	34300	67302	-33002	42681	78535	-35864	43150	73310	-30160
ROK	6126	7148	-1022	7005	9036	-2031	8574	11346	-2772	9446	13294	-3848
Total	41607	108794	-28580	46609	82097	-35488	57456	97011	-39548	60070	95822	-35752

	1997 Expt	1997 Imp	1997 B of Tr	1998 Expt	1998 Imp	1998 B of Tr	1999 Expt	1999 Imp	1999 B of Tr	2000 Expt	2000 Imp	2000 B of Tr
China	9168	13482	-4314	9204	11212	-2008	26407	19184	7223	33783	24985	8798
Japan	42009	71264	-29263	34717	46693	-11976	37629	51244	-13615	51982	61404	-9422
ROK	10668	14857	-4189	7813	9267	-1454	10878	12110	-1232	14145	14471	-356
Total	61845	99603	-37766	51734	67172	-15438	74914	65338	-7624	99910	100860	-950

Source: Asean Secretariat, Jakarta.

The above shifting pattern in ASEAN trade relations with the three East Asian economies implies the increasing extent of intra-industry trade with the region and the emergence of a regional production network. This phenomenon is more distinctive in the case of ASEAN's trade with Japan where electrical equipment, computer and machinery together contributed more than 70 per cent of ASEAN exports to, and imports from, Japan.

In the case of ASEAN-China and ASEAN-ROK, trade in these products is also high, which, however, do not reflect a strong regional production network emerging among ASEAN, China and ROK. Most of the machinery and electrical appliances exported by China to ASEAN are those for general or special uses. On the other hand, a substantial part of the machinery and electrical appliances that China imports from ASEAN are electronic components and devices. For example, of the US $ 2.88 billion worth of machinery and electrical appliances that China imports from Malaysia, more than half of them were kinescope, transistors and integrated circuits, and more than 40 per cent were machinery and electrical appliances.

However, recent trend suggests the possibility that China is emerging as major trade and production hub for the East Asian region, drawing in imports on the basis of China's own domestic demand as well as inputs for the production of its exports to the US and other developed market. [1]

---

[1] For a more elaborate discussion on this, see World Bank, *Looking Beyond Short-terms shocks*, *East Asia and Pacific Region*, April 2003.

Table 8a Major ASEAN Export to China(%)

HS chapter	Sector	1993	2000
85	Electrical equip.	6.01	31.77
84	Computer/machinery	6.39	16.63
27	Lubricants/fuel/oil	32.30	13.17
38	Misc. chemical products	0.61	5.68
44	Wood	22.64	2.75
29	Organic chemical	1.52	2.10
48	Paper and paper board	0.47	1.86
15	Fats and oils	8.38	1.78
37	Photographic goods	0.01	1.34
	Total	78.33	77.08

Table 8b Major ASEAN Import from China(%)

HS chapter	Sector	1993	2000
85	Electrical equip.	11.08	35.96
84	Computer/machinery	9.70	15.69
27	Lubricants/fuel/oil	8.98	4.75
52	Cotton	5.59	2.56
90	Optical/medical instruments	1.03	2.24
88	Iron and steel	2.09	2.13
10	Cereal	3.74	2.08
39	Plastics	0.84	1.84
71	Jewellery	0.12	1.39
28	Inorganic chemicals	2.98	1.39
	Total	46.15	70.03

Table 9a Major ASEAN Export to Japan(%)

HS chapter	Sector	1993	2000
85	Electrical equip.	13.06	26.02
27	Lubricants/fuel/oil	28.15	23.08
84	Computer/machinery	7.49	18.8
44	Wood	11.72	3.44
3	Fish	7.29	2.86
89	Ships, boats	0.01	2.08
94	Furniture	2.03	1.68
39	Plastics	0.75	1.86
26	Ores	2.18	1.61
87	Cars, trucks and autos	0.29	1.35
	Total	72.97	82.78

Table 9b Major ASEAN Import from Japan(%)

HS chapter	Sector	1993	2000
85	Electrical equip.	30.00	34.57
84	Computer/machinery	23.88	23.39
87	Cars, trucks and autos	11.65	8.61
88	Iron and steel	5.45	5.1
39	Plastics	3.29	3.87
90	Optical/medical instrument	3.68	3.67
73	Articles of iron or steel	3.42	2.12
29	Organic chemical	1.95	1.88
91	Jewellery	0.36	1.45
40	Rubber	0.97	1.03
	Total	84.65	85.69

Table 10a Major ASEAN Export to ROK (%)

HS chapter	Sector	1993	2000
27	Lubricants/fuel/oil	36.44	30.86
85	Electrical equip.	9.99	26.15
84	Computer/machinery	7.79	17.16
44	Wood	17.17	2.04
26	Ores	0.89	1.70
29	Organic chemical	1.48	1.54
38	Misc. chemical products	1.70	1.34
39	Plastics	0.53	1.04
40	Rubber	2.61	1.14
74	Copper	1.27	1.23
	Total	79.87	84.20

Table 10b Major ASEAN Import from ROK(%)

HS chapter	Sector	1993	2000
85	Electrical equip.	30.39	43.55
84	Computer/machinery	11.96	11.25
27	Lubricants/fuel/oil	4.74	6.20
29	Organic chemical	2.43	4.73
39	Plastics	6.04	4.47
88	Iron and steel	8.70	4.33
87	Cars, trucks and autos	0.98	2.60
89	Ships, boats	0.87	1.91
73	Articles of iron or steel	3.37	1.76
55	Man-made staple filament	5.05	1.32
	Total	74.53	82.12

There are several reasons for the rapid growth of ASEAN-East Asia trade during the 1990s, some of which have been discussed earlier. One important factor was the dynamism of the economies in the region as reflected in the rapid growth rate of the real GDP in most regional economies.

Another factor was the falling MFN tariff rates in most economies in the region, particularly in ASEAN and China. At the beginning of 1993, China reduced its tariff on 3,371 import items and abolished import controls on more than 367 commodities. At the 1995 APEC Summit, China's President Jiang Zemin further made a commitment to cut average tariffs to 15 per cent by 2000. This new liberalization effort includes substantial tariff cuts on 4,998 tariff lines. China has also eliminated quotas, licensing and import controls on 176 tariff lines, or more than 30 per cent of commodities subject to these restrictions. As part of China's commitment for its accession to the WTO, it has agreed to make further cuts in tariffs and NTBs. Table 11 provides data on the weighted average tariff rates for 2001, and the agreed Chinese bound tariff rates reported in the Protocol of Accession to be implemented starting from the date of accession. The decline in China's average tariff rate between the time of its accession and the final year is expected to be from 13.7 per cent to 5.7 per cent.

Table 11 Post-Accession Reduction in Weighted Tariff Rates for China's Main Imports[a]

Product group	Tariff rate	
	2001(MFN)	Final[b](bound)
Cereal grains	91.1	3.0
Oil seeds	96.9	3.9
Beverages and tobacco products	57.8	10.4
Electronic equipment	10.6	2.3
Vegetable oils and fats	39.3	10.2
Wood products	10.0	3.4
Paper products, publishing	9.3	3.3
Crops	21.7	8.4
Textiles	20.5	8.7
Plant-based fibers	84.3	37.7
Motor vehicles and parts	31.6	14.1
Dairy products	19.0	8.9
Vegetables, fruit, nuts	25.9	12.6
Machinery and equipment	13.4	6.6
Meat products	18.6	9.9
Sugar	77.9	43.8
Processed rice	114.0	65.0
Paddy rice	114.0	65.0
Wheat	114.0	65.0
Ferrous metals	9.1	5.2
Chemical, rubber, plastic products	14.1	8.1
Forestry	2.3	1.3
Food products	16.8	9.8
Fishing	14.2	8.5
Metals	7.0	4.2
Wearing apparel	23.8	14.9
Leather products	11.6	8.0
Meat	14.1	9.9
Transport equipment	5.0	3.6
Metal products	9.7	7.4
Mineral products	14.4	11.4

Petroleum, coal products	8.4	6.7
Manufactures	19.5	15.8
Animal products	9.4	8.0
Average of above	14.6	6.1
All goods	13.7	5.7

Source: UNCTAD, Trade Analysis and Information System (TRAINS) database, based on WTO figures.
 a. Weighted by China's imports of relevant items in 2000.
 b. At the end of the transition period.

Similar trade liberalizing processes have been taking place in ASEAN in the context of the Uruguay Round commitments, as well as in the AFTA process. Table 12 shows ASEAN post UR-MFN tariff rates. It ranges from as low as 3.12 per cent in the case of Brunei to 43.18 per cent for Thailand. Tariff rates for Malaysia, Indonesia and Philippines were less than 10 per cent, while Singapore is a tariff free city-state.

Table 12 Average MFN Tariffs

Sector	Brunei Darussalam	Indonesia	Malaysia	Myanmar	Philippines	Thailand
Live Animals	0.00	4.74	3.96	8.12	20.00	49.28
Fruits and Vegetable Product	0.00	4.63	2.45	7.50	11.19	48.27
Fats and Oils	0.00	4.86	2.11	2.05	8.45	31.35
Prepared Foodstuffs	0.05	17.57	10.85	13.43	18.76	49.91
Mineral Products	0.00	4.05	2.04	1.42	3.54	18.05
Chemicals	0.64	5.76	1.86	2.34	4.06	32.23
Plastics	2.14	11.14	15.05	2.65	8.43	46.13
Hides and Leather	1.36	6.25	6.91	7.28	8.42	46.67
Wood and Wood Articles	10.44	3.42	1.42	11.21	11.73	36.59
Pulp and Paper	0.00	6.94	9.51	2.78	8.61	32.34
Textiles and Apparel	0.44	13.90	16.70	10.54	18.24	72.07
Footwear	5.33	16.54	19.25	7.41	15.47	79.64
Stone/Cement/Ceramics	0.65	7.26	16.91	3.68	11.01	47.38
Gems	2.41	10.76	2.87	13.65	7.07	33.4
Base Metal and Metal Articles	0.12	9.70	9.36	3.18	8.14	25.37
Machinery and Electrical Appliances	9.22	4.86	8.12	2.77	5.68	36.25
Vehicles	21.24	39.28	52.55	4.68	11.48	47.57

Optical, precision & musical instruments	7.79	7.38	1.82	5.84	4.60	36.75
Arms	0.00	9.29	15.00	9.47	19.00	37.65
Miscellaneous Manufactured articles	2.26	14.70	14.64	7.15	11.23	53.28
Antiques and works of art	0.00	12.86	1.96	4.25	15.00	31.67
AVERAGE	3.12	9.34	9.42	5.55	10.08	43.18

A number of the ASEAN countries have also embarked on deregulation and liberalisation measures over the 1990s.

☐ Brunei's applied tariff rates are low, averaging 3.1 per cent in 2000, zero for agriculture, and 3.6 per cent for non-agricultural products.

☐ Indonesia has undertaken a significant reduction of applied tariff rates, with the lowering of rates going well beyond its WTO commitments. Applied MFN tariffs have been reduced from an un-weighted average of about 20 per cent in 1994, to 9.5 per cent in 1998. Further unilateral tariff cuts are scheduled up to 2003 in accordance with a clearly defined program of tariff reduction. By 2003, the maximum applied tariff for nearly all products will not exceed 10 per cent. Already in 1998, tariffs on goods items, have been reduced to a maximum of 5 per cent.

☐ Malaysia has cut its import tariff by almost one half since 1993, reducing protection for most agricultural and manufactured goods. The average applied tariff rate has declined from 15.2 per cent in 1993, to 8.1 per cent in 1997. Furthermore, whereas only 13 per cent of tariff lines were exempt from import duty in 1995, over half of all lines now bear duty-free applied rates.

☐ In the Philippines, tariffication and reduction in tariff over the past six years have significantly opened the economy. Applied tariffs were more than halved between

1992 and 1999 from 26 per cent to just over 10 per cent. The Philippines is in the midst of a tariff rationalisation program that will in effect create a uniform tariff structure for manufactured products of no higher than 5 per cent.

☐ For Thailand, applied MFN tariff rates averaged 18 per cent in September 1999, compared with 23 per cent in 1995. Tariff peaks were reduced to 60 per cent down from 100 per cent in 1995.

IV. The ASEAN Free Trade Area (AFTA)

Arguably, the decision taken during the Fourth ASEAN Summit in 1992 to establish the ASEAN Free Trade Area (AFTA) by the year 2008 is the most significant and ambitious step taken by ASEAN so far in terms of regional economic integration. The six original founding members, Indonesia, Malaysia, the Philippines, Singapore, Thailand, and Brunei signed the treaty in Singapore that decides to establish AFTA. In mid-1995, Vietnam gained admission as the seventh member of ASEAN. Laos and Myanmar followed suit two years later in 1997 with Cambodia joining to bandwagon in 1999.

The main calculus behind the creation of AFTA was the laying of a framework and forum for ASEAN member-states to cooperate with each other whilst moving towards deeper economic integration not only among themselves but also with the world. AFTA's creation will also help member-economies to lock-on and manage trade reforms more effectively to meet the WTO initiatives collectively. The ASEAN economies that are primarily export-oriented already figure as the central entity in regional trade platforms involving Asia-Pacific economies. Nevertheless, the purpose of AFTA is not simply to promote an increase in intra-regional trade. By increasing and facilitating the free flow of goods within the ASEAN region, the AFTA is also expected to promote a greater degree of market integration.

The critical tools used to promote trade and liberalization within the region is through the elimination of intra-regional tariffs and the limitation of non-tariff barriers (NTBs). ASEAN's approach to liberalisation is one of "open regionalism". This may be characterised as the promotion of regional trade expansion through facilitation and the reduction in the official barriers to regional trade through multilateral reductions in protection. Simply put, it is regionalism with a global orientation (Piei & Abubakar 1998). Apart from promoting and enhancing trade, the AFTA framework also endeavors to promote greater intra-ASEAN investment and foreign direct investment in the region. Simultaneously, AFTA has, since 1995, gone beyond being a traditional Preferential Trading Arrangement and expanded and deepened into other important aspects such as the development and integration in "non-border" areas of co-operation. This is expected to further strengthen the links among ASEAN national markets (Chee 1997). Ultimately, it is also hoped that the region's attractiveness for trade and foreign investment will increase, and thus augment ASEAN's competitive edge as a production base geared for the world market.

The main mechanism for the implementation of AFTA is the Common Effective Preferential Tariff (CEPT). The CEPT is an agreed effective tariff that is preferential to ASEAN member-states, and is to be applied to goods that have been identified for inclusion under the CEPT scheme originating from member-states. To be eligible, several criteria need to be fulfilled, namely, that

- The product has to already be included in the "Inclusion List" of the CEPT scheme of both the exporting and the importing countries. All other categories of products including those in the "Temporary Exclusion List" will not

be eligible.
- The tariff rate in the exporting country for the same product must be at or less than 20 per cent. However, if the tariff in the exporting country is above 20 per cent, concessions can only be given when the CEPT of the importing country is also above 20 per cent.
- The product in question must be of ASEAN origin and it must have at least 40 per cent domestic ASEAN content. This refers to a single country or cumulative ASEAN content.

The original schedule required the CEPT tariffs to be reduced to between 0−5 per cent within 15 years, i. e. by 2008, while non-tariff barriers were to be eliminated beginning from 1 January 1993. In September 1994, ASEAN agreed to accelerate the establishment of AFTA by reducing the initial time frame from 15 to 10 years. Under the 1994 amended timetable, the full realisation of AFTA with tariffs falling between zero and 5 per cent was expected by the year 2003 for the original ASEAN five: Indonesia, Malaysia, Thailand, Singapore and the Philippines as well as Brunei. The deadline for Vietnam was 2006 and for Myanmar and Laos, 2008.

To help ameliorate the effects of the regional crisis and to speed up the recovery efforts, ASEAN members announced a further acceleration of the AFTA schedule during the 6th ASEAN Summit in Hanoi in December 1998. The six original signatories have agreed to advance the implementation by one year from 2002 to 2003. The six also agreed to achieve a minimum of 90 per cent of their total tariff lines with tariffs between 0−5 per cent by the year 2000. In theory, this would account for 90 per cent of total intra-ASEAN trade (ASEAN Secretariat 1999). At the same time, each member-state would individually commit to achieve a minimum of 85 per cent of the Inclusion List with tariffs of 0−5 per cent by the year 2000. Following this, there is to be an increase to a minimum of 90 per cent of the Inclusion List in the 0—5 per cent tariff range by 2001. By the year 2002, 100 per cent of the items in the Inclusion List would have tariffs of between zero and 5 per cent (with some flexibility). It was not until the Singapore meeting in late 1999 that the target of zero tariffs as the ultimate target of AFTA was explicitly endorsed. At this meeting, the Ministers agreed "to eliminate import duties on all products and to target to achieve this objective by 2015 for the six original members and by year 2018 for the new members of ASEAN". [1] Furthermore, as a first step towards this ambitious goal, they agreed that the six original members would eliminate tariffs on 60 per cent of their products by the year 2003.

What has been the progress in this direction so far? As of 11 April 2002, the CEPT Scheme had covered 98.09 per cent of all tariff lines for the ASEAN-6. Average tariff rates on these products have fallen to 3.89 per cent, which is well in advance of the agreement that 85 per cent of the Inclusion List will have tariff of 0—5 per cent. (Table 13 and 14). For the four new members of ASEAN, about half of their total tariff lines (49.94 per cent) are in the Inclusion List, 46.88 per cent of total tariff lines are in the TEL, 2.18 per cent of the total tariff lines are in the GEL, and 1.02 per cent of the total tariff lines are in the Sensitive List.

Progress in the level of deepening notwithstanding, tariff reductions under the CEPT scheme alone may not be sufficient to enhance intra-ASEAN trade if other non-tariff barriers (NTBs) remain in place. This is because the existence of NTBs may limit or perhaps negate the trade liberalizing effect of the CEPT mechanism. To address this issue, the CEPT agreement call on mem-

---

[1] These target dates were further accelerated to 2010 for the ASEAN 6 and 2015 for the new members of ASEAN.

ber countries to eliminate quantitative restrictions with respect to products under the CEPT scheme in addition to other non-tariff barriers on a gradual basis within a period of five years, respectively.

Table 13 CEPT Product List for the Year 2002

Country	Inclusion List (IL)	Temporary Exception List (TEL)	General Exception List (TEL)	Sensitive List (SL)	Total
Brunei	6276	0	202	14	6492
Indonesia	7176	21	68	4	7269
Malaysia	8867	233*	63	73	9236
Philippines	5606	35	16	62	5719
Singapore	5821	0	38	0	5859
Thailand	9104	0	0	7	9111
Total ASEAN-6	42850	289	387	160	43686
Percentage	98.09	0.66	0.89	0.37	100.00
New Members of ASEAN:					
Cambodia	3115	3523	134	50	6822
Laos	1247	2142	74	88	3551
Myanmar	2387	3017	47	21	5472
Vietnam	3573	1007	196	48	4824
Total	10322	9689	451	207	20669
Percentage	49.94	46.88	2.18	1.00	100.00
Total ASEAN-10	53172	9978	838	367	64355
Percentage	82.62	15.50	1.30	0.57	100.00

Source: ASEAN Secretariat.
* Covers group of automotive products whose inclusion being deferred to 2005.

Table 14 ASEAN: Average CEPT, 1999—2003

Country	Year 1999 Tariff Lines	Year 1999 Average	Year 2000 Tariff Lines	Year 2000 Average	Year 2001 Tariff Lines	Year 2001 Average	Year 2002 Tariff Lines	Year 2002 Average	Year 2003 Tariff Lines	Year 2003 Average
Brunei	6264	1.55	6264	1.26	6264	1.17	6264	0.96	6273	0.96
Indonesia	6931	5.36	7176	4.76	7176	4.36	7176	3.71	7176	2.18
Malaysia	8374	3.22	8417	2.79	8417	2.6	8417	2.43	8417	2.06
Philippines	5431	7.36	5431	5.88	5431	5.24	5431	4.95	5431	3.79
Singapore	5739	0	5772	0	5772	0	5772	0	5772	0
Thailand	9062	9.58	9067	7.29	9067	7.26	9067	5.98	9067	4.63
ASEAN-6	41801	4.8	42127	3.89	42127	3.67	42127	3.18	42136	2.41
Cambodia	–	–	3115	10.39	3115	10.39	3115	8.89	3115	7.93
Laos	1247	7.54	1247	7.07	1247	6.58	1247	6.15	1247	5.66
Myanmar	2356	4.45	2356	4.38	2356	3.32	2356	3.31	2356	3.19
Vietnam	3570	7.09	–	–	–	–	–	–	–	–
ASEAN-4	7173	6.3	6718	7.67	6718	7.2	6718	6.42	6718	5.85
Total ASEAN-10	48974	5.02	48845	4.41	48845	4.16	48845	3.63	48854	2.88

V. ASEAN-East Asia Investment Relation

ASEAN had been the top 10 regional FDI destinations in the 1990s, albeit up to the point when the crisis hit the region. The original 5 member countries i. e. Indonesia, Malaysia, Thailand, Singapore, and to a lesser extent the Philippines, had been in the top ten FDI receiving countries during the 1990's. Table 15 shows the net FDI inflow into ASEAN (on a balance of payment basis) between 1995 — 1999. It is observed that the extra-ASEAN FDI had been more significant than intra-ASEAN investment flows. It can be observed that inflow of total, intra- and extra-ASEAN investment had contracted sharply in 1998 and 1999 (the years immediately after the crisis hit the region). The intra-ASEAN investment share of ASEAN's total investment had contracted from as much as 10.7 per cent to 7.2 per cent. In 2000, though the regional economies have shown some recovery, and while global FDI flows increased to US $ 1,270 billion compared with US $ 1,075 billion in 1999, investment inflows into ASEAN remained on a declining trend at 5.8 per cent to US $ 13.8 billion compared with US $ 14.7 billion in 1999. In contrast, China and Taiwan recorded an increase in inflows of FDI to US $ 40.7 billion and US $ 4.9 billion respectively. FDI into ROK recorded a marginal decline to US $ 10.2 billion.

Table 15 ASEAN Net FDI on a Balance of Payment Basis (US $ million)

	Intra ASEAN	Total Extra ASEAN FDI	Total ASEAN FDI	Share of Intra-ASEAN FDI in Total FDI
1995	4,653.0	16,668.0	21,321.0	21.8
1996	2,777.7	23,238.4	26,016.0	10.7
1997	5,537.5	22,597.5	28,135.0	19.7
1998	2,019.8	17,575.2	19,595.0	10.3
1999	1,217.5	15,693.5	16,911.0	7.2

Source: ASEAN Secretariat; ASEAN FDI Database.

Table 16 shows the stock of FDI in the period 1980—1999. It is observed that the stock of FDI in the region had grown tenfold from US $ 24 billion in 1980 to US $ 249.8 billion in 1999. The bulk of the inflows were absorbed by Singapore, Indonesia, Malaysia and Thailand. Together they accounted for 88 per cent of ASEAN FDI. By the end of 1999, ASEAN share of Asian FDI has been showing a sharp decline since the crisis struck to about 29.5 per cent in 1999.

Table 16 Inward Foreign Direct Investment Stock in ASEAN (US $ billion)

	1980	1990	1998	1999
ASEAN	24.0	89.9	232.6	249.8
Brunei	0	0	1.0	1.0
Cambodia	-	0.2	0.7	0.6
Indonesia	10.3	68.8	68.2	65.2
Laos	0	0.14	0.472	0.551
Malaysia	5.2	10.3	45.2	48.77
Myanmar	0	0.1	2.1	2.4
Philippines	1.3	3.3	9.3	11.2
Singapore	6.2	28.6	82.4	79.4
Thailand	1.0	8.2	20.5	26.5
Vietnam	0	294	13.4	15.1
South, East and South East Asia	58.8	181.4	673.9	769.5
Asia	56.7	211.6	741.3	846.7
Developing Countries	131.2	377.4	1,241.0	1,438.5
ASEAN's share of South, East and South East Asia FDI Stock (%)	0.7	9.6	34.5	32.5
ASEAN's share of Asia FDI Stock (%)	42.3	42.5	31.4	29.5
ASEAN's share of Developing Countries FDI Stock (%)	19.7	23.8	18.7	17.4

Source: ASEAN FDI Database.

Table 17 shows the inflow of FDI into ASEAN by country of origin in the period 1985—1999. The US, Europe and Japan remained the major source of FDI for ASEAN. Together, they contributed more than 60 per cent of the total FDI to ASEAN. However, since the crisis, inflows of FDI from Japan had declined sharply from as much as 21.0 per cent in 1997 to 5.4 per cent in 1999. The share of the three East Asian economies in total ASEAN FDI inflows reduced accordingly to just 9 per cent in 1999, from as much as 24.1 per cent in 1997.

However on a cumulative basis, the share of the three East Asian economies in ASEAN FDI stock from 1995 to the first half of 2002 remains substantial at 19.2 per cent, higher than the US at 12.9 per cent.

Table 17 Net FDI Inflow to ASEAN by Country of Origin (%)

	1995	1996	1997	1998	1999	1995—1st half of 2000
USA	14.4	15.0	9.3	12.2	15.4	12.9
Europe	23.5	30.0	22.4	23.5	33.2	26.2
Japan	19.5	19.6	21.0	13.2	5.4	15.7
ROK	2.3	2.1	2.9	4.6	2.8	2.8
China	0.6	0.4	0.2	1.5	0.8	0.7
Total (US$ billion)	21.3	26.0	28.1	19.6	16.9	112.6

VI. The Potential Effects of The EAFTA

Based on our discussion in the previous section on the economic features of the ASEAN countries and its linkages with the three East Asian economies, it can be concluded that the proposed EAFTA will make both good political and economic sense. The reasons for this are as follows:

Increased Bargaining Power

The proposed FTA will strengthen the bargaining position of the region, particularly ASEAN, as ASEAN countries would be able to negotiate as a collective, both regionally and multilaterally in areas of common interest to them. Indeed, the use of regional integration to strengthen the bargaining power of members against a perceived stronger negotiating partner is based on the belief that there is strength in members. A prime example is the EEC, whose formation is believed to have been partly motivated by the desire to increase the member countries' bargaining power against the US. Needless to say, one of the prime objectives of the formation of ASEAN, and AFTA, is to enable the consolidation of its regional bargaining position in its dealings with stronger economies and regional grouping. As a group, ASEAN has managed to negotiate better deals from its negotiating counterparts, something that could not have been achieved if individual member countries negotiated individually.

Signalling the Region's Policy Credibility and Commitment to Reform

The proposed EAFTA will also serve as a signalling device as to the region's policy credibility and commitments to reform. It would send a strong message to other regions, and sub-regions, of each of the EAFTA member country's strong commitment to policy reform including trade liberalization, and thus enhance its position as a credible trade partner. Such a commitment also signals to current and prospective investing firms the advantages of locating their long-term investments in an area committed to open markets and stable macroeconomics.

From the perspective of ASEAN, there is an urgent need to regain, and to enhance foreign investor's confidence in the stability and credibility of policies of member countries in the region. The need is even stronger now than ever before, especially since the advent of the ASEAN economic crisis, which had badly damaged the region's economic standings.

Preparation for Bolder Reforms and Future Challenges

Membership in the proposed EAFTA would prepare prospective member countries in the region to undertake even bolder policy reforms, and confront the challenges of other countries and regional groupings in the future. Country experiences have shown that the first steps toward undertaking policy reforms are often the most difficult, as they are usually strongly resisted by those with vested interests. The fact that policy reform in the EFTA is circumscribed within a limited number of member-countries would help to overcome the initial difficulties of undertaking the reform. Furthermore, an FTA with China would enable ASEAN member countries to reap an "early harvest" of China's post-accession commitment to liberalise its economy, and this would place ASEAN member countries in a better stead compared to the rest of the world in their economic relationship with China. The fact that the proposed EAFTA would also include two members of the OECD countries, Japan and ROK, will give ASEAN member countries an invaluable experience in their future dealings with the rest of the OECD members. In short, all these will prepare and enhance member countries' confidence to embark on bolder policy reforms in response to the onslaught of globalization and liberalization process of the world economies.

Market Enlargement

The proposed EAFTA would lead to an expansion of ASEAN's market size as producers could pool together the markets of the other three East Asia economies. The combined EAFTA market would be about US $ 6868.1 billion, which is about 12 times the current market of ASEAN, that is about US $ 570 billion.

A better measure of the market potential of the EAFTA is the size of the "effective demand" that would be created. This can be gleaned from the per capita income levels of the member countries as shown in Table 1. It is estimated that China would be the country that would provide most of the additional markets for ASEAN, considering that its population is six times of Indonesia with per capita income that is 10 per cent of Indonesia. Effectively, this means having seven Indonesia instead of just one in ASEAN/AFTA.

Trade Creation and Trade Diversion

These are the traditional static effects of a regional economic integration. Trade creation refers to the shift in expenditure or imports of a member country from more expensive domestic sources to a cheaper source within the region. The creation of more trade also refers to the addition and increased variety of exports to other member countries. These exports may be new and non-existent before the integration due to high and restrictive tariffs in the importing member countries. Trade diversion, meanwhile, refers to the shift in imports from a cheaper source outside the region to a more expensive source within the region. Trade creation is welfare enhancing, while trade diversion causes deterioration in the welfare of the importing member countries.

Intuitively, the creation of an EAFTA would be dominantly trade creating as far as ASEAN is concerned. The scope for trade creation is larger than in the case of ASEAN/AFTA, because EAFTA would include lower cost producing countries in a wide range of products, particularly Japan, and to a lesser extent, ROK and China. Conversely, the scope for trade diversion resulting from EAFTA is smaller than in the case of AFTA since the latter would include larger and more developed member countries.

Efficiency and Enhanced Competitiveness

With the formation of the EAFTA, and with the trade barriers among member countries eliminated, competition among enterprises in member countries would increase, thus promoting specialisation, efficiency, productivity and economic welfare. Not only would competition be intensive between and among enterprises of member countries, but strategic alliances between them would also be created in many sectors. The surviving enterprises might become globally competitive too.

Effects on the Volume and Pattern of Investment

With the removal of barriers to trade, and eventually, of barriers to capital flows within the region, this would result in a more conducive investment climate within the region. There will be more certainty and uniformity in investment policies within the region, besides having an enlarged regional market. All these would be important factors in attracting investors to the region and having them invest. A more efficient pattern of production would emerge, drawn along the lines of comparative and competitive advantages.

As the EAFTA would comprise of member countries lying across a spectrum of factor endowments and economic development levels, production rationalisation would thus take place in consideration of such differences in factor endowment as well as in effective demand across member countries. This could effectively spur growth in agriculture, manufacturing and services. As a result, the proposed EAFTA could have profound implications on investment activity in the region.

The Economic Cost

While the effects of the EAFTA are generally beneficial, it is nevertheless expected to bring with it attendant costs. In particular, the preferential reduction of trade barriers among members of the FTA can bring with it some diversion of trade as explained earlier. From the perspective of ASEAN, the choice is between trade diversion resulting from AFTA only, and trade diversion resulting from ASEAN's integration with Japan, ROK and China in EAFTA. Theoretically, trade diversion resulting from EAFTA should be smaller than those resulting from AFTA. Indeed, the scope for trade diversion is smaller, but

—the bigger is the regional integrated economies

—the higher the intra-regional trade is vis-à-vis its extra regional trade

—the more developed are the new members of the regional economic integration

—the lower the cost of production in member countries compared with those in non-member countries.

Based on our earlier discussion, EAFTA fulfils all the above criteria. Hence, trade diversion would be small and could be kept minimal by taking some pre-emptive measures.

Decline in Tariff Revenues

The reduction of tariff barriers against member countries following the formation of the EAFTA may lead to some loss in government revenue in some member countries. This will occur as tariff revenues previously collected from import (from non-members) declines as imports are diverted to members receiving preferential treatment at low or zero tariffs.

Within the ASEAN countries, the most affected countries would be the new members, Cambodia, Laos, Myanmar and Vietnam. This is mainly due to their high differential between MFA and CEPT tariff levels. However, this does not constitute real economic losses because it simply amounts to redistribution of welfare to consumers who now may be able to enjoy a lower price for imported goods. Moreover, ASEAN's experience in implementing AFTA has shown that these countries have managed to mitigate these problems by looking for alternative source of revenue elsewhere in the economy. For example, Cambodia used to receive 56 per cent of its total tax revenue from customs duties prior to joining AFTA, two thirds of which were levies on imports from the other ASEAN countries. However, membership in ASEAN/AFTA gave the Cambodian government the impetus to introduce a value-added tax in 1999. This has likewise been the experience of other ASEAN countries in the wake of the AFTA implementation. Likewise, the same experience will take place resulting from the formation of EAFTA.

Adjustment Costs due to EAFTA

Adjustment costs " encompass a wide variety of potentially disadvantageous short-term outcomes that might result from trade liberalization which may include a reduction in employment and output, the loss in industry-specific and firm-specific human capital, and macroeconomic instability resulting from balance of payment difficulties or reduction in government revenue. " It must be acknowledged that the formation of EAFTA would result in a dislocation in member economies as proven in the case of AFTA. But these effects would occur as a result of any other policy changes undertaken by an economy such as trade liberalisation, and its long-term effect is shown to be relatively small. More advanced member countries may even provide technical assistance and aid to help the affected countries in their effort to readjust to new economic and trade regimes, as was the practise by more advanced ASEAN countries when implementing the AFTA programme. Moreover, the adjustments undertaken by the less-developed member countries would be done more easily and quickly by being members of the EAFTA, compared to them undertaking the reforms individually.

VII. The Architecture of the East Asia Free Trade Area

In the event that ASEAN and the three East Asia economies, China, ROK and Japan agree to establish a free trade area, there are several modalities to choose from. These include:
- [ ] A region-wide FTA involving all the thirteen countries concerned
- [ ] An EAFTA comprising a network of FTAs: ASEAN-China FTA, ASEAN-Japan FTA, ASEAN-ROK FTA, Japan-China FTA, Japan-ROK PTA, and China-ROK FTA
- [ ] An EAFTA involving ASEAN and North East Asia FTA similar to the proposed ASEAN/AFTA-CER FTA.

Needless to say, the first modality is the first best option, as it would involve region-wide economic integration of thirteen separate entities into a single and unified market. The gains from such a comprehensive liberalization, to the region as well as to individual member countries, are expected to be large, while the adjustment process easier, and less costly. Though this choice of regional integration is the most difficult to achieve at the moment, it must be adopted to be the ultimate modality to strive for in the long run.

The second modality is to "weave a web of free trade agreements and areas together across the thirteen economies to finally form a huge East Asia Free Trade Area". Altogether, it would involve six FTAs. To start with, there is already a strong commitment to create an ASEAN-China FTA in 10 years' time, and there are good prospects for an ASEAN-ROK FTA to follow soon. The signing of a bilateral free trade agreement (BFTA) between Japan and Singapore may act as catalyst for the other ASEAN countries to negotiate an FTA with Japan either individually or as a region as explained earlier. By doing so, it may neutralise whatever advantages and preferences Singapore may be enjoying in Japan's market, and hence eliminate the bias against them. This phase of the EAFTA evolution is progressing well with ASEAN appears to act as the "hub" in its relation with the individual Northeast Asian countries: China, Japan, ROK.

A more difficult phase is to carve-out three more FTAs among the three East Asian economies. The first one is a Japan-ROK FTA. This initiative, which has already been announced, is potentially the most influential one of the three possible bilateral FTAs among the East Asian economies. The timing is most opportune given the current improvement in the bilateral relationship between the two economies. There have been suggestions that the Japan-ROK FTA "should logically be extended to include China as well because it otherwise would create serious political tensions". The inclusion of China would effectively rule-out the need to create bilateral FTAs (the China-Japan FTA and China-ROK FTA). Indeed, this would transform the exercise in the direction of a bigger undertaking, that is, the formation of a

North East Asian sub-regional arrangement that would eventually be linked to the one already in existence, the ASEAN/AFTA. This represents the third route that may be pursued.

Irrespective of the modality to be preferred modality, several parameters governing the proposed framework of co-operation need to be clearly spelt-out and adopted. These include, among others, the time frame of implementation, guiding principles, scope and coverage, special and differential provisions.

Time Frame

The time frame for implementation will need to consider existing benchmarks. On the one hand, there is the APEC vision to create free trade in the area by 2010 for developed countries and 2020 for developing countries. The proposed EAFTA needs to achieve liberalization of goods earlier than that which has been agreed upon under APEC, or else this initiative will be made redundant by the latter. This means that the developed countries of EAFTA, Japan, ROK and possibly Singapore, should proceed at a faster pace than APEC i.e. earlier than 2010, while the remaining countries should proceed not later than 2020. For the ASEAN-6, this should not be much a problem because under AFTA they are targeting CEPT zero tariff by 2010. Subject to any new arrangements pertaining to AFTA[①], the pace of liberalization of EAFTA should not normally go beyond the pace of liberalization to which ASEAN members have already agreed under AFTA i.e. elimination of tariff by 2010 for ASEAN-6 and 2015 for the new members. Consideration is to be given to the CLMV countries that need more time to adjust to the required market-opening policies. Hence, they should be accorded some amount of flexibility and differential deadlines in their liberalization com-

---

[①] Presently, there is intense discussion on the initiative to form the ASEAN Economic community by year 2020 proposed by Singapore Prime Minister, Goh Chok Tong. This will involve natural extension of the AFTA process.

mitments.

Scope

The EAFTA should be as comprehensive as possible to cover trade in all goods, services, investments, tariff liberalization, non-tariff barriers, technical barriers to trade, and mutual recognition arrangements (MRAs). Other areas could possibly be included as and when the need arises. This is to ensure that the FTA is trade creating, and hence would lead to efficiency gains for the region as a whole, and the member countries individually.

In the case of trade in goods, agriculture will be one sector that could pose some problems[①] due to its sensitivities in almost all economies, except for Singapore. The ASEAN/AFTA approach in phasing in the agricultural products into its CEPT scheme may be used as a model for the three East Asian countries to adopt. Under the AFTA, agricultural raw materials and unprocessed agriculture produce are categorized into two: sensitive and highly sensitive unprocessed agricultural products (UAPs). All sensitive UAPs (altogether 181 tariff lines) would have to be included by 2005, and their tariff rates to be reduced to 0 — 5 per cent by 2010. Meanwhile, the highly sensitive UAPs, which are relatively few in number, need to be phased in by 2005 and their terminal tariff are allowed to be greater than 5 per cent by 2010. As for rice, which is considered as highly sensitive in most ASEAN countries, the indicated terminal tariff would be less than 20 per cent.

Tariff

Subject to the time frame discussed earlier, the overall objective is to achieve free trade in goods by 2010 for the ASEAN 6

---

① The issue on agriculture will be most critical in the case of ASEAN-Japan FTA but less so in the case of ASEAN-China FTA since most of the "down payment" offered by China involved agricultural products.

and China, Japan and ROK and 2015 for the new members of ASEAN. As a guide, ASEAN could consider extending the AFTA tariff rates to the three East Asian countries (China, Japan and ROK) and the latter would progressively reduce tariff for ASEAN from the conclusion of negotiation, reaching free trade by 2005. For Japan, and to a lesser extent ROK, the fact that they are developed economies makes them in a better position to achieve free trade vis-à-vis ASEAN at an earlier date. For the new members of ASEAN, the rest of the EAFTA would consider to offer them a special preference similar to the ASEAN Generalised Scheme of Preference for their products to enter the rest of the EAFTA.

Rules of Origin

To avoid the possibility of trade deflection, FTAs normally adopt rules of origin (ROO) which specify the degree of value added the goods must embody before they can be considered as a regional product which entitled them preferential treatment when traded within three FTAs. In the case of AFTA, the ROO is 40 per cent domestic and/or regional cumulative content for all goods and for all member countries. It is too simplistic and favors the more developed member countries.

In the case of the EAFTA, ROO of 40 per cent is too low as input from Japan, China and ROK will be considered as local or regional input. A higher percentage of regional content is preferred, and it should be varied by the type of goods traded, and by the country that produced the goods. Sensitive products, where there is greater possibility of trade deflection to occur, are assigned a higher percentage of local/regional content. Similarly, more developed countries like Japan, ROK and Singapore may also be assigned a higher percentage of regional content.

Non-tariff Barriers

Under the AFTA process, member countries are obliged to eliminate all NTBs, upon enjoyment of the CEPT treatment.

Similar rulings need to be instituted in FTAs with the three East Asian countries.

Technical Assistance

The EAFTA would need provisions on technical assistance particularly from the more developed members. Such technical assistance should cover the following areas:

- technical assistance in the development, strengthening and diversification of the production and export bases of the new members of ASEAN in particular
- assisting of the ASEAN new members in their capacity building
- facilitating the transfer of know-how to the ASEAN countries

It is to be acknowledged that the more developed members of the EAFTA have been the major providers of technical assistance to the less developed members of ASEAN either bilaterally, or through collaboration with ASEAN and other multilateral agencies, particularly in the Greater Mekong Development Projects. With the establishment of the EAFTA, this initiative would be enhanced further in a sustainable manner.

Trade Facilitation

The EFTA should include trade facilitation activities to enhance the effect of the trade liberalization process. Trade facilitation activities are already underway in AFTA, as well as in the APEC. What is needed is to ensure that these activities are strengthened so as to bear some tangible benefit in the short term. These activities include harmonization of customs nomenclature and procedures, harmonization of standards, MRAs, and SPS Conference etc.

Investment

The EAFTA should contain a framework of investment

principles and rules that would increase and secure capital flows to and within the region. This aspect has already been taken care of in the case of ASEAN under its Framework Agreement of the ASEAN Investment Areas (AIA, 1988) whereby all barriers to investment in ASEAN are to be removed by 2010. Non-ASEAN investors would enjoy the same privileges by 2020. The ultimate aim is to promote the ASEAN region as a single international destination for investment. To accommodate the non-ASEAN members of EAFTA, the implementation could be accelerated, and in return the latter could consider reciprocal arrangement for the ASEAN investors.

There are other aspects that need to be covered by the proposed EAFTA, but they are beyond the scope of this paper. These include among others such matters concerning the inclusion of the services sectors, intellectual property rights, e-commerce, etc.

Conclusion

This paper has highlighted salient features of the economic relationship between ASEAN and the three East Asian economies, China, ROK and Japan for the last decade or so. It has showcased the growing strength of economic interdependencies within, and among, members of the regional economies concerned, and the further scope for greater regional economic integration that exists. All the member economies have benefited from this development, and more gains are expected if regional economic co-operation strategies are to be pursued via the EAFTA proposal.

This paper has also outline the possible modalities of the proposed EAFTA as well as it objectives, principles and coverage and several special provisions that need to be instituted for the efficient implementation of the proposed EAFTA.

References

Framework Agreement on Comprehensive Economic Cooperation between the Association of South East Asian Nations and the People's Republic of China, ASEAN Secretariat, Jakarta, 2002.

Harry Harding, "International Order and Organisation in the Asia-Pacific Region", Robert S. Ross (ed.), *East Asia in Transition: Towards a New Regional Order*, Institute of South East Asian Studies (ISEAS), Singapore, 1995.

Mohd. Haflah Piei, "Steps Towards Economic Integration: The ASEAN Free Trade Area", *Panorama* 2/1999, Konrad Adenauer Stiftung, Manila.

Mohd Haflah Piei and Syarisa Yanti AbuBakar, "Promotion of Trade and Investment in ASEAN: Policies and Result", MIER, Kuala Lumpur, 1998.

Simon Tay, Jesus Estanislao and Hadi Soesastro (eds.) *"A New ASEAN in a New Millennium"*, Centre for Strategic and International Studies, Jakarta, 2000.

UNCTAD/UN, *"Trade and Development Report, 2002"*, United Nation, New York, 2002.

East Asian Cooperation: The ASEAN View

Gloria O. Pasadilla[1]

Introduction

This paper is one ASEAN national's reflection on the current developments in integration in the East Asian region. The basis for such a reflection is primarily, economic, particularly, trade. Admittedly, the ASEAN grouping and all the recent forms of integration encompass a far larger scope than merely trade among members. For instance, ASEAN cooperation covers environment, anti-terrorism, anti drug trafficking, as well as monetary and financial cooperation. And, from its original inception, ASEAN was built to address peace and security concerns in the Southeast Asian region, not primarily to tackle trade issues. Unlike the EU which started out as a way to address economic coordination, particularly, Iron and Steel production between France and Germany,[2] subsequently moving towards more and more political integration, ASEAN began for an expressed political purpose — to solve territorial and political dis-

---

[1] Gloria O. Pasadilla, Senior Fellow, University of Asia and the Pacific and Philippines Institute for Development Studies, Manila, the Philippines.

[2] Much of the economic integration in Europe, however, had an underlying political objective of avoiding the repeat of European wars that arose, primarily, from German and French rivalry.

putes peacefully. Economics and trade discussions are figured more prominently only much later, after the Cold War security issues have abated.

Despite its narrow scope, reflection on ASEAN and a future East Asian integration from the economic prism offers an illuminating perspective. In the first place, economic imperatives, not political ones, are driving ASEAN and East Asian to bond together in a stronger fashion, not to cut itself off from the rest of the world, but to lessen the region's dependence on the US and EU markets and to rely more on a diversified and strong Asian regional market. Other economic push are likewise affecting the Asian integration, in particular, the current trends of regionalism elsewhere as well as the slow pace of multilateral efforts. North America, Africa, and Europe are trying to integrate their economies more and more, forcing Asians to, likewise, look more inwardly. The improved living standard apparently caused by the EU integration also adds to the attractiveness of similar integration projects in East Asia. Lastly, the last Asian crisis also fostered a more inward, akin to soul-searching, look at themselves as a region, and revitalized a desire to build a stronger regional capacity to help each other out in the next crunch time.

All these incentives driving greater East Asian cooperation are economic. The region has little of the political motivations that drive Europe to unite, namely to prevent wars by increasing interlocking economic interests, and more recently, to be able to break the hegemony of the United States. Asia also has less cultural and historical ties that can aid greater unification. Unlike Europe that shares a common deep Christian root, history and culture, and is relatively homogeneous in living standards, Asia is very diverse in culture, religion, language, historical experience, ethnicity, and levels of development. What is uniting them and driving the Asian integration process are, fundamentally, economic considerations.

If, then, economics is the driving force behind greater East Asian cooperation, it stands to reason to evaluate the economic logic that is influencing the process. Since economics is about tradeoffs and of benefits and costs, the paper's reflection on East Asian integration will therefore discuss these potential benefits and costs under different scenario, in particular, under different possible hub-and-spoke trading arrangements with Japan or China or ROK, and/or various combinations of multilateral agreements. In the next section, it will first discuss some selected historical landmarks in the formation of the ASEAN as a regional organization to trace its progressive evolution from being a regional forum for security issues, to a more integrated regional market and Free Trade Area. Next, it shifts to the economics of the hub-and-spoke phenomenon and multilateral-like agreements. The paper then shifts to a political economy discussion of the potentially important role of ASEAN for an East Asian FTA to come about. It discusses the questions and problems that beset ASEAN member nations that prevent it from playing an even more constructive and indispensable role in the East Asian region.

I. The ASEAN Evolution: ASEAN, AFTA, and East Asian FTA

From its modest beginning of providing a regional framework in which disputes could be dealt with peacefully and without resort to force, ASEAN continues to evolve into a major influence for greater regional cohesion not only for Southeast Asia but also for the entire East Asia. This section briefly sketches the major milestones in the evolution of ASEAN.

The Beginnings and Enlargement

ASEAN was founded on August 8, 1967 amidst gloomy circumstances: Indonesia had just emerged from a period of confrontation with Malaysia and Singapore; Malaysia and Singapore had just been through an acrimonious separation, and the Philippines were pursuing its claim to Sabah, a part of Malaysia (Severino, 2002a). Around the same period, communism and the "free world" was competing for followers in the region. Thailand was bordered by communist Cambodia and Vietnam and was, itself, threatened within by communist insurgency in the Northeast. China was in the throes of the Cultural Revolution; Vietnam was at war; and Myanmar did not want to have anything to do with international organizations. All in all, a good part of Asia was in turmoil and threatened by communism.

In response to this situation, the five countries of Indonesia, Malaysia, the Philippines, Singapore, and Thailand formed ASEAN. The "Bangkok Declaration", which the ministers of these countries signed, emphasized the "desire to end external interference and take primary responsibility in regional affairs." The association was, thus, a hedge against further embroilment in the rivalries of powers, particularly Communist China and the US. Interestingly, from its foundation, ASEAN was declared open for membership to all countries in Southeast Asia, even as the region was then divided between five ASEAN members and the rest.

In 1976, after the end of the Vietnam War, ASEAN leaders established the ASEAN Secretariat to improve coordination among ASEAN members, and signed the Treaty of Amity and Cooperation (TAC). This treaty enshrined one of ASEAN's fundamental principles—that of non-interference in each other's internal affairs. This principle was an important reason for the other Southeast Asian nations to join the young regional grouping.

In 1984, Brunei Darussalam joined ASEAN immediately after its independence from the UK. In 1995, Vietnam, still under a communist system, was also admitted, heralding a new era in Southeast Asia in which ideological and political differences were no longer considered a hindrance to regional cooperation (Chalermpalanupap, 2002). Laos and Myanmar (formerly, Burma) joined ASEAN in 1997, and Cambodia in 1999. With the last membership of Cambodia, all nations of Southeast Asia finally came under one ASEAN roof.

Thus, in its first 25-year history, ASEAN sought to stabilize the region. It consolidated its foundations and processes, provided a framework and an environment for peaceful relations among its members, and took a leading part in the management of the new situation that emerged from the Vietnam War (Severino, 2002a).

> **Box 1 Selected Historical Highlights of ASEAN**
>
> *A. On ASEAN Formation*
>
> 1967 ASEAN was founded. Founding members: Indonesia, Malaysia, Philippines, Thailand, and Singapore. Important document: Bangkok Declaration.
> 1976 ASEAN Secretariat was established. Spelled program of action to include political, economic, social, cultural, information, security. Treaty of Amity and Cooperation (TAC) was signed.
> 1984 Brunei Darussalam joined ASEAN.
> 1995 Vietnam joined.
> 1997 Laos and Myanmar joined.
> 1999 Cambodia joined. All Southeast Asian countries are now ASEAN members.
>
> *B. ASEAN Free Trade Area*
>
> 1992 ASEAN endorsed AFTA. Important document: Framework Agreement on Enhancing ASEAN Economic Cooperation.
> 1994 Agreement to accelerate realization of AFTA from 15 years to 10 years by 2003. First ASEAN Regional Forum.
> 1995 Accelerated tariff reduction to 2002. Abolition of tariff by 2010 for first 6 members, by 2015 for newer members.
>
> *C. East Asian FTA*
>
> 1997 First ASEAN +3 Summit in Malaysia, followed by successive ASEAN+1 Summit. Common theme of summits: cooperation between ASEAN-Japan, ASEAN-ROK, and ASEAN-China, to become building blocks for regional cooperation in East Asia.
> 1998 Hanoi Summit. Agreement to form East Asia Vision Group (EAVG).
> 1998—2001 EAVG worked to discuss future cooperation in East Asia. Submitted recommendation in 2001.
> 1999 East Asia Study Group (EASG) was formed to study practical ways and means to deepen and expand existing cooperation. Assess EAVG Recommendation. Prepare Action Plans.

Growth in Economic Interdependence

By the 1990s, with the end of the Cold War, with China rapidly opening itself up to the world economy, and with globalization gathering momentum, ASEAN's response was to make itself into a free trade area, by reducing and eventually abolishing tariff and non-tariff barriers to trade among themselves. Thus, ASEAN Free Trade Area (AFTA) was initiated in 1992. Unlike the ASEAN Preferential Trade Agreement in 1977, the

AFTA Common Effective Preferential Tariff (CEPT) Scheme encompasses a far larger scope. Not only does it include a greater number of products subject for lower tariffs, but it also includes provisions for the elimination of non-tariff barriers, quantitative restrictions, and other cross-border measures. As a result, in 2003, tariffs of roughly 82.46% of tariff lines dropped to no more than five percent in the first six ASEAN members that, not coincidentally, are the region's leading trading nations. Average tariffs in these six economies are as low as 2.27% (see Table 1). By 2010, all tariffs are expected to disappear. The newer members, meanwhile, have been given a longer period (until 2015) to comply with the Common Effective Preferential Tariff (CEPT) Scheme. Delays in the inclusion of products in the AFTA scheme or suspensions of AFTA concessions are governed under stringent conditions. ①

Several factors helped in the formation of the AFTA. Some were external, like the growing trend in regionalism elsewhere, particularly NAFTA and EU integration, which prompted Asia to likewise look inwards. But internally, the region had also undergone a transformation, from being highly export dependent on markets outside the region, to being more economically interdependent. Starting in the 1980s, intra-ASEAN trade has grown steadily. For most countries, exports to and imports from other ASEAN countries, in terms of percentage of total, have increased in the 1990s (see Table 2).

---

① The AFTA CEPT is dubbed as WTO-plus in the sense that the liberalization commitments of countries have gone beyond what has, so far, been agreed upon in the multilateral setting.

Table 2 Intra-ASEAN Trade (% of Total)

	Exports to ASEAN			Imports from ASEAN		
	1991	1999	2000	1991	1999	2000
Brunei	18.33	15.16	29.48	36.15	62.44	50.06
Indonesia	11.45	16.71	17.52	9.86	19.84	20.23
Malaysia	29.33	23.5	24.87	20.08	23.53	20.01
Philippines	7.21	14.21	15.71	9.45	14.61	15.79
Singapore	23.33	25.14	27.31	19.1	23.54	24.72
Thailand	11.7	16.6	21.80	12.78	15.49	16.92
Vietnam	18.03	15.03	-	13.07	25.8	-

Source of Basic Data: PC-TAS, NAPES Database and ASEAN Secretariat

Much of this growth in intra-ASEAN trade is largely attributed to the growth in intra-firm trade among Transnational Corporations (TNCs) operating in the region. In the second half of 1980s, Japanese TNCs feared the erosion of their competitiveness in global trade because of surging wage rates and the yen currency appreciation. To preserve their lead, they moved some of the production processes from Japan, particularly those that were more labor-intensive and a few capital- and skill-intensive ones, to the Newly Industrializing Economies (NIEs) and then to Southeast Asia, where wage rates were relatively lower. These different production segments were then linked together through international subcontracting or outsourcing arrangements, creating a highly vertically integrated process of production within the region. Thus, a Japanese car export to the US, may have part of the wheels and tires manufactured in Malaysia, its radio produced in Singapore, and perhaps assembled in the Philippines. US TNCs, likewise, eventually adopted the same production strategy, fuelling further increase in intra-regional trade. The desire to have an optimal procurement system for the vertically integrated companies greatly influenced the motivation behind the development of the ASEAN Free Trade Area (AFTA). With the reduction of trade barriers, intra-regional trade more than doubled from $ 44. 2 billion in 1993 to $ 97. 8 billion in 2000. The logic of increasing liberalization has been extended to services trade. In 1995, ASEAN concluded the Framework Agreement on Services (AFAS). So far, the third package of specific sector commitments has been submitted. But agricultural products remain a subject for further liberalization as well as other sensitive sectors not previously integrated in the Inclusion List of countries under the CEPT program.

On to East Asian FTA?

While ASEAN members have laboriously made concerted efforts to unify Southeast Asian nations, they have never lost sight of the need to engage their external partners, particularly Japan, China, and ROK. ASEAN has had dialogue with Japan since 1973, with ROK since 1989, and with China since 1991. The three countries joined ASEAN in launching the ASEAN Regional Forum (ARF), an ASEAN Dialogue with all its Partners,[1] in 1994. In 1997, the historic inaugural meeting of ASEAN + 3 Summit took place , which was followed by three successive ASEAN + 1 summits. The different bilateral Joint Statements expressed agreement on the need to consolidate their close economic relations by promoting trade and investment, facilitating market access, and other various modes of economic cooperation. They also contained recognition that the stability and prosperity of Northeast and Southeast Asia are closely interlinked.

The East Asia Vision Group (EAVG), composed of academics and other non-government official experts and representatives from each of the ASEAN member countries, was set up in

---

[1] This includes Australia, Canada, EU, Japan, ROK, New Zealand, US, China, Russia.

1998 to discuss the future of cooperation in East Asia and to submit recommendations for the 2001 Summit. Likewise, an official East Asia Study Group (EASG) composed of senior officials and the ASEAN Secretariat was set up in 2000 to assess the recommendations of EAVG, to explore practical ways and means to deepen and expand the existing cooperation in East Asia, and prepare concrete measures and action plans.

Interestingly, the EAVG study was entitled: *Towards an East Asian Community: Region of Peace, Prosperity and Progress*. One of its major recommendations is the establishment of an East Asian Free Trade Area (EAFTA), starting with an interim step of linking existing free trade areas in East Asia together. It also recommended the evolution of ASEAN + 3 Summit to East Asian Summit and the institutionalization of the East Asia cooperation process to create regular channels of communications and cooperation. Implicitly, the evolution to the East Asian Summit seems to entail the creation of an East Asian Community as a new regional organization (Chalermpalanupap, 2002).

The EASG recommended 26 measures selected from the EAVG recommendations. It included the formation of EAFTA and the evolution of ASEAN + 3 Summit into an East Asian Summit as long-term measures. It also recommended the formation of an East Asia Forum, an East Asia Business Council and a network of East Asian eminent intellectuals, and the promotion of East Asian studies as part of the short-term measures.

Summing up, from an association designed to address peace and security problems in the region, ASEAN has evolved into a more closely integrated Free Trade Area, and might yet evolve into a larger East Asian Community. The underlying driving force for East Asian integration is economics: large Chinese market, greater leverage in multi-polar world, fear of US trade deficit backlash, regionalism in other parts of the world.

Whether East Asia would be like the EU is, at least at this point, a moot question. Nevertheless, though East Asia is yet far from looking like the EU, domestic and external forces, as well as the logic of globalization, are likely going to make East Asia resemble EU more closely than it does today (Severino, 2001). But with it come the corresponding benefits and costs.

II. Hub-and-Spoke Regionalism: Potential Benefits for ASEAN

Since the East Asian FTA is a long-term goal, the more immediate concerns at this time are the almost simultaneous bilateral trading arrangements that are being discussed and negotiated between individual ASEAN countries with Japan and/or China, or bilateral trade agreements between Japan and ROK, which portend to be the beginning of the larger EAFTA. But this different set of negotiations is leading to some sort of a hub-and-spoke trading arrangement with one country (the hub) having many different bilateral arrangements with many individual countries (spokes). This section analyses the economic benefits from this type of arrangement.

As in most other types of analysis of preferential trade, the framework shows that welfare effects are, theoretically, ambiguous. Positive gains depend largely on the increased market access in partner economies as well as on the ability, particularly of small ASEAN economies, to take full advantage of the market access opportunities. The challenge, therefore, is on the productive capacities of individual economies to supply those markets. Otherwise, most of the benefits of various regional or bilateral trading arrangements in East Asia, discounting the unambiguous consumer benefits, will redound more to the advanced economies because of their high production capabilities.

To start with, considering that Japan is already aggressively pursuing bilateral trade arrangements with each of the original

ASEAN, the section first analyzes the effects of a hub-and-spoke arrangement in which Japan is the hub and the ASEAN 6[①] are the spokes. What are the benefits to the individual spokes, as well as the hub? Next, we analyze what happens if the spokes also form an FTA among themselves. Note that this case is similar to forming a multilateral FTA between ASEAN countries and Japan. Then, it looks at the benefits from a "two-hub arrangement" (ASEAN-China and ASEAN-Japan FTA, but without a China-Japan bilateral agreement). Finally, it considers the benefits of a multilateral East Asian free trade agreement[②].

Japan as Hub, ASEAN as Spokes

The general framework of analysis is based on Baldwin and Wyplosz (2003) diagrams which highlights the discriminatory effect of preferential liberalization, i.e., the essential tradeoffs between volume effects and terms-of-trade loss from a free trade area[③]. The framework assumes a three-country world: Home, Partner, and Rest of the World (ROW). Home and Partner engage in preferential trade between them, and the welfare effects are illustrated in Figure 1. The curves are the import demand function in Home and the two-supply function in Partner and ROW. Without tariffs, domestic price is where importing supply, which is equal to the sum of ROW and Partner's export sup-

---

[①] Brunei, Indonesia, Malaysia, Philippines, Singapore, and Thailand.

[②] The analysis in this section would be the same if any other country, say ROK instead of China, were the alternative hub.

[③] This tradeoff is preferred to Viner's trade diversion/trade creation phraseology because the latter fails to capture all the welfare effects of discriminatory tariff liberalization. In particular, the trade diversion-trade creation term is slightly misleading (suggesting trade volumes are the key even though they refer to price changes) (Baldwin and Wyplosz, 2003). But the term remains an "effective tool of focusing policy makers' attention on the ambiguous welfare effects of preferential trading arrangements." (Panagariya, 1999)

ply (not shown in diagram) cuts import demand. With most-favored-nation (MFN) tariff, domestic price in Home is P' (which is higher than tariff-free price not shown in diagram) while the border price (or the price faced by both ROW and Partner) is P'-T. Now, if Home and Partner agree to have bilateral free trade, the result is an increase in imports and conflicting border price effects, which becomes the source of welfare ambiguity[①].

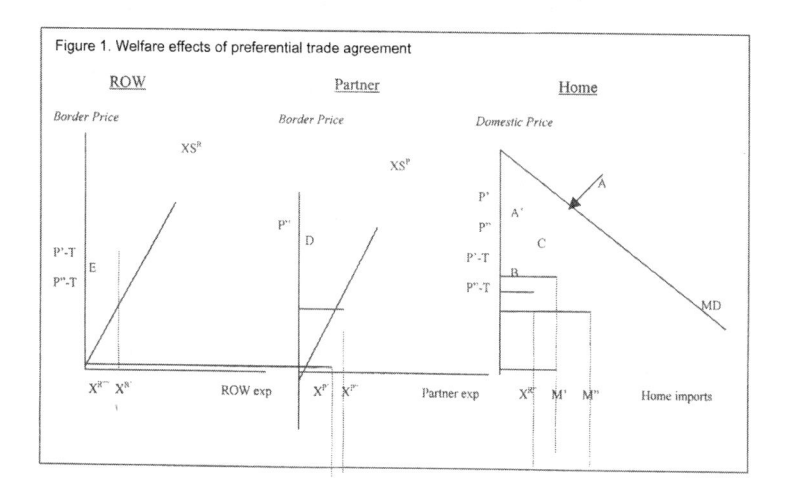

Figure 1. Welfare effects of preferential trade agreement

Based on Figure 1, the welfare change for Home, on the import side, is represented by area A which comes from increased imports from M' to M'' (volume effect), hence is positive[②]. Moreover, border price with respect to ROW drops from P'-T to P''-T, thus represents an additional gain for Home. The idea be-

---

① The Baldwin-Wyplosz framework assumes symmetric-size markets. The ambiguity in welfare effect tends to disappear for Home if it partners a low-cost country.

② Note that area A' is additional consumer surplus but since it is equivalent to the tariff revenue loss, it does not add to overall welfare for Home.

hind this is that ROW is forced to lower its prices to $P''-T$ to be able to compete with Partner in Home market, thus making their goods cheaper for Home. The total area B represents the lower border price for all the imports from ROW, XR''. However, for the remaining imports from Partner, $M'-XR''$, Home pays a higher price of P'' instead of the $P'-T$ previously, hence takes a loss of C. Thus, the total net benefit on the import side is $A+B-C$. Note that the border price effect does not apply to $M''-M'$ units because these were not imported before the preferential trade agreement. There is, thus, no point in comparing prices for these units pre-and post-PTA.

On the export side, assuming symmetric markets and same tariff levels, Home, likewise, gains access to Partner market, equivalent to Partners' access to Home market. Now, Partner increases exports from XP' to XP''. Moreover, it receives a higher price for those exports from $P'-T$ to P''. Thus total benefit on the export side is area D. In sum, net welfare change for both Home and Partner is equal to $A+B-C+D$. This net welfare change is either positive or negative depending on the areas A, B, C and D, which in turn, depends on the slopes of import demand and supply.[①]

Benefits for Hub

How does this analysis apply to Japan and individual ASEAN countries' bilateral trade arrangements?[②] One thing sure is that, if others form a bilateral agreement, it does not make sense not to form bilateral agreements with the hub as well. In the diagrams, notice that the ROW, the excluded country, loses through reduced import volumes and lower border prices, equivalent to twice the area of E because it loses in both Home and Partner markets. Welfare of the excluded country,

---

[①] Ibarra-Yunez (2003) arrived at similar conclusion using a different framework. In essence, he argues that increased welfare from bilateral trade agreement comes from: 1) increased profit abroad due to market access; and 2) domestic consumer surplus due to lower prices. Moreover, these two tend to outweigh the loss in tariff revenue and domestic profit reduction that results from greater competition at home and lower domestic output. The fact that the positive effect (from increase in consumer surplus and higher profits abroad) is counterbalanced by reduced domestic profits and tariff revenues means that there is a limit to networking or that there is an optimal number in a regional trading arrangement. This type of literature usually leads to the conclusion of an optimal number of trading blocs and/or size of the trade bloc.

Actually, welfare effects of regional arrangements, and bilateral arrangements for that matter, are typically ambiguous at the theoretical level. Many questions are quantitative rather than qualitative, as sketched in the framework. That is why most researchers make use of methods like Computable General Equilibrium(CGE) models to assess relative benefits and costs of entering into such trade agreements. See, for instance, Harrison, et. al., (2001)in the case of the impact of Chile's manifold trading agreements. However, the exercise in this paper is very useful in understanding some important intuition on the tradeoffs from these trade agreements.

[②] In the foregoing, much of the emphasis is on goods (and services) trade. Admittedly, additional economic argument for RTAs is the creation of knowledge capital and investment flows when bilaterals emerge, but these are not reckoned in the framework discussed. These additional benefits from investments and knowledge capital flows definitely add to the reasons on why bilaterals have flourished over the past few years since NAFTA.

therefore, is unambiguously reduced. This creates a "domino effect" of bilateralism in that once some countries form bilateral arrangements, others tend to follow suit in order not to be closed off from its former trading partners' market. The implication is that since Singapore and Japan started on preferential trading arrangement, it is almost sure that other bilateral arrangements would be linked between Japan and other ASEAN countries for fear of trade exclusion.

For the hub country, i. e. Japan, the trade off is between the benefits from the free market access in each of its partner spoke country and the loss in the domestic market caused by increased competition as well as by the terms of trade deterioration (i. e. higher post-integration border price). Note that the benefits of Japan as hub come not only at the expense of the ROW (EU and US, for example) but also at the expense of its other spoke countries that do not have bilateral relations among themselves. Thus, if the Philippines and Thailand, for instance, do not have a bilateral trading arrangement, the Philippines (Thailand) will be considered as part of ROW in the Thai (Philippines) market as far as Japan-Thailand (Japan-Philippines) bilateral agreement is concerned.

Benefits for Spokes: Substitute vs. Complementary Agreements

Like the hub, the spoke country considers the same benefits (access) and loss (higher border prices) from the PTA (i. e. area $A+B-C+D$). However, in addition, its benefits tend to be further eroded for each new addition of a spoke, particularly if the new arrangement is a so-called *substitute* agreement. A *substitute* agreement is when a new spoke produce goods that are substitutes for those produced within the FTA (Kowalcyk and Wonnacott, 1992). Thus, if Japan obtains bilateral agreements with each of the ASEAN countries, the individual countries' benefits are reduced each time a new spoke is added. Considering that ASEAN countries tend to produce and export similar goods, the implication is that the benefits from each country's bilateral agreement with Japan will diminish as each new trading agreement is concluded by another ASEAN country with Japan.[①] That is, Singapore's benefits from Japan-Singapore agreement may be reduced after Japan signs a separate agreement with the Philippines, or with Malaysia, through a strategy called "additive regionalism".

However, so far as agreements are *complementary* in that imports from new spokes produce resources not previously available within the Free Trade Area, each newly concluded bilateral trading agreement with Japan can increase the benefits of the existing spokes. Thus, one can think of the vertically integrated production in the ASEAN, benefiting from each additional Japanese hub-and-spoke arrangement. Since each additional component for production enjoys free market access in the hub's market, these components can be exported to the hub and from the hub, re-exported to another spoke country. Such re-routing through the hub can reduce production cost in each of the spokes, assuming minimal transportation cost and very liberal rules of origin agreement. Furthermore, if income of both the hub and the new spoke increase as a result of a PTA, even if that agreement were a substitute agreement with respect to the original spoke PTA, it could become complementary if exports of existing spokes increase as a consequence. Thus, in the Japan-Singapore case, Singapore, as the original spoke, can gain from the possibility that an agreement between Malaysia and Japan can increase the income of both countries, which consequently increas-

---

[①] Another way by which various other bilaterals can reduce the initial spokes' benefits (and the hub's) is through the increased administrative complications that come from the labyrinth of trade restrictions, particularly when rules of origin are inconsistent with one another.

es Singapore's exports to both.

In sum, the addition of each new spoke, in the case of substitute FTA, can erode the benefits of the original spokes' FTA with the hub. But, if incomes in the new spoke and the hub increase that induce an increase in the exports of the original spokes to both countries, the substitute FTA may yet turn out to be a complementary FTA. But if each new additional hub-spoke arrangement turns out not to be complementary and diminish the benefits accruing to earlier spoke partners, does it make sense to enter into an FTA as one of the first few spoke countries? The answer, given our framework, remains yes. The reason is that, even in the case of pure substitute agreement, it may still be better to participate in the FTA as a spoke in a hub-and-spoke system than being an outsider to the trade agreements. As long as there is, on the whole, net benefits from free trade with the hub, regardless of how many spokes end up joining in, it is preferable to be inside the hub-and-spoke arrangement than out of it.

The one important caveat is that the benefits which the spokes can derive from the FTA arrangement depend not only on the sufficient market access obtained in new markets but, more importantly, on whether that potential market access is actually taken advantage of. For ASEAN countries with poor productive capacities, this is the crucial challenge because the enlarged foreign export market made possible by trade agreements could remain under-exploited as a result of poor infrastructure support, low productivity, and unsupportive government institutions. If this happens, the regional trading arrangement would not bring about much higher profits abroad which could counterbalance the reduced domestic profits in the home market that results from opening it up to more foreign competition. Consumers, on the other hand, are definitely benefited by lower prices. Yet, since producers are better organized than consumers, producers' clam-

or and complaints about the adverse effects of free trade agreements on their total profits tend to downplay the overall benefits of FTA. This is one reason why, at times, developing countries are ambivalent about preferential trading arrangements.

AFTA: Spokes Forming a Bloc

What happens when the spokes, themselves, form a trading arrangement among themselves? In the case of ASEAN, how does the formation of the ASEAN Free Trade Area (AFTA) affect the hub-and-spoke arrangement centered on Japan? Closing the loop of bilaterals can substantially transform a hub-and-spoke arrangement to a multilateral FTA with Japan. Of course, in this case, the multilateral rules of origin would need to be reformulated and made consistent with one another.

Assuming that the hub is a higher cost producer, the spokes can restore some of the trade they used to have with each other that might have been switched to the hub as a result of the bilateral agreement. Moreover, both gain access to cheaper input that can allow them to compete better with the hub. So, while both spokes' benefit and the previous advantage (from volume) enjoyed by the hub can be reduced as a result of bilateral agreements among the spokes. But if the hub is a low-cost producer, there will be no trade between the spokes that can be switched back. In this case, a low-cost hub will not be negatively affected by a preferential trade agreement among its spokes.

Certainly, the hub gains more in a hub-and-spoke arrangement than in a multilateral FTA (i.e. in a situation where all the spokes also form an FTA among themselves) because of the preferential market access it gets in each spoke market. With the spokes forming an FTA among themselves, the hub has, essentially, more competitors in each spoke market. The positive note is that the income of spoke countries may increase under such multilateral FTA, thereby increasing hub's exports in each of these markets. Moreover, for both hub and spokes, a multilateral agreement would be less costly. In a hub-and-spoke system, the administrative costs are high because each has to keep track of all the rules of origins negotiated in the different bilaterals, and particularly so if those bilateral agreements do not have consistent rules of origin. Likewise, transport costs can be higher in a hub-spoke system if spokes, to avoid high tariffs in a country with which it has no FTA agreement, end up re-routing its exports to that country through the hub[1].

Thus, in sum, the welfare of both spokes and hubs may increase under the framework of one integrated agreement. Why, then, do countries not engage in multilateral agreements straightaway, instead of negotiating several bilateral agreements? One reason is that bilaterals have the advantage of enabling countries to tailor an agreement to their own special needs, making deeper liberalization possible. To illustrate, the Mexico-US agreement was far more liberalizing than the Uruguay Rounds Agreement; the same with the Japan-Singapore Agreement, which contains not only goods liberalization but also investments and competition provisions. In contrast, in multilateral agreements, the agenda may be set or heavily influenced by third countries with other problems that may be unrelated to the problems of another country. Countries in multilateral agreement may not also share the same sense of urgency regarding particular issues. An example is the "convoy" problem in multilateral agreements in which the pace of the entire trade bloc tends to be determined by its most hesitant member. Particularly, in the ASEAN context in which decision making is done by consensus, the convoy problem can backstop greater liberaliza-

---

[1] Though, admittedly, well-designed rules of origin can prevent this from happening.

tion in the entire region as a whole. In all these possibilities, bilaterals may offer a superior arrangement than regional agreements.

In the above analysis, we started off with bilaterals in a hub-and-spoke arrangement that eventually turn into a multilateral agreement when the spokes also form bilaterals among themselves. However, in the ASEAN context, we observe a different sequence of trade arrangements. In particular, ASEAN countries already have a regional FTA in existence, the AFTA, while the bilaterals are just coming in. In other words, the spokes already have existing FTAs, while the hub-spoke system has still to be formed, with Japan as purportedly the center. How does a different initial condition affect the welfare analysis for the participants in the trade agreements?

The actual situation is similar to a backdoor accession by Japan to an existing FTA via bilateral arrangements with each of the members. In this case, the spokes (especially ASEAN-5) compare the benefits of gaining access to the Japanese market with the losses from having to share its original preferential market in ASEAN with Japan. If a Member reckons that the net benefit is positive, it agrees to a bilateral agreement. Japan, on the other hand, compares the cost of opening up its own market to the benefits of getting improved access to ASEAN's preferential market. Arguably, in Japan's reckoning, positive net benefits only come from improved market access in ASEAN-5, rather than from the entire ASEAN-10, hence it pursues bilateral agreements only with these five countries.

In terms of benefits, however, the analysis remains broadly similar. The hub (Japan) still competes with other spokes in ASEAN preferential market and thus benefits less from it compared to a situation in which its spokes do not have their own bilateral agreements. Yet, at the same time, it benefits from the higher income in each of its spoke market, which results from their own independent bilateral agreements. The spokes, too, benefit from its bilateral agreement with the hub, but increases its overall benefit if it also forms bilateral agreement with the other spokes.

China as Another Hub[①]

If China forms separate bilateral trading arrangement with each ASEAN country, it gets the same benefits that Japan could get as a hub, namely preferential market access in each of the ASEAN countries it signs an agreement with. In the three-country framework discussed earlier, China is certainly better off negotiating bilateral trade agreements than be excluded in the ASEAN markets. The spoke partners from ASEAN, on the other hand, would enjoy free market access in the large home market of China as well as that of Japan. Yet, again, the challenge here is whether ASEAN countries have sufficient capacity to supply the markets that are opened for them by the trade agreements.

That China becomes another hub like Japan clearly reduces the benefits of Japan as hub, in the same way that spokes' benefits are reduced by each new addition of a *substitute* agreement. But if the agreements of ASEAN with China are complementary to that of Japan-ASEAN, then Japan's benefits from its hub-spoke arrangement with ASEAN countries are increased with China's new hub-spoke arrangement in the region. The question is whether China-ASEAN agreements would be substitute or complementary agreements with Japan-ASEAN trade agreements. The answer is likely yes, if only for the fact that access to the large Chinese market can increase the income of ASEAN

[①] This analysis as well as that of the next section on the EAFTA can easily be extended to ROK.

and thus, consequently, increase exports of Japan to the ASEAN spoke economies. Conversely, Japan's bilateral agreements with ASEAN countries, can be complementary to the China-ASEAN agreements and are thus beneficial for China, as well. In addition, considering the difference in production structure of China and Japan, the ASEAN-China trade agreements might be complementary to Japan-ASEAN, in the sense that previously unavailable imports in the Japan-centered ASEAN trade agreement become available if China-ASEAN agreement exists. Furthermore, if those imports are inputs to Japanese production, Japan enjoys additional benefits from the China-ASEAN agreement.

East Asian FTA

If China and Japan (and for that matter, ROK), likewise, form a bilateral agreement, then the loop is closed for the region to have, essentially, a regional trading arrangement (RTA) or a multilateral agreement among East Asian economies. ASEAN countries' advantage as "hub" to the two countries is reduced, assuming that rules of origin are reformulated to be consistent with one another. But everyone is eventually better off, including ASEAN, because of the resulting increase in regional trade. An East Asian FTA, therefore, should, theoretically, result to higher welfare for all[①].

III. ASEAN Role in East Asian Integration

While the above analysis shows that Japan and China's engagement in the region bring economic benefits and is, consequently, a fundamental driving force that can steer greater inte-

---

[①] Albeit, the impact to each individual economy will vary and will greatly depend on how well each is able to take advantage of a growing export market.

gration, these two economies are, at the same time, political rivals that are vying for leadership position within East Asia. Japan has, so far, been the leading economic power in Asia and the one that has influenced industrial development and economic growth in the region. But its decade-long recession is weakening its edge. It also has to deal with its "history" problem as well as complications brought about by individual Asians' claims for compensation for wartime sufferings.

China, on the other hand, has had phenomenal export and income growth, even during the Asian crisis. It is a source of cheap labor and is a large domestic market by itself, thus attracting more investments than the NIEs or ASEAN. With its preferential trading arrangement with the rest of the region, it has the opportunity to replace Japan as the Asian leader that can influence global economic agenda. But, at the same time, China is still perceived as a security threat: its military expenditures have been expanding and the issues related to Taiwan remains like the sword of Damocles' hanging over Asian peace and stability. China is also seen as a competitor of ASEAN not only in many export products but also in attracting foreign direct investments (FDI). Thus, ASEAN is also wary of China.

With Japan and China political rivalry as a backdrop, ASEAN and even ROK has an important role to play to glue all the countries together into the East Asian FTA. It has been said that what Asia lacks is leadership of the kind that France and Germany played in the EU, or US in the NAFTA, because China and Japan have their own image and domestic economic problems. Still, ASEAN can play the important role of a broker, a benign mediator if you will, for the EAFTA to move progressively beyond political statements. After all, wasn't it the ASEAN's initiative that made the historical first ASEAN + 3 Summit possible in 1997? The fact is that, given Asian culture, a leader of the western type would also likely not be accepted in

Asia. Rather, a quiet, less threatening one would do a more effective job. ASEAN, in this sense, fits the bill because Japan and China both trust ASEAN and see in it no threat. Because it has no ambition for political hegemony, it has no ambition to dominate but rather to become partners in Asia. But can ASEAN rise to this challenge?

"ASEAN" Way

Soesastro (2002) describes the ASEAN way as a "non-confrontational attitude, a willingness to see the point of view of another, a conscious refrain from exerting influence or coercion over other member states and a willingness to be patient and persevere in reaching consensus." It reflects conventions, culture and customs prevailing in Member States, where the way of dealing with one another is through a manifestation of goodwill and the slow winning and giving of trust.

With the hindsight of history, the ASEAN way, though slow and time consuming, has served the organization well in solving problems, harmonizing diverging interests, and managing conflicts among member states. From the beginning, by not forcing its incredibly diverse and mutually suspicious members into legally binding standards, and relying rather on informal agreements, the ASEAN has, over the years, done a remarkable job of moving its members from animosity and distrust to close cooperative relationship. It is interesting to note that even the 1967 Bangkok Declaration upon which ASEAN was founded was a mere two-page Declaration and certainly was no Treaty of Rome (Severino, 2001b).

But would this evolutionary approach, relying on patient consensus-building to arrive at informal understandings or loose agreements, work for the EAFTA? Already, the ASEAN way of consensus-based decision-making has frustrated APEC efforts to speed up the pace of trade liberalization. What more for EAFTA with the even deeper political ramifications it implies. The perception outside the region is that consensus-based decision-making has become a weakness limiting the growth of ASEAN as an organization, and diminishing its potential of effectively brokering the EAFTA.

If ASEAN were to take an effective lead in bringing forth the EAFTA, one solution is to adopt a more flexible approach, relying perhaps on a "coalition of the willing" to set the pace for the rest of the region, or alternatively, changing the decision process to majority voting. But, so far, there is reluctance to change the "consensus" process.

Diversity of Membership

ASEAN's diverse membership also makes greater integration with East Asia difficult. Not only do members have different levels of economic development, they also have widely divergent political systems. Some are democratic and prosperous, while others are still partly socialist and very poor. Some, like Singapore, are relatively pro-globalization, while others are hesitant to give out more and more trade commitments. ASEAN countries also have varied strategic and security concerns. With diverse levels of economic development, extensive trade liberalization even among ASEAN members is difficult; what more with the richer East Asian countries. The lack of relative economic homogeneity is compounded by the respective internal instability in individual ASEAN country, which diverts priority away from regional integration efforts. So then, if ASEAN, could somehow not put its own house in order, how can it lead the formation of EAFTA?

Loose Institution

ASEAN's ambivalence towards institutionalization is another characteristic that hampers its potential leading role in the EAFTA. Within ASEAN itself, it operates mostly through *ad hoc* understandings and informal procedures rather than within the framework of binding agreements, which are arrived at through a formal process (Severino, 2001b). The ASEAN process mostly involves numerous meetings at different levels (heads of states, ministers, senior officials, committees), which usually reach informal understandings that are not legally binding. Thus, "regional economic integration seems to have become stuck in framework agreements, work programs and master plans" (Severino, 1999).

However, since AFTA, ASEAN has increasingly relied on more legally binding agreements, for instance, the ASEAN Framework Agreement on Services (AFAS), or the e-ASEAN framework agreement. This has come from the growing realization that closer regional economic integration requires commitments that are clear, firm, and enforceable, and thus need to be based on binding legal foundations. This also helps in the policy lock-in by member countries because non-fulfillment of country commitments could possibly imply some form of sanctions. [1] For instance, if a country retreats for its tariff liberalization commitments, other countries can demand compensations or can retaliate in some forms. It is likely that the developing rules-based regime in trade will gradually extend to other areas of ASEAN cooperation, particularly those relating to transnational problems as marine environment, the preservation of biodiversity, money-laundering, drug trafficking, etc. (Severino, 2001b).

Institution-wise, ASEAN is devoid of a body like the European Commission to implement its programs and to ensure compliance with such agreements and measures, or the European Court of Justice to adjudicate ASEAN disputes. The Indonesia-based ASEAN Secretariat has no supranational authority or re-

---

[1] Even though, thus far, there is no effective trade dispute settlement system in ASEAN similar to that of the World Trade Organization (WTO).

sponsibility, unlike the European Commission. Negotiations with ASEAN, properly speaking do not take place with the ASEAN Secretariat, but with each individual country because ASEAN is not represented by a monolithic body. ASEAN is rather a loose voluntary organization of sovereign states that have not yielded their sovereignty to a central authority.

Yet for closer economic integration, countries may have to yield some degree of sovereignty, the ASEAN Secretariat would have to be allowed to wield some extent of supranational authority, and more binding agreements rather than informal understandings may be needed to manage the integrated economy and the problems that transcend national boundaries. The question is whether its members have the vision and political courage to take that leap.

Integration of the Spirit

Greater institutionalization of ASEAN to manage the integration process, in turn, requires greater mutual trust among ASEAN members. Trust would grow through a deep sense of community and popular support for regionalism. However, the rich diversity of cultures has not yet allowed the region to feel one. A change of mindset, of thinking regional rather than each nation to its own, is what is required. To this end, initiatives on various regional co-operations in culture, regional education exchange network, and cultural exchange can help towards improving a sense of a regional identity.

Conclusion

ASEAN is an important regional organization. It had achieved several milestones, remarkable for an organization originally conceived to be only a talking shop for resolving security issues in a peaceful way. It is making efforts towards greater integration of its economies through the AFTA. ASEAN may not be economically important compared to China or Japan but, politically, it has a potentially vital role as mediator or broker of a far bigger and more challenging economic integration—that of the entire East Asian economies.

But ASEAN needs to rise up to the challenge. Several factors hamper it from exercising this important role in East Asia namely, its slow decision-making process, its lack of centralized institutions with supranational authority, its diversity and lack of unity.

The current phenomenon of hub-and-spoke bilateral trade agreements between individual ASEAN and Japan or China offers potential net benefits, particularly when positive investment effects form part of the reckoning. But the benefits for all countries would be bigger still if the region forms an FTA.

Given the difficulties in the formation of the EAFTA, the bilateral agreements could become the building blocks for East Asian regional integration. Since bilateral arrangements are carefully designed so that no particular challenge is too overwhelming, political resistance towards larger trade arrangements in East Asia can be overcome. The successful experience of relatively easy reforms could change expectations and open up opportunities for more difficult reforms down the road (Munakata, 2002)[①].

To a certain extent, there are also a way of going around the

---

[①] It should be noted, however, that a common framework for all ASEAN is needed, if they have to go via bilaterals. Otherwise there will be a complete tangled-up spaghetti arrangement, especially in the Rules of Origin. So far Singapore has been the pioneer but it is not advisable for other ASEAN to follow the model because Singapore is *sui generis*—it has no agriculture interests and has the administrative capacity to handle the details in complex FTA negotiations. Other ASEAN countries do not have the same financial and human resources as Singapore.

slow decision process that marks the "ASEAN way". Since the bilateral arrangements are between two countries that are willing and able to commit and accept trade concessions in each other's market, these agreements create some sort of "coalition of the willing" that can, eventually, set the pace of integration for the rest of East Asia. Bilateral trade agreements can increase the pressure on other hesitating economies to soon follow suit because delays mean that they could find themselves excluded from a rapidly integrating market. With the "domino effect", the coalition of the willing can then, eventually, embrace the entire region.

References

Andriamananjara, S. 1999. "On the Size and Number of Regional Integration Arrangements: A Political Economy Model", *World Bank Policy Research Working Paper 2117*. May.

Austria, M. 2003. "East Asian Regional Cooperation: Approaches and Processes", Philippine Institute for Development Studies Discussion Paper. March.

Baldwin, R. and C. Wyplosz. 2003. *The Economics of European Integration*.

Chalermpalanupap, T. 2002. "Towards an East Asian Community: The Journey has Begun", paper presented at the Fifth China-ASEAN Research Institutes Roundtable on Regionalism and Community Building in East Asia, HongKong, 17—19 October.

Harrison, G., T. Rutherford, and D. Tarr. 2001. "Chile's Regional Arrangements and the FTAA: The Importance of Market Access", *World Bank Working Paper*. April.

Ibarra-Yunez. 2003. "Spaghetti Regionalism or Strategic Foreign Trade: Some Evidence from Mexico", *NBER Working*

Paper # 9692. May.

Kowalczyk, C. and R. Wonnacott. 1992. "Hubs and Spokes, and Free Trade in the Americas", *NBER Working paper* # 4198. October.

Lee, C. 2000. "Northeast Asian Economic Cooperation: The Need for a New Approach", *NIRA Review*, Autumn.

Lloyd, P. 2002. "New Regionalism and New Bilateralism in the Asia-Pacific", *ISEAS Visiting Researchers Series* No. 3.

Munakata, N. 2002. "Whither East Asian Economic Integration", *RIETI Discussion Paper Series* 02-E-007.

Panagariya, A. 2000. "Preferential Trade Liberalisation: The Traditional Theory and New Developments", *Journal of Economic Literature* 38: 287-331.

Schiff, M. and A. Winters. 2002. "Regional Cooperation and the Role of International Organizations in Regional Integration", *World Bank Policy Research Working Paper 2872.* July.

Severino, R. 2002a. "The Three Ages of ASEAN." Lecture delivered at Harvard University, 3 October.

——. 2001. "Will ASEAN Be like the EU?" Remarks delivered at the European Policy Center, Brussels, 23 March.

——. 2001b. "The ASEAN Way and the Rule of Law", Address of the ASEAN Secretary-General at the International Law Conference on ASEAN Legal Systems and Regional Integration. Kuala Lumpur. September 3.

——. 1999. "No Alternative to Regionalism", interview with Panorama Magazine. August.

Soesastro, H. 2002. "Lessons from ASEAN Institution", paper presented at the Annual APEC Study Center Consortium Conference, "From the Asian Financial Crisis to a Global Recession: Towards a More Proactive Role of APEC", Merida, Mexico, 22—24 May.

Making ASEAN as a Close Partner: Comparing China and Japan

Zhang Yunling [①]

Introduction

ASEAN combined by 10 South East Asian countries has become a highly integrated region in East Asia through AFTA and other regional cooperation and integration arrangements. The newly signed document by ASEAN leaders in Bali, Indonesia in October, 2003 would lead ASEAN toward a more integrated community. China[②] normalized its relations with Southeast Asian countries only until early 1990s. Economic linkages used to be very weak. But trade between the two sides has been developed very fast in recent years. What is significant is that the two sides signed the framework document for close economic partnership in 2002, and the document for a strategic partnership in 2003, which set a firm foundation for future close economic, as well as political cooperation.

Japan as the largest economy in East Asia has been one of the most important economic partner of ASEAN. Japan provides an important market for ASEAN and its investments are consid-

---

① Zhang Yunling, Professor, Director of Institute of Asia-Pacific Studies, Chinese Academy of Social Sciences.

② Herein, China refers only to Mainland China.

ered as a key factor in ASEAN's manufacturing industry. Nevertheless, due to the economic trouble, both Japan's trade and investment with ASEAN have been declined. Efforts have been made by Japan to strengthen its relations with ASEAN through many arrangements, including FTA or close economic relation arrangement (CER). It seems that Japan intends to re-enhance its relations with ASEAN in face of a changing situation.

Regionalism in East Asia is emerging. It has achieved progress by formulating the process of "10+3" (ASEAN plus China, Japan and ROK). But for regional free trade arrangement, it started only from a multi-layered process. ASEAN is a pathfinder in this direction through its AFTA. China becomes active to engage in regionalism after joining WTO. China's first move is to sign an agreement with ASEAN for an FTA within 10 years. However, an FTA with ASEAN is not the end of its interest in regionalism. China has strong interest to promote a larger based East Asian FTA and a real community in a longer term.

Japan is a key factor in any regional arrangement. Japan has moved in a new direction by initiating and concluding bilateral FTAs, but "a comprehensive deal is not on with Japan because of agriculture"[1]. It seems that Japan will try to conduct negotiations with some more developed economies, like ROK, Thailand, Malaysia, etc. after Japan-Singapore CEP and still needs time to move to an East Asian strategy on FTA.

It is crucial that China and Japan can cooperate in East Asian integration and cooperation. The common interest is growing between the two countries through economic integration. But political will is needed for two countries to work together based on a new consensus.

---

[1] Peter Drysdale & Kenichi Ishigaki, 2001, p. 5.

I. Comparing Economic Relations of China and Japan with ASEAN

China-ASEAN

China and ASEAN trade started from a very low level. But it has been grown fast and now they have become very important trade partners. Currently, ASEAN is China's 5th largest trade partner, and China is ASEAN's 6th largest partner. Since early 1990s, the average annual growth rate in trade between ASEAN and China has been more than 20%, higher than the average of the growth rate at the same period. For most years since early 1990s, China has trade deficit, i. e. import more than the export.

ASEAN used to be one of the major FDI sources for China. But FDI flow to China has been slowed down, especially after 1997 due to the financial crisis. ASEAN accounts for 11% of FDI flow to China in 1997, only 4.9% in 2001 due to the impact of financial crisis. However, China's investment in ASEAN is still small compared to ASEAN investment in China, only 0.65 billion US dollars by the end of 2001. But it is expected that China's investment in ASEAN will increase significantly in the coming years. Besides, China has large contracted projects in ASEAN, total value is more than 12 billion US dollars by the end of 2001.

A striking phenomenon in China-ASEAN trade relations is that China has become a major market for ASEAN's exports. ASEAN countries benefited largely from China's phenomenal growth since China's imports from ASEAN have grown faster than from the rest of the world. With economic growth, it is expected that China will increase its gross imports by a rather big margin.

Figure 1 Trend of China and ASEAN Trade (in billion dollars)

Source: ASEAN secretariat, China International Trade Statistics.

The trade between China and ASEAN still has a clear complementary nature. Among China's increasing import products, many of them are specially relevant to ASEAN: rice, palm oil, rubber, chemicals, textiles, pulp and paper, petroleum products, telecommunications, machinery and electrical appliances, grain and oil processing products, etc. The trade figure of 2002 showed that China becomes ASEAN's most promising market for export. ASEAN becomes the fourth largest partner for China's import after Japan, Taiwan and EU. This reflects a fact that ASEAN benefits significantly from an economically booming China.

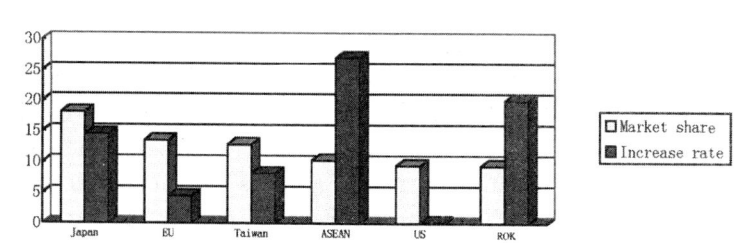

Figure 2 China's Import Distribution in 2002

Source: http://www.moftec.gov.cn

ASEAN used to be one of China's important sources of FDI. But 1997 financial crisis largely reduced ASEAN's capacity to invest in China. However, China's investment in ASEAN is still very limited, the total amount until 2001 only less than 5 billion US dollars, though the potential is promising if following current China's economic trend.

Figure 3 Share of ASEAN in China's FDI Inflow

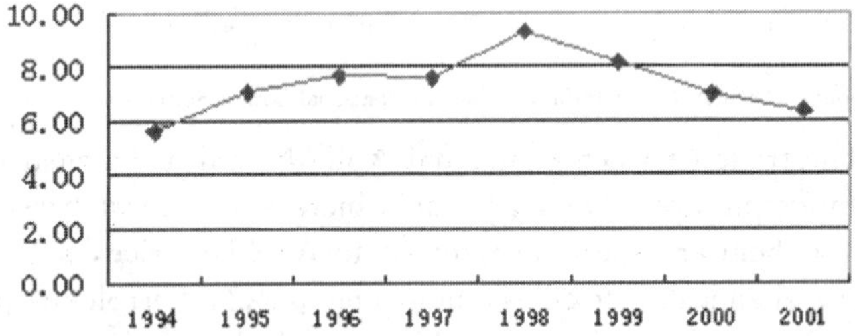

Source: Yearbook of China Statistics, 1995, 1997, 2002.

Japan-ASEAN

Japan is the second largest trade partner of ASEAN after the United States. From 1993—2001, the share of Japan's trade with ASEAN or ASEAN with Japan was almost equally about 15%. However, this general figure does not fully reflect the nature of Japan-ASEAN economic relations. Japan provides a large market share for ASEAN's external trade, but the share has been declined, either export or import.

From 1994, ASEAN side always has had large trade deficit with Japan, i.e. Japan exports more than imports.

It is interesting to compare China with Japan. In early 1990s, China's market share for ASEAN is very marginal, but till 2001, China's import from ASEAN is almost the same as Japan's import from ASEAN. After financial crisis, from 1998—2001, China's trade deficit with ASEAN is 14.6 billion US dollars, while Japan's trade surplus with ASEAN is close to 23 billion US dollars.[1]

Figure 4 Japan's Export and Import to ASEAN from 1993—2001 (In billion US dollars)

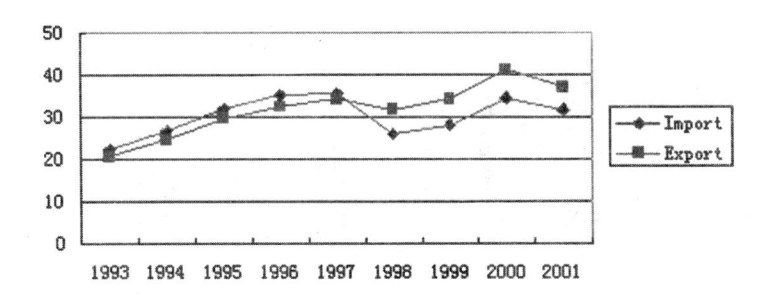

Figure 5 Japan Market Share for ASEAN Export and Import (% of total)(1993—2001)

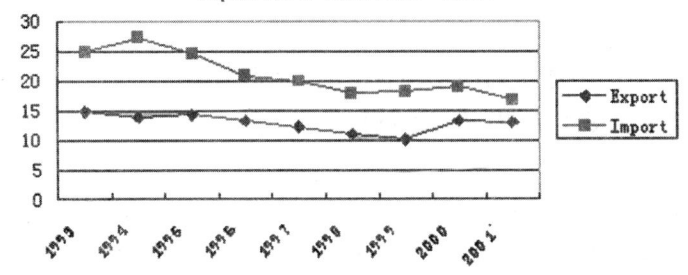

Japan has made substantial investments in ASEAN, accounting for 18.4% of total FDI into ASEAN in year 2001. Japanese investments have played an important role in developing ASEAN's modern manufacture industries, especially the export industries. However, although ASEAN has always been a major destination for Japanese investors, over the last decade, Japan's investment in ASEAN has been slowdown, as a result, the share of total investments into ASEAN decreased from about 28% in

---

[1] ASEAN statistics, http://www.aseansec.org.

1991 to 18.4% in 2001. ①From the comparison we can find that Japan is still an important economic partner, but its role and position has been changed, which is the result of its economic difficulty and also the outcome of China's rising.

Figure 6　Japanese FDI share in ASEAN from 1995—2001

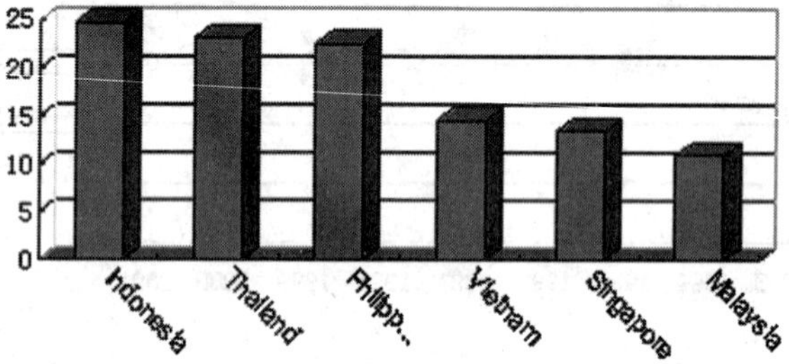

Note: Japanese FDI in Laos, Cambodia and Myanmar still marginal.
Source: UNTADC.

II. Comparing Cooperation of China and Japan with ASEAN

Both China and Japan have made great efforts to promote economic cooperation with ASEAN. China and ASEAN cooperation started mainly from 1990s and have quickly developed recent years while the cooperation between Japan and ASEAN began much earlier, but slowed down after the financial crisis and new efforts have been made to strengthen it. Both China and Japan emphasized that either China-ASEAN FTA or Japan-ASEAN CEP "would boost the future development of an economic area covering East Asia".

The Cooperation Between China and ASEAN

The cooperation between China and ASEAN can be traced

---

① Joint report of the ASEAN-Japan closer economic partnership expert group, 2002, p.1.

to 1991 when Foreign Minister Qian Qichen was invited to attend opening session of the 24th ASEAN ministers meeting in Kuala Lumpur. He expressed China's interest in strengthening cooperation with ASEAN for mutual benefit. In 1993, ASEAN and China agreed to establish two joint committees for economic and trade cooperation in science and technology. At the same time, ASEAN and China agreed to engage in consultations on political and security issues of common concern at the senior officials level. In July 1996, China was accorded full dialogue partner status. In 1997, China and ASEAN established the ASEAN-China Joint Cooperation Committee (ACJCC) and ASEAN-China Cooperation Fund. China participates in a series of consultative meetings with ASEAN, which includes the ASEAN Regional Forum (ARF), the Post Ministerial Conferences (PMC) 9+1 and 9+10, the Joint Cooperation Committee (JCC) Meeting, the ASEAN-China SOM Consultations and the ASEAN-China Business Council Meeting.

At the Eighth ASEAN-China Summit in Phnom Penh on 4 November 2002, China and ASEAN signed the "Framework Agreement on Comprehensive Economic Co-operation between ASEAN and China" which provides the groundwork for the eventual establishment of an ASEAN-China Free Trade Area (FTA) by 2010 for the older ASEAN members and 2015 for the newer members. The Trade Negotiating Committee (TNC) was established in May 2002 for negotiating a comprehensive agreement. It is expected that the negotiation for a free trade area would be concluded by 30 June 2004. Cooperative activities between China and ASEAN have been expanding in the five priority areas, namely agriculture, information and communications technology, human resource development, two-way investment, and Mekong River Basin development. The two sides signed a Memorandum of Understanding on Agricultural Cooperation. The areas of cooperation include forestry, livestock production, fisheries, biotechnology, post-harvest technology and the field harmonization of quarantine measures and standard conformity of agriculture products.

Development cooperation between the two sides has been progressing at a considerably fast pace especially with the establishment of the ASEAN-China Working Group on Development Cooperation (ACWGDC) in May 2002. The cooperation also is in the frameworks of the Greater Mekong Sub-region (GMS), ASEAN Mekong Basin Development Cooperation and the Mekong River Commission. Between May 2002 and March 2003, ASEAN and China have implemented 14 projects in the areas of science and technology, ICT, agriculture, transport, social development, HRD, and mass media. More projects covering ICT, HRD, science and technology, investment, transport, academic exchange, SME, environment, and cultural sectors are expected to be implemented. In 2003, China and ASEAN signed a Memorandum of Understanding on Cooperation on Information and Communication Technology. [1]However, as a developing economy, China has played a very important role in assisting ASEAN economic development and the cooperation between the sides is still limited. Along with the closer economic integration, the cooperation will be further developed more on a institutionally arranged base.

Importantly, China-ASEAN cooperation goes beyond economic area. In 2002, with signing of "Framework Agreement on Comprehensive Economic Co-operation", the Leaders also adopted the "Joint Declaration of ASEAN and China on Cooperation in the Field of Non-traditional Security Issues","Declaration on the Conduct of Parties in the South China Sea" aiming at "promoting a peaceful, friendly and harmonious environment in the South

---

[1] http://www.aseansec.org: ASEAN China Dialogue, p. 3; http://www.mof.gov.cn.

China Sea between ASEAN and China". In 2003, China formally signed "Treaty of Amity and Cooperation in Southeast Asia (TAC)", and a document for the strategic partnership, which provides a good foundation for improving political cooperation in the future.

However, China-ASEAN cooperation and integration is not an easy course. As acknowledged that "the extent and level of cooperation rests on the presence of two vital ingredients: political will and a deep pool of knowledge and mutual understanding". [1]

The Cooperation Between Japan and ASEAN

Japan and ASEAN started their formal cooperation in 1977 when they decided to establish a forum for cooperation. In 1987, the two sides announced "a new partnership toward peace and prosperity".

In 1997, Japanese Prime Minister Ryutaro Hashimoto announced his "Hashimoto Doctrine" and called for developing a "broader and deeper partnership" and "broader and deeper exchanges at the top and all the other levels".

Japan has participated in a series of consultative meetings with ASEAN which includes the ASEAN Regional Forum (ARF), the Post Ministerial Conferences (PMC) 9+1 and 9+10, ASEAN Economic Ministers-Ministry for International Trade and Industry (AEM-MITI) Consultations, ASEAN-Japan Forum, Senior Economic Officers-Ministry for International Trade and Industry (SEO-MITI) Consultations, Joint Planning Committee (JPC) Meeting, ASEAN-Japan Economic Council (AJEC), ASEAN-Japanese Businessmen's Meeting (AJBM). The ASEAN-Tokyo Committee also assist in conducting and maintaining the dialogue with Japan. Regular Dialogue meetings

---

[1] Lim Swee Say, "ASEAN and China: The Challenges of Cooperation", *Reader*, Singapore Institute of International Affairs, Vol. 2, No. 2, 2002, p. 6.

such as the AEM-MITI Consultations and the ASEAN-Japan Forum are now held annually. Japan also participates in the ARF.

In addition to being one of ASEAN's most important economic partners, Japan is a major contributor to development cooperation. Japan has provided technical assistance to ASEAN through several programs, such as the Japan-ASEAN Cooperation Promotion Program (JACPP), the Intra-ASEAN Technical Exchange Program (IATEP) and the Japan-ASEAN Exchange Program (JAEP).

In 2002, Japanese Prime Minister Koizumi visited a number of ASEAN countries and put forward "Koizumi Initiative", which is made up of three pillars: filling economic gaps and enjoying prosperity, reassuring human dignity, and fostering democratic and stable governance.[1] He also proposed several initiatives for cooperation, including the designation of 2003 as the Year of ASEAN-Japan Exchange, reinforced cooperation in education and HRD, solidifying the security relations between Japan and ASEAN, the ASEAN-Japan Comprehensive Economic Partnership (CEP). The ASEAN-Japan Summit, held in Phnom Penh on 5 November 2002, issued a Joint Declaration endorsing the development of a framework for Comprehensive Economic Partnership, including elements of a possible FTA by 2012. Another big step was made when Japan initiated the Japan-ASEAN Summit in Tokyo on December 11－12, 2003. The two sides reaffirmed close economic partnership and identified more than 100 projects for cooperation through the action plan. This shows that Japan has made more efforts to reinforce close relationship with ASEAN, which has been negatively effected by the financial crisis in 1997 and Japan's economic slow down.

---

[1] Yoriko Kawaguchi's policy speech, "Building Bridges toward Our Future: Initiating for Reinforcing ASEAN Integration", June 17, 2003.

To compare the cooperation of China and Japan with ASEAN, we may find that Japan had longer history than China in proceeding economic cooperation and Japan's role is much larger in providing economic assistance to ASEAN. However, China is moving fast in promoting cooperation with ASEAN, and China has broader programs than Japan in making ASEAN as a partner.

III. China and Japan in Regional Integration and Cooperation

China and Japan have their different interests and strategies in developing economic relations with ASEAN. ASEAN is the direct close neighbor for China. China emphasizes its interests with ASEAN on a comprehensive dimension. This is why China takes ASEAN as an integrated region. ASEAN as a stable region and a cooperative relationship will well serve China's interest in creating a peaceful environment, which is crucial for its transition toward the modernization. China-ASEAN relationship starts and develops from a new foundation, while for Japan, ASEAN is firstly a big market and also strategic navigation route. Japan already built up close relationship with ASEAN countries in the past. Japan now wants to renew its existing relations through the new efforts.

However, it is important to recognize that the two countries can find more interactions and common interests in their relation with ASEAN. From a broad perspective, especially from the angle of emerging East Asian regional cooperation, we may identify three ways of interactions and possible cooperation:

FDI Driven Interactions

Japanese FDI has created a large network for economic exchange within ASEAN and ASEAN with outside market through import and export. Following increasing Japanese FDI in China, this network has been enlarged into a Japan-China-ASEAN structure. After the financial crisis in 1997, we have witnessed a trend of reallocation of Japanese FDI, less to ASEAN, more to China. This reallocation has created a new network between China and ASEAN through production network of Japanese companies. The real story behind fast increase of ASEAN exports to China is a reflection of this new network, i. e. increasing exchanges of parts and components between Japanese investors in China and ASEAN. This China-Japan-ASEAN economic angle has made the three sides more integrated ever.

For example, during 1996—2001, ASEAN exports of computer components, machinery and electrical equipments to China increased sharply. This reflects a new trend of China-ASEAN economic relations, i. e. China's role as market is increasing. Japanese FDI reallocation is not a zero sum game to ASEAN.

Figure 7   ASEAN Exports of Computer, Machinery and Electrical Equipments to China(In million US dollars)

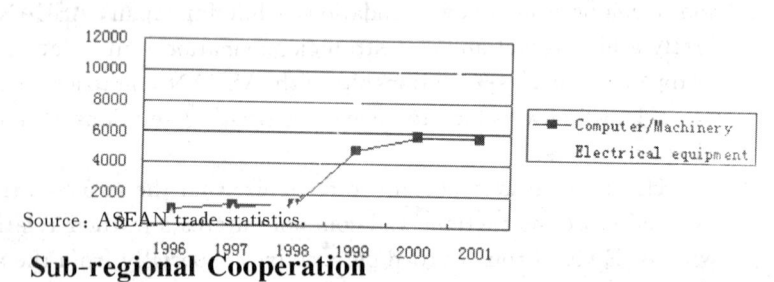

Source: ASEAN trade statistics.

Sub-regional Cooperation

China and Japan may find more common areas in the sub-regional cooperation with ASEAN. Currently, the major area for cooperation is Great Mekong Sub-regional project/ (GMS). ASEAN adopted its basic framework of Mekong Basin development cooperation in 1996 aiming at "strengthening the interconnections and economic linkages between the ASEAN member countries and the Mekong riparian countries". ①This project become an important project for "10 plus 3" cooperation, which both China and Japan participated.

GMS provides an important opportunity for China and Japan to cooperate together. Geographically, China is directly linked to the Mekong Basin area and has strong interest to participate and make contribution. Japan has been the largest donor to less developed countries, like Cambodia and Laos and played important role in assisting their economic development. Thus, China and Japan should not be competitors in participating this project.

Japan is currently supporting two flagship projects in this area. One is the East-West Corridor which will benefit Vietnam, Laos, Thailand and Myanmar, and the other is the second East West Corridor which connect Cambodia with its neighbors. A bridge was completed in 2000 which is called "Kizuna bridge". ②

The two countries have been cooperated in improving infrastructure of the region, like Kunming-Bangkok high way and other projects. So that, the sub-regional cooperation may become a platform for China and Japan to work together with a complementary feature of their roles to play. ③This of course needs good will and also good coordination in a one integrated regional framework of the cooperation.

East Asian Cooperation

East Asian cooperation as a formal process started from 1997 as a reflection of the financial crisis. This process has been developed well. Politically, it is under "10 plus 3" formula, with informal leaders' meeting and several ministers' meetings. Eco-

---

① Basic Framework of ASEAN Mekong Basin Development Cooperation, Kuala Lumpur, 17 June,1996.

② Yoriko Kawaguchi's policy speech, "Building Bridges toward our Future: Initiating for Reinforcing ASEAN Integration", June 17,2003.

③ "China-ASEAN Economic Relations: View from China's Understanding", 2003, *Study Group Report*, CASS, p.76.

nomically, it is still following a multi-layered structure, with different efforts by different parties, like Japan- Singapore FTA (JSEPA), Japan- ASEAN CEP, China-ASEAN CEP and FTA, as well as China-Japan-ROK CEP etc. It seems that time is still needed before these multi-layered processes can be integrated into one unique East Asian approach and finally move toward an East Asian identity. EAVG called on an East Asian Community building in 2001. The author proposed an early establishment of an Organization of East Asian Cooperation (OEAC) to coordinate and integrate East Asian cooperation process. [1]

China and Japan are considered as two key players in developing and realizing East Asian cooperation and integration. Both China and Japan have participated "10 plus 3" process and a special "Northeast Asian 3" dialogue. It seems that while China and Japan share some common interests in developing East Asian cooperation, some differences are there. As for China, it becomes active to promote an EAFTA as early as possible. China-ASEAN FTA may be used as a pathfinder to forge EAFTA. This is why China even supports an early arrangement of trilateral FTA in Northeast Asian region though it is the weakest among three countries. It is wrong to think that China's move intends to reduce Japanese interests in ASEAN and to exclude Japan from East Asia. [2]

Japan has shown a different approach. Its near future effort seems to be focused on the bilateral, rather than the regional. After the conclusion of JSEPA, Japan concluded Japan-ASEAN CEP (JACEP) in 2002, but intends to negotiate bilateral FTA

---

[1] Zhang Yunling, *East Asian Cooperation: Progress and Future*, World Affairs Press, Beijing, 2002, p. 6.

[2] It was said that Japan's rapid pursuit of JACEP was in response to China-ASEAN FTA and it was out of fear that relative gains would otherwise shift against Japan in East Asia. Jiro Okamoto (ed.), *Whither Free Trade Arrangements?* IDE, JETRO, 2003, Tokyo, p. 246.

only with more developed economies of ASEAN, like Thailand, Malaysia, The Philippines, etc., rather than with the whole ASEAN. In Northeast Asia, Japan's first priority is to complete CEP with ROK, rather than a trilateral one. ① As for EAFTA, the government policy has not been made clear yet though experts urged government to adopt a more active policy to it and to establish an East Asian Economic Community (EAEC) in 2007. ②A good news from Japan-ASEAN Summit in Tokyo on December 11—12, 2003 is that they will cooperate to "seek to build an East Asian community which is outward looking, endowed with the exuberance of creativity and vitality and with the shared spirit of mutual understanding and upholding Asian traditions and values, while respecting universal rules and principles." ③This is the first time in a Japanese official document to identify the East Asian Community building as a goal.

How to make China and Japan cooperate and move to an integrated direction? Although their current priorities are different, shared interests can be found for the two countries since both of them emphasize the importance of East Asian cooperation. This of course needs real cooperation between China and Japan, i.e. a real partnership in promoting East Asian cooperation. East Asian cooperation process may provide an important platform for China and Japan to improve their bilateral relations and identify their common interests.

As a matter of fact, East Asian cooperation and integration is a comprehensive process including economic, political, social, as well as cultural progresses. It is for sure that cooperation of China and Japan in East Asian community process needs strong

---

① Perspective on East Asian FTA, JETRO, March, 2003, p. 37.
② According to the report, 40 Japanese leading experts put forward a policy report and called on establishing EAEC. *World Weekly (in Japanese)*, July 8,2003.
③ *Tokyo Declaration for the Dynamic and Enduring ASEAN-Japan Partnership in the New Millennium*, December 12,2003.

political will and spirit from both sides. It seems that this political foundation is still very weak and to some extent, also very vulnerable. The first weakness is the bilateral relationship due to the historical legacy and security concerns. The second weakness is the trust in engaging regional activities, both sides consider the other side as the competitor. In order to make the two as the real partners in forging East Asian cooperation and integration, we have to overcome some political barriers if we achieve an economically free East Asian region and finally moving toward a real community.

It is recognized that "regionalism is on the rise in East Asia",[1] but it is still in the early stage. China has taken an active attitude policy in participating and promoting the regional cooperation, especially the East Asian cooperation. Starting from economic cooperation, China hopes that this process will move to the other areas, including political, security, social and cultural areas. Prime Minister Wen Jiabao called a comprehensive cooperation during the latest "10 + 3" leaders' meeting in Bali, Indonesia in October of 2003.[2] As a regional cooperation process, China surely welcomes an active Japanese role. A closer Japan-ASEAN relationship is helpful for the East Asian region. As a matter of fact, China- ASEAN and Japan-ASEAN relationship are quite complementary. China and Japan should work together to play the leading role in this process, which is essential to overcome the " leadership gap" in this region. Both China and Japan need new mindset in moving to this direction.

---

[1] Chia Siow Yue, "Regional Economic Cooperation in East Asia: Approaches and Process, in *East Asian Cooperation: Progress and Future*, World Affairs Press, 2003, p. 37.

[2] "Wen Jiabao Called on Strengthening East Asian Cooperation", *People's Daily*, October 8, 2003.

The Economic Rise of China: A Catalyst for East Asian Economic Integration

John Wong[①]

Introduction

The Chinese economy, following its successful economic reform and open-door policy, has experienced spectacular growth for over two decades. In the process, China's economy has also become more closely integrated with its East Asian neighbours. In the short run, China's dynamic economic growth and its integration process carry both positive and negative spill-over effects on the region. Over the longer run, the economic rise of China can be seen as not only a new engine for the region's economic growth, but also a powerful force for integrating the East Asian economies. In recent years, China has been the main driving force behind East Asia's regional trade interdependence, as most East Asian economies have already experienced the largest percentage-point increases in their export to China.

Initially, Japan and the four East Asian NIEs (newly industrialized economies) of ROK, Taiwan, Hong Kong and Singapore tended to capture most of the benefits from China's open-door policy by trading with and investing in China. As China

---

[①] John Wong, Research Director of East Asian Institute, National University of Singapore. He is grateful to Ms Sarah Chan for updating the statistical tables.

continued to press ahead with its export-oriented development strategies, it started to cast a large shadow on its ASEAN (Association of Southeast Asian Nations) neighbours to its south, many of which have economies that compete with China in attracting FDI (foreign direct investment) and in exporting manufactured products to the same third-country markets.

To allay ASEAN's growing apprehension of China, Beijing took the initiative to arrange an FTA (free trade agreement) with ASEAN, which would operate to increase the region's trade and investment to the benefits of both sides. Signed in November 2002, this landmark China-ASEAN FTA deal has put great pressures on Japan and ROK to follow suit by intensifying their economic relations with ASEAN under the proposed cooperation umbrella of the "ASEAN + Three" (ASEAN with China, Japan and ROK) scheme. With China as a rising regional political and economic power, its FTA initiative with ASEAN has thus sparked off the process towards the New-Age economic integration in East Asia.

I. The Economic Rise of China

China's economy grew at an average rate of 9.5% for the period of 1978—2002. Whereas the 1997 Asian financial crisis brought down many Asian economies, the Chinese economy was hardly affected by the crisis as it continued to grow at 8.8% in 1997 and 7.8% in 1998. After the crisis, while economic growth in most of Asia had fallen to low or negative rates and the world economy at large was creeping into recession, China's economy alone was still steaming ahead with strong growth. China chalked up 7.3% growth for 2001 and 8% for 2002. ①Recently, China has shown that its economy after the SARS could bounce back in growth much faster and stronger than other Asian economies, which were brought down by such an external shock.

China has been much less affected by the global economic downturn and other external shocks, mainly because over 80% of China's economic growth is generated by domestic demand (i. e. domestic consumption and investment). However, China's exports have also been growing rapidly, averaging at 17% for the past two decades, from US $ 9.8 billion in 1978 to US $ 326 billion in 2002. By 2002, China has become the world's 4th largest exporting nation after USA, EU and Japan. ② For foreign direct investment (FDI), China has become the world's most favored destination in comparison with all other developing countries since 1993. From 1988 to 2001, China's realized FDI grew at an average rate of 23% per annum. By the end of 2002, China had attracted a total of US $ 621 billion FDI. In fact, China in recent years has captured about half of all FDI in Asia. Not surprisingly, over 80% of the world's 500 largest companies have set up businesses in China. ③

In all, China's total nominal GDP in 2002 has breached the 10 trillion yuan (US $ 1.2 trillion)——or more than twice the combined GDP of Indonesia, Malaysia, the Philippines, Singapore and Thailand. China is already the world's sixth largest economy. In terms of purchasing power parity (PPP), the

---

① See "GDP Set for 8% Growth", *China Daily* (Beijing, December 31, 2002). Also John Wong, "China's Economy in 2002 and Outlook for 2003", *EAI Background Brief* No. 143 (Singapore, East Asian Institute, 2 January 2003).

② News article, accessed from http://news.Xinhuanet.com/fortune/2003-01/09/content-684846.htm website.

③ "China Trade Surplus Adds up to US $ 13.3 Billion", *The Standard* (Hong Kong), July 12, 2002.

Chinese economy today is already the world's second largest after the USA—one needs, of course, to be aware of the problem of overstating China's real GDP by the PPP measure. ①

Indeed, as a result of its rapid industrialization progress, China has fast become the world's foremost manufacturing base. In 2001, China produced 160 million tons of steel; 40 million sets of color TV, 13 million refrigerators, 18 million air-conditioners, 2.7 million automobiles and 8 million PCs. ② In 2002, China became the world's fifth largest automobile manufacturer with a total output of 3.3 million units. ③By mid-2003, China surpassed the USA as the world's largest telephone market (238 million fixed lines and 235 million mobile phones)④Also by mid-2003, China's registered Internet users reached 68 million to form the world's second largest "Web population". ⑤Above all, on account of its strong external balance, China's foreign exchange reserves recently soared to US $346 billion, as the world's second largest. This has led to mounting international pressures on China to revalue its Renminbi. ⑥

Accordingly, the meteoric rise of China's economy has sud-

---

① World Bank, *World Development Report 2000/2001* (New York: Oxford University Press). Also, *Mingpao* (Hong Kong), September 20, 2000.
② National Bureau of Statistics, *China Statistical Yearbook 2002*; article accessed at www.cinanews.com.cn/n/2002-02-06 website.
③ "Car Industry Needs Sober Minds", *China Daily*, (July 17, 2003).
④ "Telephone Users in China Number 472 Million", *China Daily* (July 24, 2003).
⑤ "China's Netizens See Rapid Growth", *China Daily* (July 22, 2003).
⑥ "Premier Wen: China to Keep RMB Rate Stable", *China Daily* (August 6, 2003).

denly become a "hot" topic in international and regional media. ① Many Asian commentators are concerned over the emergence of China as a potentially disruptive force to the Asian economic growth. Others even point a finger at China for their own economic woes, including the accusation of China exporting deflation to them. Even the Japanese have started to show anxiety over China's recent dynamic industrial expansion. The famous Japanese economist Kenichi Ohmae even used a sensational title "Asia's next crisis: 'Made in China'" to talk alarmingly about the rise of China. ②According to Japanese estimates in 2001, as shown in Chart 1, about one in two of the world's motorcycles, one in three of the world's air-conditioners and one in four of the world's color TVs were manufactured in China. China is indeed already producing more cell phones, more desktop computers and more DVD players than Japan. ③ Not surprisingly, many Asian economies, particularly the smaller ASEAN countries are watching the rise of China with apprehension.

II. East Asian Growth and Interdependence

China's economic performance in the past two decades has

---

① China's emergence as the world's manufacturing powerhouse after two decades of dynamic growth has invited worldwide prominent attention. The international media have recently portrayed China's economic resurgence as an economic threat. David Roche, a famous Wall Street economist, commented on China being a source of current global recession with its mass production of a wide range of low-priced manufactured products for the world market. Early this year, Japan's *Nikkei Weekly* reported about China setting pace in markets for commodities around the world. The Chinese media and academia have since come out to defend China's position.

② "Asia's Next Crisis: 'Made in China'", *The Strait Times* (Singapore, August 2, 2001).

③ See "China Takes Production Lead as Foreign Firms Set up Shop", *The Nikkei Weekly* (August 6, 2001).

indeed been breathtaking. Viewed in the overall East Asian context, however, China's hyper-growth is actually not so exceptional. Nor is it unprecedented, as many other Asian economies have experienced such high growth before the emergence of China.

East Asia (EA) is commonly defined to comprise Japan, China, the four Newly Industrialized Economies (NIEs) of ROK, Taiwan, Hong Kong and Singapore, and the four ASEAN countries of Indonesia, Malaysia, the Philippines, and Thailand—the original ASEAN members. ① Situated on the western rim of the Pacific, many of these East Asian economies (EAEs) have displayed dynamic growth for a sustained period until 1997 when they were hit, in varying degrees, by the regional financial crisis. The World Bank in its well-known study referred to their high growth phenomenon as the "East Asian Miracle". ②

Why have the EAEs been able to sustain high growth for so long? The EAEs have generally committed a high proportion of their GDP (at around 30%) to domestic investment during their critical periods of industrial take-off. Furthermore, their equally high levels of domestic savings largely matched their high levels of gross domestic investment. ③In short, high investment, as the single most important neo-classical explanation of high growth, has worked on these EAEs much like a "virtuous circle": high rates of investment induce high export growth, and then high GDP growth, high savings and finally high investment again.

---

① Singapore is historically and geographically an integral part of Southeast Asia, and politically a member of ASEAN. However, economically and socially, Singapore is more akin to the other East Asian NIEs, and hence commonly labelled as one of the four East Asian NIEs.

② *The East Asian Miracle*, Oxford University Press, New York, 1994.

③ See World Bank, *World Development Report* (various years) and Asia Development Bank, *Asian Development Outlook* (various years), which provide data on investment and savings rates of the EAEs for various years.

Other explanations include intensive human resource development for certain resource-poor EAEs. In terms of policy, the EAEs share the salient common feature of operating effective export-oriented development strategies, as reflected in their generally high export-GDP ratios and their relative high shares in the world export markets. Their export orientation has thus propelled them to high growth through reaping the gains from international trade and specialization. [1]

Historically speaking, the EA growth process is marked by three waves. Japan was the first non-Western country to become industrialized. Its high growth dated back to the 1950s after it had achieved its rapid post-war recovery, and carried the growth momentum over to the 1960s and much of the 1970s. Japan's economic growth engine was initially based on the export of labour-intensive manufactured products; but it was soon forced by rising wages and increasing costs to shed its comparative advantage for labour-intensive manufacturing in favour of the four NIEs, which started their industrial take-off in the 1960s. These four NIEs, once dubbed "Asia's Four Little Dragons", were arguably the most dynamic economies in Asia, as they had sustained near double-digit rates of growth for three decades, from the early 1960s to the 1980s. The rise of the NIEs constituted the second wave of the region's growth and integration.

By the early 1980s, high costs and high wages had also caught up with these four NIEs, which had to restructure their economies towards more capital-intensive and higher value-added activities by passing their comparative advantage in labor-intensive products to the late-comers of China and the four ASEAN economies and thereby spreading economic growth to the latter.

---

[1] For further discussion of this topic, see John Wong, "The East Asian Phenomenon and the Implications for Economic Development", in Basant K. Kapur, et. al. (eds.), *Development, Trade and the Asia-Pacific*, Essays in honour of Professor Lim Chong Yah, Prentice Hall, Singapore, 1996.

In this way, China and some ASEAN economies were able to register high growth through the 1980s and the 1990s. Many Japanese scholars like to depict this pattern of development in Asia as the "flying geese" model. [1] (See Table 1).

During the past two decades, the Chinese economy on account of its successful market reform has consistently chalked up near double-digit rates of growth while at the same time many ASEAN economies due to a number of institutional and structural constraints were losing some of their former growth dynamism. How far does the rise of China today constitute the third wave of the region's growth and integration? This is actually the gist of this article, and it will be expounded in the following sections.

Suffice it to say that the dynamic EAEs that are also open and outward-looking are bound to produce greater economic interaction with each other. Thus, an important feature of these EAEs is their growing economic interdependence. The EAEs, despite their inherent political, social and economic divergences, can actually economically integrate quite well as an informal and loosely constituted regional grouping. This is essentially the underlying meaning of the "flying geese" principle. Thus, Japan is obviously the natural economic leader of the group and has in fact been the prime source of capital and technology for other EAEs, first the NIEs and then China and ASEAN. The resource-based ASEAN-four complement well with the manufacturing-based NIEs while both are also complementary with the more developed Japanese economy. Then the huge potential of China, with its vast resource base and diverse needs, offers additional opportunities for all.

---

[1] The "flying geese" concept of development was originally coined by a Japanese economist, Kaname Akamatzu. ("A Historical Pattern of Economic Growth in Developing Countries", *Developing Economies*, No. 1, March/August, 1962).

Not surprisingly, the EA region has already developed a significant degree of economic interdependence as manifested in its fairly high level of intra-regional trade. As shown in Table 2, the EA region in 2001, despite the general economic slowdown in the EA region, still absorbed 41% of China's total exports; 43% of ROK's, 49% of Taiwan's, 52% of Hong Kong's, 54% of Singapore's, and 44% of the average of the ASEAN-4, though only 39% of Japan's—still unusually high for Japan as a global trading power.

Table 2 also describes the process of EA's growing export dependence over the past two decades, which shows that Japan's export orientation has over the years made a highly remarkable shift towards greater regional focus, with its export share to the EA region increasing from 22% in 1980 to 39% in 2001. The four NIEs have similarly made significant shifts in the same period by re-orienting their exports towards the region, mainly as a result of the opening up of China: ROK from 24% to 43%, Taiwan from 41% (1992) to 49%, Hong Kong from 23% to 52%, and Singapore from 40% to 54%. China, on the other hand, has moved in the opposite direction by slightly reducing its export dependence on the region, as China's exports in recent years were geared more to the US and EU markets, while the ASEAN-4 have similarly shown a slight reduction of export dependence on the EA region, from 51% in 1980 to 44% in 2001.

Apart from intra-regional trade, intra-regional foreign direct investment (FDI) flows have also operated as a powerful integrating force for the EA region, especially since a great deal of regional FDI is trade-related in nature. The EAEs, as essentially open and outward-looking economies, are highly dependent on foreign trade and foreign investment for their economic growth. In particular, both China and ASEAN have devised various incentive schemes to vie for FDI, which is generally treated not just as an additional source of capital supply but, more importantly, as a means of technology transfer and export market development.

Initially, western capital dominated the EA region's FDI scene. Then came the Japanese capital as the second wave, particularly after the early 1980s. In the 1990s, the region witnessed a new but no less significant trend associated with increasing FDI flows from the NIEs to ASEAN and China. The NIEs, having transformed themselves from capital-scarce to capital-surplus economies, become a new source of capital outflow to other less developed EA economies, thereby forming the third wave. Driven by rising costs and higher wages, the NIEs were relocating their labor-intensive manufacturing facilities to ASEAN and China with lower production costs, much like what Japan had done earlier. In this way, trade and FDI, often closely interrelated, have operated as a powerful integrating force for the EA region. And once again, China is at the center-stage of the region's FDI interflow.

China in recent years has become the most favored destination of all developing economies for FDI. As can be seen from Table 3, the EA region, especially Hong Kong, Taiwan, Japan, Singapore and ROK, accounted for an overwhelming share of FDI inflow to China. Such regional predominance has been declining in recent years, as China has made efforts to attract more technology-intensive FDI from North America and the EU. By 2000, the East Asian share of FDI in China declined to 55%, down from 88% in 1992. Nonetheless, the rise of China has completely altered the FDI landscape in the EA region.

III. China: A New Source of Growth and Integration

Suffice it to say that China's economic growth fits in quite well with the overall EA growth patterns. Since the EA region absorbs about 50% of China's exports and supplies three-quarters of China's FDI, it is not hard to see that China's rapidly growing economy since 1978 has impacted significantly on many EAEs to each other's advantage. On the one hand, China has been able to harness the region's vast trade and investment opportunities to facilitate its own economic growth. At the same time, China's economic growth and increasing integration with the region also provide new opportunities to enhance the region's overall growth potential and new impetus for regionalism.

However, the actual impact of the fast-growing Chinese economy on the EAEs is quite uneven. China's dynamic economic growth has produced both positive and negative effects for the individual EAEs in the region. By and large, Japan and the four NIEs have been able to capture most of the benefits arising from China's open-door policy by exporting more high-tech products and by investing in China, as shown in Table 3.

Accordingly, as shown in the trade matrix of Table 2, for the past two decades, Japan's share of exports to China almost doubled from 3.9% in 1980 to 7.7% in 2001; ROK's share from no direct trade in the 1980s to 12% in 2001; Taiwan's share also from zero direct trade in the early 1980s to 22% in 2001; Hong Kong's share from 6% in 1980 to a stunning 37% in 2001; and Singapore's share from 1.6% to 4.4%. In time to come, these five economies, which are inherently complementary with China, are set to grow even more closely integrated with China. Hong Kong today and to some extent, Taiwan have already become highly dependent on China for their economic growth.

It is thus sufficiently clear that China has been operating as a kind of locomotive for the economic growth of the EAEs. Even the ASEAN-4, which exported very little to China before 1980, also saw their export share to China more than tripled from 1.1% in 1980 to 4.4% in 2001. Table 4 provides more compelling evidence to this argument. In showing China's role in the changes of East Asian export dependency in recent years, Table

4 also brings out most vividly China's growing market potential for the exports from other EAEs. Thus, between 1995 and 2001, China as an importer provided the largest market share increase for Japan, ROK, Taiwan, Singapore, Indonesia, Malaysia, and Thailand; and the second largest market share increase for the Philippines. Because of its vast domestic market, China has clearly become an important engine of East Asian intra-regional trade growth.

IV. Competitive Pressures on ASEAN

However, the economic relations between China and the ASEAN-4 tend to be more competitive than complementary at their present stages of economic development. In many ways, China's dynamic economic growth has created strong competitive pressures for these ASEAN economies, which are vying for FDI with China as well as competing head-on with China's manufactured exports in the developed country markets. [1]

The 1997 Asian financial crisis, in slowing down the economic growth of the ASEAN-4, has also delayed their economic integration process with other EAEs, particularly China. By the end of 1999, two years after the outbreak of the crisis, the ASEAN-4 managed to bounce back in positive growth, in the form of a "V-shaped recovery" as a result of the recovery of their stock markets, increased exports and greater exchange rate stability. [2] However, their recovery processes were soon disrupted with the onset of the global economic downturn and other external shocks, bringing about a smaller second "dip" (Chart 2). Under the circumstances, the rise of China has inevitably pre-

---

[1] For further discussion of this topic, see Prakash Loungani, "Comrades or Competitors? Trade Links between China and Other East Asian Economies", *Finance & Development* (June 2000).

[2] "Asia's Astonishing Bounce-back", *The Economist*, August 21—27, 1999.

sented the ASEAN-4 with formidable external challenges.

The Sino-ASEAN economic relations are actually quite complex, and a more detailed examination of this topic is in order. Initially, China's success in economic reform and development had produced very little impact on the ASEAN countries to its south. Sino-ASEAN trade was very small and in fact constitutes only a small proportion of each other's total trade. Even by the early 1990s, when massive FDI began to flow into China, there is no evidence that China had "sucked" in a lot of capital from the ethnic Chinese in Southeast Asia. [1]

The picture has radically changed since the second half of the 1990s. While many ASEAN economies continued to be plagued by persistent economic crises and domestic political instability, China has been relentless in its pursuit of economic modernization. This has resulted in further narrowing the development gaps between ASEAN and China. In fact, the ASEAN region now risks being left behind by China's rapid economic development.

Specifically, the change in China's export structure carries the most serious implications for the ASEAN economies. When Deng opened up China in 1978, half of China's exports were made up of primary commodities like mineral and agriculture products. Today, manufactured products constitute about 90% of China's exports. Before 1995, traditional labour-intensive manufactures like textiles, clothing and footwear (TCF) used to dominate China's export structure. (Chart 3). All developing economies have gone through the stage of exporting such traditional labour-intensive manufactured exports. Hence China's TCF exports were not much a real "threat" to ASEAN's own exports, especially since many of ASEAN's TCF export items to

---

[1] See John Wong, "Southeast Asian Ethnic Chinese Investing in China", *EAI Working Paper*, No. 15, October 23, 1998.

developed countries are protected by the Multi-Fiber Arrangement (MFA) system. [1]

In recent years, the composition of China's manufactured exports has experienced even more significant changes, marked by the rise of non-traditional items like machinery, electronics, and other hi-tech products. [2] China's rapid expansion of such non-traditional exports is clearly posing serious challenges for the ASEAN-4, which are directly competing with China in the third country markets, particularly the USA.

As China is now a WTO member, Sino-ASEAN export competition in such non-traditional items as electrical machinery and electronics products is expected to grow even more intense in the future. As illustrated in Chart 4, although the electrical and electronic exports of the ASEAN-4 and the NIEs combined are higher than China's, China is rapidly taking on these Asian competitors as evident in its increasing share of the US market for these products over the years.

In 1990, for instance, China's share of the US electronics market was only around 2% but this share has now increased to 9.7% by 2000, comparable to 8.4% for Taiwan and 9.8% for ROK, and higher than the ASEAN-4 countries —9.2% for Malaysia, 1.02% for Indonesia, 3.0% for the Philippines, and 4.5% for Thailand. China is set to overtake both the NIEs (which are relocating their production bases to China) and the ASEAN-4 whose export competitiveness is rapidly eroded by

---

[1] World trade in textile and apparel was previously governed by the MFA system that permitted the use of quotas without compensation. On 1 Jan 1995, the MFA was replaced by the Agreement on Textiles and Clothing (ATC), which applies to all WTO members.

[2] John Wong and Sarah Chan, "China's Rapidly Changing Export Structure", *EAI Background Brief No.* 85, Singapore, 9 April, 2001.

China's growing strength in these non-traditional items. ①

What made China different from ASEAN is the fact that China has by far a much larger pool of both skilled as well as non-skilled labour. China also has a large domestic market for all sorts of products, from high-tech to low-tech, to take advantage of the economies of scale effect. With lower average and marginal costs generated as a result of high-volume production, China is thus able to enjoy its natural cost advantage compared to ASEAN and other smaller developing countries. Furthermore, for both China and ASEAN, a high proportion of these non-traditional items are produced under OEM (original equipment manufacturing) arrangements whereby large multinational companies (MNCs) use China (and ASEAN) as a platform to process products for exports. Where sharp cost gaps occur, these multinationals may simply cut back their production facilities in ASEAN and move them to China. Hence a negative impact on ASEAN's own FDI and manufactured exports.

There is, of course, also a complementary angle to the Sino-ASEAN economic relationship. As the Chinese economy continues to grow, it will also increase demand for exports from ASEAN, particularly for its primary commodities and natural resources. This is why several ASEAN countries, particularly Malaysia and Thailand, are taking a positive view that the rise of China also means the emergence of a potentially new locomotive of economic growth for the ASEAN region. ② In 2002, China im-

---

① China's top electric appliance maker, Haier, for instance, has penetrated the US market to compete against entrenched foreign firms on the basis of price and quality. It has established a plant in the US to manufacture consumer electronics like refrigerators and air-conditioners. *Far East Economic Review*, 29 Mar 2001.

② This is actually happening now, as argued in the most recent UN report "World Economic Situation and Prospects 2003" that China has become a "bit of an engine for the whole Asian region" by picking up Japan's slack. See "An engine for Asian region", *China Daily* January 11, 2003.

ported much more from ASEAN than ASEAN from China, indicating that China can be a huge potential market for ASEAN's goods. Many ASEAN countries, particularly Malaysia, Thailand and Vietnam, also witnessed a sharp rise of tourist arrivals from China. Even more significantly, China's outbound FDI to the ASEAN countries has been steadily increasing in the past few years. In 2001, Premier Zhu Rongji urged Chinese domestic enterprises to adopt a "going outside" (outward-looking) strategy. While most Chinese enterprises have been attracted to Latin America, North America and Europe, there is increasing interest in investing within East Asia. [1] Despite all these trends and developments, the rise of China, on balance, still poses a real challenge to the ASEAN-4, at least in the short run.

V. China's FTA Initiative

Mindful of ASEAN's growing apprehension of the disruptive effects and consequences of its economic rise, China in recent years has been under mounting political pressures to improve its overall relations with its ASEAN neighbours to its south. During the 1997 Asian financial crisis, Beijing's steadfast refusal to devalue its Renminbi so as not to aggravate this regional crisis was widely appreciated as a good political gesture by ASEAN. But the single most important initiative ever undertaken by China to upgrade its long-term political and economic relations with the ASEAN region is China's celebrated FTA (free trade agreement) scheme.

At the ASEAN-China Summit in November 2000, Chinese Premier Zhu Rongji proposed the creation of a free trade area be-

---

[1] For more detailed information on this subject, see John Wong and Sarah Chan, "China's Outward Direct Investment: Expanding Worldwide", *China, an International Journal*, Vol. 1, No. 2, September 2003.

tween China and ASEAN within 10 years. On November 4, 2002, China and the ASEAN countries signed a landmark framework agreement in Cambodia to establish an FTA by 2010. ① The formation of the China-ASEAN FTA signifies the creation of an economic region of 1.7 billion consumers with a combined GDP of US $2 trillion. It offers an effective means for smaller ASEAN states to overcome its disadvantage of smallness by pooling resources and combining markets. This will in time lead to greater economic integration between China and ASEAN, clearly a kind of win-win situation for both sides. ②

In the short run, however, ASEAN has to deal with the initial risks of the FTA in connection with the potential trade diversion effect and related structural adjustment. ③ In general, the FTA scheme will give rise to uneven distribution of costs and benefits among different industries, different sectors, and even among different ASEAN countries. This means that adjustment costs are likely to be asymmetrical among the ASEAN states, i. e. some will be more adversely affected than the others. Adjustment costs will be even more asymmetrical between China and ASEAN. Individual ASEAN economies, being essentially small-

---

① The framework agreement signed by the eleven nation states sets out a road map for trade liberalization in goods and services for most countries by 2010 and for the less developed ASEAN nations (namely Cambodia, Laos, Myanmar and Vietnam) by 2015.

② For further discussion of this topic, see John Wong and Sarah Chan, "China-ASEAN Free Trade Agreement: Shaping Future Economic Relations", *Asian Survey*, Vol. XLIII, No. 3, May/June 2003.

③ Trade diversion occurs when members of a free trade grouping trades more among themselves than with other non-member countries, due to a lowering of tariffs or non-tariff barriers within the FTA. Structural adjustments occur because when intra-regional barriers are dismantled, industries will expand in some countries and contract in others as industries relocate in response to differences in factor endowments. The costs of adjustment resulting from such relocation of economic activity can be asymmetrical since some economies will incur higher costs in the short run than others.

er, are likely to incur higher costs of adjustment than China. ① In any case, as China is bracing itself for the challenges arising from its WTO membership, its FTA arrangements with ASEAN will therefore incur little additional costs. ②

After the initial process of adjustment, individual ASEAN economies will need to develop their own niches in their economic relations with China. With China continuing its dynamic economic growth, opportunities will arise for the ASEAN countries to exploit China's growing market so as to capture the spillover of its growth. Apart from its primary commodities, ASEAN's resource-based products will be in great demand in China. China is such a vast and disintegrated market that East China, South China and Southwest China individually can offer different opportunities to ASEAN producers. Beyond merchandise trade, FTA also promotes trade in services. China may generally have strong comparative advantage in manufacturing because it can enjoy the economies of scale, which, however, may not apply to many service activities. In fact, a lot of China's service activities, on account of their socialist legacies, are known to be more backward than those in ASEAN. ③

Above all, as the FTA scheme is gradually phased in over

---

① China's economy is much larger than the individual ASEAN countries; as such, it is able to absorb the adjustment costs relatively better than the ASEAN economies, particularly when the Chinese economy is rapidly growing and developing.

② This is quite self-evident as China is restructuring its economy to meet the challenges of WTO. China has already implemented structural reforms to strengthen its domestic industries to meet the competition from foreign investment. In the long term, when the FTA between China and ASEAN is realised within ten years, there will be considerably less additional costs for China since it would already have reformed most of its economy to better adjust to the challenges arising from the FTA with ASEAN.

③ See John Wong &. Ruobing Liang, "China's Service Industry (II): Gearing Up for WTO Challenges", *EAI Background Brief No. 163* (Singapore, 28 July 2003).

the years, multinationals in the region will take steps to restructure their supply chains and rationalize their production networks by taking China and ASEAN together as kind of a single market. This will eventually lead to a redistribution of regional FDI as a result of the reshuffle of regional production networks. The new regional production patterns will be based on a bigger and more diverse market. In short, both trade and FDI in the region should continue to grow under the impact of the FTA. This will certainly be a boon to both China and ASEAN.

VI. A Breakthrough for ASEAN+3

Politically, China depends on the FTA to stabilize and improve its long-term relationship with ASEAN. Successful implementation of this scheme will lead to much more prominent Chinese political and economic presence in the ASEAN region. In the meanwhile, even as some ASEAN members may remain doubtful of potential benefits accruing to ASEAN arising from the China-ASEAN FTA arrangements that are underway (e. g. the "early harvest program" for reducing tariffs of certain agricultural products), what is most significant is that the scheme has already occupied center stage in the EA region's future economic integration endeavor.

As already discussed in the foregoing sections, the EA region, despite its dynamic growth performance and its relatively high degree of economic interdependence, remains a weak and loosely constituted economic grouping with very few formal economic cooperation arrangements. ASEAN is the only institutionalized regional body, in addition to the rather limited bilateral FTA arrangement between Japan and Singapore—Japan and ROK are also in the final stage of entering into a general, development cooperation kind of FTA.

For more than three decades of its existence, however,

ASEAN has made little progress in terms of substantive regional economic integration. It may be noted that Third World countries have never experienced smooth going in their attempts to achieve economic integration. This explains why in the past so many regional cooperation schemes in Latin America and Africa had collapsed one after another. ASEAN is perhaps the only regional body in the developing world that has continued its "active existence" for more than three decades. ASEAN has survived primarily because of its so-called "ASEAN Way" of cooperation, which emphasizes consensus building, non-intervention, minimal institutionalization and open-ended cooperation projects. [1]

Nonetheless, without effective regional institutions and with only few formal cooperation programs, the EAEs have been unable to achieve further progress towards higher levels of economic integration. In fact, for years the EA region has prided itself on having this kind of market-driven but slow-moving "open regionalism", which was widely regarded as best suited for the region's political and economic realities. In recent years, however, the 1997 Asian financial crisis along with EU's success in its new integration initiatives and the rise of NAFTA has provided a new impetus and new demand for regionalism among many EAEs. Since the EA region is but a larger mirror image of ASEAN in terms of political, economic and social heterogeneity, ASEAN's past experiences in accommodating such inherent regional differences are considered useful and relevant. Hence the notion of extending ASEAN's basic regional cooperation process to the rest of the EA region through the "ASEAN+3" arrangement, i. e. ASEAN's cooperation arrangements with China, Japan and ROK.

Viewed in this larger context, China's FTA initiative with

---

[1] For further discussion, see John Wong, "ASEAN's Experience in Regional Economic Cooperation", *Asian Development Review*, Vol. 3, No. 1, 1985.

ASEAN not only marks the most important first step in the "ASEAN+3" endeavor but in fact also plays a crucial catalyst role in galvanizing the EA region towards the New-Age economic integration. Since China is a rising regional political and economic power, its FTA move is widely seen to be carrying profound geo-political implications for the region, thereby prompting similar responses from Japan and ROK. Indeed, in November 2002, Japan and ASEAN signed a joint declaration to draw up a general framework for FTA in ten years, which will comprise Japan's bilateral FTA arrangements with individual ASEAN member countries. In the meanwhile, Japan, China and ROK have agreed to initiate a joint study on possible Northeast Asian economic cooperation. Taiwan is particularly keen to conclude FTA with ASEAN countries for both political and economic relations. It is still uncertain if the future involvement of Taiwan and Hong Kong in the region's FTA process is to be included in the "ASEAN+3" (with Taiwan and Hong Kong as, politically speaking, Chinese territories), or under a new " ASEAN + 5" scheme, as proposed by Japan.

Suffice it to say that once China has fired the first shot, East Asian economic regionalism has taken a new turn. If the past ASEAN cooperation experiences are to go by, East Asian economic integration is destined to be a long, drawn out process, At the same time, the spate of new developments in recent years has shown that East Asian economic integration is no longer an abstract notion, but something that is achievable so long as the EAEs can maintain their steady economic growth. In this regard, China is an important source for both economic growth and integration in East Asia.

Table 1 China's Performance Indicators In East Asian Context

	Population (Mn)	GNP per-capita (US$)	PPP estimates of GNP per-capita (US$)	Growth of GDP(%)									Annual Export Growth (%)	Mfg exports as % of total exports	Exports as % of GDP
	2000	2000	2000	1960-70	1970-80	1980-90	1990-2000	1998	1999	2000	2001	2002*	1990-2000	1999	2000
China	1,261	840	3,940	5.2	5.5	10.1	10.3	7.8	7.1	8.0	7.3	8.0	15.6	88	26
Japan	127	34,210	26,460	10.9	4.3	4.0	1.3	-1.1	0.8	1.5	-0.4	-0.3	4.6	94	10.8
NIEs															
ROK	47	8,910	17,340	8.6	10.1	9.4	5.7	-6.7	10.9	9.3	3.0	6.2	16	91	45
Taiwan	22	14,188	n. a.	9.2	9.7	7.9	6.3	4.6	5.4	5.9	-1.9	3.5	7.9	n. a.	55
Hong Kong	7	25,950	25,660	10.0	9.3	6.9	4.0	-5.3	3.0	10.5	-0.2	2.3	8.4	95	150
Singapore	4	24,740	24,970	8.8	8.3	6.6	7.8	-0.1	6.9	10.3	-2.0	2.2	11.2	86	179
ASEAN-4															
Indonesia	210	570	2,840	3.9	7.2	6.1	4.2	-14.2	0.8	4.8	3.3	3.7	5.4	54	39
Malaysia	23	3,380	8,360	6.5	7.9	5.3	7.0	-7.4	6.1	8.3	0.4	4.0	12	80	125
Philippines	76	1,040	4,220	5.1	6.0	1.0	3.3	-0.6	3.4	4.4	3.2	4.6	7.3	41	56
Thailand	61	2,010	6,330	8.4	7.1	7.6	4.2	-10.5	4.4	4.6	1.8	5.0	9.5	74	66

Notes: (1) 2002 GDP growth figures for China, HK, Taiwan, Thailand, Singapore and Indonesia are official figures; the rest are estimates from Asian Development Bank.
(2) 1998—2001 GDP growth rates extracted from *Regional Outlook: Southeast Asia*, 2003—2004.
(3) Per capital GNP figure for Taiwan extracted from *Statistical Yearbook of the Republic of China*, 2001.
(4) Average annual GDP figures for Taiwan from 1980—90 and 1999—2000, respective years from 1997—2001 from *Statistical Yearbook of ROC*, 2001.
(5) 1996—2002 GDP growth rates for Japan represent real GDP growth rates.
(6) Average annual export growth for Singapore calculated from data provided by *EIU*; that of Taiwan from Ministry of Economic Affairs website.
Sources: *World Development Report* 1995; *World Development Report* 2000/2001; *World Development Report* 2002; World Bank website; ISEAS, *Regional Outlook: Southeast Asia* 2003—04; Taiwan Ministry of Economic Affairs, www.moea.gov. tw; *EIU* DataServices; *Statistical Yearbook of the Republic of China*, 2001.

Table 2(A) East Asian Trade Dependency, 1980–2001

Share of Total Exports Destined For (%)

East Asian Economy	Year	Total Exports (US $ million)	Japan	China	ROK	Taiwan	Hong Kong	Singapore	ASEAN-4	East Asia
Japan	1980	130,441		3.9	4.1	–	3.7	3.0	7.0	21.7
	1988	264,856		3.6	5.8	–	4.4	3.1	4.9	27.2
	1992	339,885		3.5	5.2	–	6.1	3.8	8.1	32.9
	1996	410,901		5.3	7.1	–	6.2	5.1	12.4	42.4
	2000	479,249		6.3	6.5	–	5.7	4.3	9.5	39.8
	2001	403,496		7.7	6.3	–	5.8	3.6	9.3	38.7
China	1980	18,099	22.3		–	–	24.1	2.3	4.3	53.0
	1988	47,540	16.9		–	–	38.4	3.1	2.8	61.2
	1992	80,517	13.8		2.9	0.8	44.2	2.5	2.8	67.0
	1996	151,197	20.4		5.0	1.9	21.8	2.5	3.4	55.0
	2000	249,297	16.7		4.5	2.0	17.9	2.3	3.7	47.1
	2001	266,620	11.0		4.7	1.9	17.5	2.2	3.8	41.1
ROK	1980	17,505	17.4	–		1.6	5.9	1.5	4.6	23.5
	1988	60,696	19.8	–		3.0	7.7	2.2	2.8	32.3
	1992	76,632	15.1	3.5		3.1	8.6	4.2	7.0	40.5
	1996	129,715	12.2	8.8		2.0	8.6	5.0	9.3	47.0
	2000	172,268	11.9	10.7		3.9	6.2	3.3	7.2	41.3
	2001	150,439	11.0	12.1		3.9	6.3	2.7	6.8	42.8
Taiwan	1980	–	–	–	–		–	–	–	–
	1988	60,667	10.9	0.0	1.4		18.9	3.1	6.9	41.2
	1992	81,470	10.9	0.6	2.3		23.1	4.0	8.3	50.1
	1996	115,942	11.8	0.6	2.3		23.1	4.0	8.3	50.1
	2000	148,321	11.2	2.8	2.6		21.1	3.7	7.4	48.8
	2001	122,866	10.4	3.9	2.7		21.9	3.3	7.2	49.4

Table 2(B)   East Asian Trade Dependency, 1980−2001

East Asian Economy	Year	Total Exports (US$ million)	Japan	China	ROK	Taiwan	Hong Kong	Singapore	ASEAN-4	East Asia
Hong Kong	1980	19,730	4.6	6.3	1.2	—		4.4	6.8	23.3
	1988	63,163	5.9	27.0	2.6	3.6		2.8	3.2	41.9
	1992	119,512	5.2	29.6	1.6	3.5		2.6	3.1	45.6
	1996	180,750	6.5	34.3	1.6	2.4		2.7	3.7	51.2
	2000	201,860	5.5	34.6	1.9	2.5		2.3	3.3	50.1
	2001	189,894	5.9	36.9	1.8	2.4		2.0	3.3	52.3
Singapore	1980	19,375	8.1	1.6	1.5	—	7.7		20.8	39.7
	1988	39,306	8.6	3.0	2.0	2.8	6.2		20.3	42.9
	1992	63,483	4.4	1.8	2.6	2.4	7.2		14.3	32.7
	1996	125,014	8.2	2.7	3.8	3.9	8.2		25.5	52.3
	2000	137,804	7.5	3.9	3.6	6.0	7.9		24.9	53.8
	2001	121,751	7.7	4.4	3.9	5.1	8.9		24.2	54.2
ASEAN-4	1980	47,100	34.5	1.1	1.7	—	1.9	11.8		51.0
	1988	80,080	19.5	2.2	2.8	2.0	2.9	9.0		38.4
	1992	112,788	21.9	2.6	2.9	3.1	3.9	13.6		48.0
	1996	204,270	17.8	3.3	3.5	3.4	5.1	14.0		47.1
	2000	269,099	16.0	3.4	3.7	4.2	4.2	12.5		44.0
	2001	250,656	16.1	4.4	3.7	3.8	4.1	11.8		43.9

Sources: IMF, *Direction of Trade Statistics Yearbook* (various issues); www.moea.gov.tw.

Note: ASEAN-5 refers to Singapore, Malaysia, Thailand, Indonesia and Philippines. East Asia comprises Japan, China, ROK, Taiwan, Hong Kong, Singapore and ASEAN-4.

Table 3 Foreign Direct Investment in China (US $ Million)

	1992 Actual Amount Invested	1992 %	1993 Actual Amount Invested	1993 %	1994 Actual Amount Invested	1994 %	1996 Actual Amount Invested	1996 %	1997 Actual Amount Invested	1997 %	1998 Actual Amount Invested	1998 %	1999 Actual Amount Invested	1999 %	2000 Actual Amount Invested	2000 %
Total	11292	100	27771	100	33946	100	42135	100	45257	100	45463	100	40319	100	40715	100
EAST ASIA	9900	87.7	23333	84	28267	83.2	32714	77.6	30389	67.1	26626	58.6	23210	57.4	22202	54.5
Hong Kong	7706	68.2	17445	62.8	19823	58.4	20852	49.5	20631	45.6	18508	40.7	16363	40.6	15500	38.1
Taiwan	1053	9.3	3139	11.3	3391	10	3482	8.3	3289	7.3	2915	6.4	2599	6.4	2296	5.6
Japan	748	6.6	1361	4.9	2086	6	3692	8.8	4326	9.6	3400	7.5	2973	7.3	2916	7.2
ROK	120	1.1	382	1.4	726	2	1504	3.6	2142	4.7	1803	4.0	1275	3.1	1490	3.7
ASEAN	271.6	2.4	1005.9	3.6	2240.6	6.6	3184.3	7.6	3418	7.6	4197	9.2	3274	8.2	2837	7.0
Indonesia	20.2	0.18	65.8	0.2	115.7	0.3	93.6	0.2	80	0.2	69	0.2	129	0.3	147	0.4
Malaysia	24.7	0.22	91.4	0.3	509.4	1.5	460.0	1.1	382	0.8	340	0.7	238	0.6	203	0.5
Philippines	16.6	0.15	122.5	0.4	201.0	0.6	55.5	0.1	156	0.3	179	0.3	117	0.3	111	0.3
Singapore	125.9	1.1	491.8	1.8	1179.6	3.5	2247.0	5.0	2606	5.8	3404	7.5	2642	6.6	2172	5.3
Thailand	84.3	0.75	234.4	0.8	234.9	0.7	328.2	0.8	194	0.4	205	0.5	148	0.4	204	0.5
USA	519	4.6	2068	7.4	2491	7	3444	8.2	3239	7.2	3898	8.6	4216	10.5	4384	10.8
Others	873	7.7	2370	8.5	3188	9	5977	14.2	8192	18.1	10729	23.6	9619	23.9	10218	25.1

Sources: *Statistical Yearbook of China (1992—2000)*; and *China Monthly Statistics*.

Table 4 China and East Asian Export Dependency, 1995—2001

Exporter	Largest Market Share Increase		Second Largest Market Share Increase	
	Importer	% Point Change	Importer	% Point Change
Japan	China	7.8	Philippines	1.4
NIEs				
ROK	China	16.5	Taiwan	1.3
Taiwan	China	13.7	Indonesia	2.6
Hong Kong	Indonesia	3.0	Hong Kong	1.7
Singapore	China	3.6	Indonesia	2.9
ASEAN-4				
Indonesia	China	5.6	Malaysia	3.0
Malaysia	China	7.8	ROK	2.1
Philippines	Taiwan	8.2	China	7.3
Thailand	China	10.1	Indonesia	2.0

Source: IMF, *Direction of Trade Statistics*, 2002.

Chart 1 China's Shares of World's Production of Some Key Commodities, 2001 (%)

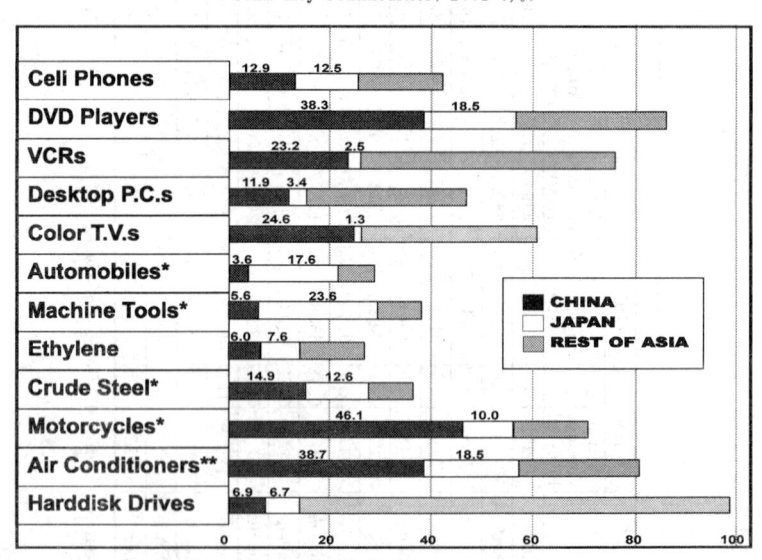

Commodity	China	Japan	Rest of Asia
Cell Phones	12.9	12.5	
DVD Players	38.3		18.5
VCRs	23.2	2.5	
Desktop P.C.s	11.9	3.4	
Color T.V.s	24.6	1.3	
Automobiles*	3.6	17.6	
Machine Tools*	5.6	23.6	
Ethylene	6.0	7.6	
Crude Steel*	14.9	12.6	
Motorcycles*	46.1	10.0	
Air Conditioners**	38.7	18.5	
Harddisk Drives	6.9	6.7	

* 2000, ** 1999.
Source: *The Nikkei Weekly*, August 6, 2001.

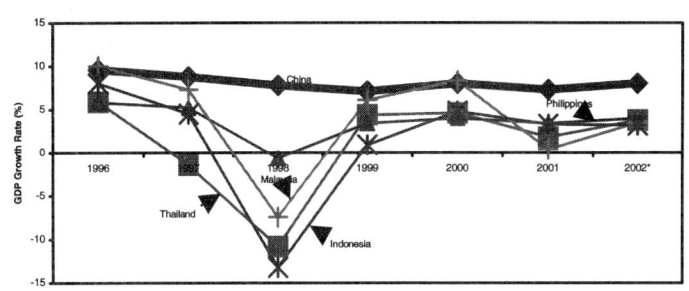

Chart 2 Crisis and Prolonged Economic Recovery of ASEAN-4

Note: * 2002 growth forecast estimated by World Bank in its half-yearly report on East Asia.
Source: World Bank, "East Asia Regional Update: Making Progress in Uncertain Times", 6 November 2002; *Asian Development Outlook 2002.*

Chart 3 East Asian Exports of Textiles, Clothing & Footwear (TCF) to US Market, 1990−2000

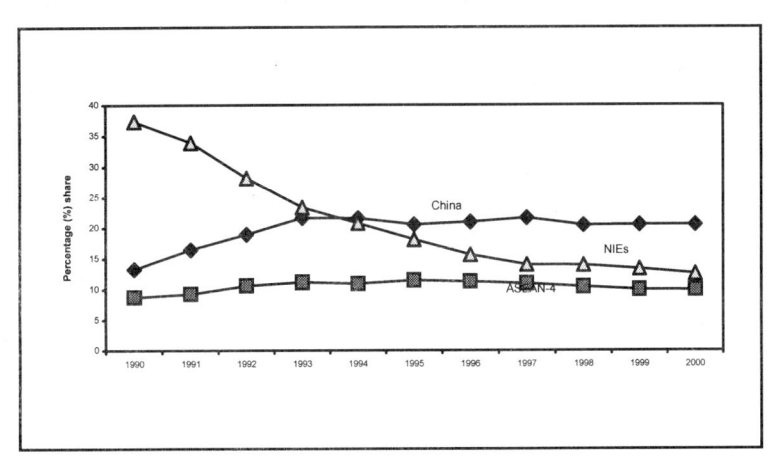

Source: US Census Bureau, US Department of Commerce.

Chart 4 East Asian Electrical & Electronics Exports to US Market, 1990—2000

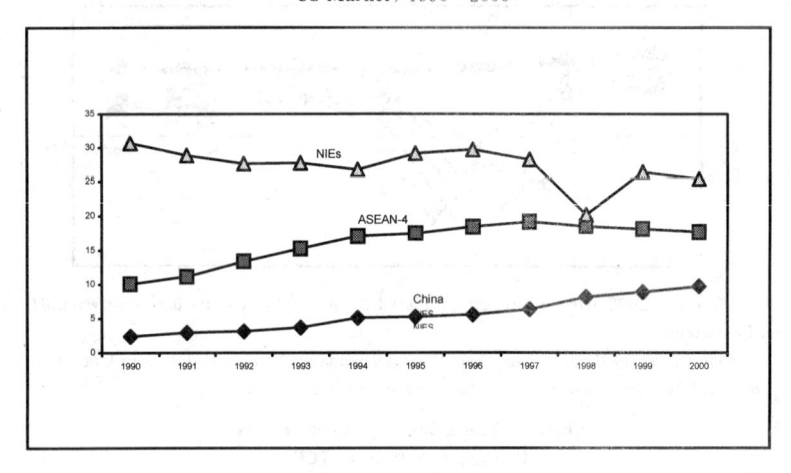

Source: US Census Bureau, US Department of Commerce.

Emerging East Asian Identification: A Cultural Perspective

Yu Xintian[①]

East Asia as a region is on rise. The concept of region not only refers to the geographic, economic and political formation, but also includes cultural identification. It is recognized that East Asian identification has already taken shape. The causes and characteristics of the identification, as well as its significance to East Asian international relations and its problems and prospects are worth an in-depth study.

I. Characteristics of East Asian Identification

Identification is a cognitive process in which the Self-Other distinction becomes blurred and at the limit transcended altogether. Collective identification merges the Self and the Other into a single identity. Collective identity involves shared characteristics, but not all shared characteristics involve identification. For example, France and Algeria both speak French, but they do not identify with each other. Collective identity, in short, is a distinctive combination of role and type identities, one with the casual power to induce actors to define the welfare of the Other

---

[①] Yu Xintian, Director, Professor of Shanghai Institute of International Studies.

as part of that of the Self, to be altruistic. Altruistic actors may still be rational, but the basis on which they calculate their interests is the group or team. [1]

The identification of East Asian countries is a kind of regional collective identification and, to a considerable extent, is related to economic globalization and regional integration. We have found regional organizations and identification of all forms in the world. East Asian identification is quite new with its birth in recent years. East Asia includes Northeast Asia and Southeast Asia. Southeast Asia was integrated through ASEAN in the 1970s and 1980s. Soon afterwards, Malaysian Prime Minister Mahathir set forth the proposal of setting up the East Asian Economic Caucus in 1991. At the time of the first Eurasian Meeting, East Asian countries especially held consultations on this proposal and naturally formed the framework of the enlarged ASEAN plus China, Japan and the ROK. East Asian regional cooperation in an embryonic form thus appeared. In the meantime, the academia in these countries explored a lot of plans and ideas for East Asian cooperation, such as China-Japan-the ROK Economic Cooperation Circle, 10+1, 10+3, Tumen River Area Development Zone and Mekong River Development Project. The Asian financial crisis in 1997 spurred the intention of East Asian countries joining hands in resisting negative effects of economic globalization, making the East Asian identification enter a new phase. Japan has signed the Free Trade Agreement with Singapore and is discussing a similar agreement with the ROK. China and ASEAN have declared that they will set up a free trade area in 2010 and China also proposed to initiate the research on China-Japan-the ROK and China-Japan-the ROK-ASEAN free trade agreements. Close economic intercourse among East Asian coun-

---

[1] Alexander Wendt, *Social Theory of International Politics*, Cambridge University Press, 1999, p. 229.

tries is unprecedented and economic interdependence among them is enhancing. Interest interrelation is the basis of regional identification, while recognition of shared interests is the key to promoting identification. 1997 financial crisis brought East Asian countries together. The regional identification was thus intensified.

East Asian cultures are rich and diversified, but in the current international system, their basic norms of behavior have accepted international standards mainly coming from the West. In the process of modernization, East Asian countries have accepted market economic principles, such as individual rights, individual values and competition awareness. For example, Malaysian Prime Minister Mahathir, who has often been criticized by westerners, repeatedly stresses the necessity of learning from western culture. He has championed Asian values does not necessarily mean that Western values are bad. As he said that we do not live in a simplistic either-or world. We live in a culture different from western one and hope cultures besides western culture are respected. Everyone should be open-minded enough to ponder other possibilities. He does not agree to call the 21st century Asian Century, advocating that this is a World Century and all countries, nations and regions enjoy same opportunities. [1] There is no need to cite the exposition of other Asian elite. The majority of them know that East Asian countries must learn from the West to give impetus to the process of modernization. As a matter of fact, Asians, like the majority of peoples of developing countries, tend to cultural relativism and want to contend for an equal position with western culture. [2]

East Asia is the converging point of Chinese cultural circle,

---

[1] Mohamad Mahathir, *A New Deal for Asia*, Peladuc, 1999, pp. 68, 135.
[2] Yu Xintian, "Outline of Research in International Culture", *Academic Quarterly of Shanghai Academy of Social Sciences*, No. 1, 1999.

Indian cultural circle and Islamic cultural circle. In their long historical intercourse, the three cultures have influenced one another, changed their respective faces and extended to include the factors of one another. The things in common among them surpass those between them and western culture. For instance, under the impact of Chinese culture and Indian culture, the formation of Islamic culture in East Asia is quite different from that in the Arabian world. The basic creed is the same, but cultural manifestations and explanations are different. Arabia lays stress on tribe, while Southeast Asia stresses family and clan, respect of parents, respect of the state and emphasis on education. Arabians advocate force and blood revenge, while East Asians praise highly harmony and peace. East Asian cultures have many common tendencies, which mainly are social harmony, cliquism resulting from clan, emphasis on education and respect of authority. They not only have exerted impacts on psychology and behavior of the broad masses of people but also have given birth to a political culture with East Asian characteristics. East Asian countries have learned from and absorbed Western values. By so doing, their native cultures have been renewed and transformed, presenting new formations. On this basis, the cultural values of East Asian elites have much commonality. David Hitchcock, former Director for East Asia and Pacific Affairs at the US Information Agency, found differences between elites of the U.S. and East Asians when he did a questionnaire. The order of societal values which East Asians think are the most important was as follows: a. an orderly society; b. social harmony; c. the accountability of public officials; d. being open to new ideas; e. freedom of expression; and f. respect for authority. But the order of the U.S. was different. a. freedom of expression; b. individual rights; c. individual freedom; d. the open debate; e. thinking for oneself; f. the accountability of public officials. Obviously, East Asians placed more emphasis on order, harmony and respect for authority, while the U.S. paid more attention to individual rights, open debate and freedom of expression. As for the most important personal values, 39% of East Asian respondents and only 19% of Americans chose "fulfilling obligations to others" while 59% of US respondents and only 33% of East Asians chose "individual achievements". And 69% of East Asians and only 15% of Americans stressed respect for learning and 48% of East Asians and only 22% of Americans emphasized self-discipline. [1] It is clear that East Asians share quite similar cultural values, which is the cultural source of the East Asian identification.

East Asian values have influence not only on the elite but also on the youth, which shows the strength of cultural inheritance and indicates the future of East Asian cultures. This is a striking characteristic of the East Asian identification. Scholars of China, Japan and the ROK made a survey of values of the youth, the result of which is very interesting. The values of the youth in these three countries have been clearly modernization-oriented. Less than 10% of the young respondents approved the traditional family with the authority of husband. More than 50% thought relations between generations to be friendly. Less than 20% held politics to be dealt with by politicians. Less than 25% considered it necessary to often extend respect to authoritative personages. Meanwhile, traditional Confucian culture exists in their values. Over 77% of respondents were proud or relatively proud of their own country and 80% of them were strongly or relatively strongly willing to serve their country. Most of them welcomed foreigners as their neighbors, which indicated openness in their private life. But the attitude to dealing with international relations is quite different according to the choice of re-

---

[1] David Hitchcock, *Asian Values and United States: How Much Conflict?*, 1994.

spondents from different countries. More respondents in China and the ROK think that national interests are the most important factor when dealing with international relations, while the proportion of respondents choosing world interests in Japan was the highest. More than 80% of the young respondents in the three countries advocated inheritance of traditional national culture but no hostility to western culture. Only less than 20% considered western culture as one making people hostile. [1]

Japan shows some difference from other East Asian countries in cultural diachronism. As is known to all, besides synchronism, culture has the feature of diachronism, that is, manifestations related to the degree of social development. In this regard, the ideological trend and value judgment of the Japanese are closer to those of western developed countries, though they also have the characteristics of Japanese culture. Other East Asian countries are closer to one another and are different from Japan in cultural diachronism. [2] For example, the Japanese youth pay more attention to global interests, while the youth in other countries lay more emphasis on national interests. This is an issue we cannot ignore in understanding the East Asian identification.

II. Significance of East Asian Identification

As Alexander Wendt pointed out that without interests identities have no motivational force, and without identities in-

---

[1] Wu Luping, et. al., *Convergence and Clash of East Asian Social Values:Comparison of Social Awareness Between the Chinese, Japanese and ROK Youth*, Social Sciences Documents Press, 2001, pp. 10-2, 144-55.

[2] Yu Xintian,"Similarities and Differences Between Chinese and Japanese Values and Their Impacts on Bilateral Relations", *Pacific Journal*, No. 1, 2000.

terests have no direction. ①Identification gives East Asian countries collective identities, guiding them to seek interests through cooperation. According to Realism, every country is egotistic and wants to pursue maximum self-interests. This is, to some extent, correct, but it cannot explain many issues such as why European countries have renounced part of their national interests to form the European Union. Interests naturally have their objectivity, but they also have subjectively recognized factors, behind which is the role of culture. The gap in strength between Japan and Malaysia is very wide and no doubt both of them seek national interests, but they are quite different in cultural psychology of cognizing and defining interests. So, in WWII, Japan invaded Malaysia, but now Japan forges friendly relations with Malaysia. National interests refer to the possibility of countries maintaining subsistence, security, development and dignity. In all these respects, identification will change people's definition of national interests and the channels of seeking national interests.

Security is the most sensitive issue. The definition of interests by East Asian countries has changed subject to identification. In fact, there still exist border disputes among East Asian countries, but they have begun to settle these disputes through peaceful consultations. If unable to resolve the disputes for a short while, they have also shelved them. Singapore and Malaysia as well as Malaysia and Indonesia have peacefully resolved their border disputes as well as other disputes. After 1970s, when rich oil was found in the South China Sea, six countries and regions respectively occupied several islands and there were signs that further actions would be taken. China and ASEAN countries agreed on a code of conduct for maintaining the status quo. The September 11 attacks again sounded a warn-

---

① Alexander Wendt, *Social Theory of International Politics*, Cambridge University Press, 1999, p. 231.

ing to East Asian countries and spurred their new understanding of nontraditional security. Terrorism, drug-trafficking, weapons-trafficking, transnational crime, AIDS and other activities have all transcended the borders, so leaders of all countries have no choice but to join hands. East Asia set up a framework of exchanging and sharing intelligence about terrorist activities and laundering. In the field of environmental protection, as the destructive smoke resulting from Indonesian burning the grass on wasteland caused other countries' economy to suffer, an agreement on cooperation in preventing the destructive smoke was signed. In 2003, when SARS indulged, leaders of China and the ASEAN met and jointly adopted effective measures to fight against the disease. They set up a fund into which China pledged US $ 1.2 million and Thailand US $ 0.25 million. At the same time, countries also reiterated their commitments to keep open their borders and economy, showing the will of enhancing mutual understanding and working together. It was at this summit that Chinese Premier Wen Jiabao declared that China decided to join the Treaty of Amity and Cooperation in Southeast Asia. The identification between China and ASEAN has further been enhanced. Pondering of nontraditional security has pushed ahead cooperation in traditional security. It is a good proof that since 2002 China has attended the Cobra Gold military exercises in Thailand as an observer.

It goes without saying that identification can promote common development. East Asia has formed multilevel and multiform cooperation mechanisms. Indeed, it is a fact that ASEAN was once worried about foreign investment transferring to China. In the 1990s, the foreign capital ASEAN absorbed accounted for 30% of that flowing into Asia, but in 2000 it dropped to 10%. Lee Kuan Yew, Singaporean Senior Minister, said that though China had absorbed more foreign capital than Southeast Asia, its economic growth would benefit countries in this region. He predicted that in the coming 30 — 50 years, Southeast Asia, China, the ROK and Japan would form a chain production and operation group, which would re-divide the Asian economic territory. This identification has produced obvious results. China's market demands have brought along East Asian prosperity. In 2001, China's trade volume with East Asian trade partners (excluding Japan) accounted for 40% of its total volume and its foreign investment from East Asia accounted for 67% of its total. When East Asia was in contact only with the U.S. and Japan, the industries in East Asian countries had the same structure and lacked horizontal contact. After China's rise, East Asian horizontal economic contacts have been greatly strengthened and endogenous economic variables are gradually becoming the leading force of development. Between 1990 and 2001, the export from Singapore, Malaysia, Thailand, the Philippines and Indonesia to China increased by 600%, while that to Japan, Europe and the U.S. only 250%. China's economic emergence will surely benefit East Asian economies. As Osamu Watanabe, Chairman of the Japan External Trade Organization (JETRO), recently pointed out that East Asian economy is rapidly developing and a new Pacific industrial zone from Japan and China to Southeast Asia is taking shape. The strategy of JETRO will no longer focus on Europe and the U.S. but transfer to Asia. Instead of complaining "China threat" and "hollowed industry", Japan is starting to upgrade the knowledge-related industries for competition and promoting economic cooperation with other East Asian countries. This is also a drastic change in interests and identification.

  The East Asian identification will further enhance the confidence of East Asian countries in success and affirmation of East Asian cultures is the motive force of promoting economic success. Max Weber summarized the Western capitalist spirit as individualism, market competition, *laissez faire* and others. However, East Asian work ethics and corporate spirit are very different. Individuals are meaningful only in organizations. Everyone must observe his/her responsibilities and obligations in the organizations and attach importance to mutual cooperation. American scholar Michael Bond investigated 40 values in 22 countries and found that East Asia placed special emphasis on respect, humbleness, frugality, willpower, sense of shame, mutual courtesy, steadiness, reputation, tradition and others. Yu Shaohua with the National University of Singapore investigated the values of enterprise managers in Singapore and Malaysia and also agreed to the interrelation between cultural background and economic development. Of course, the importance of political system and economic structure is not excluded. Samuel P. Huntington affirmed East Asian cultures' role in economy in his new work. He found that around 1960 the economic level and structure of the ROK was similar to Ghana. Thirty years later, the ROK became an industrial giant in the world, while Ghana's per capita GNP was only one fourteenth of the ROK. There were many reasons, but culture was an important factor. [1] In the same work, three scholars from developing countries maintained that poverty, autocracy and injustice in Africa and Latin America had resulted from traditional cultural values. [2] Although after the East Asian financial crisis many people denied East Asian cultures and their values, a lot of experts have strengthened positive evaluation of East Asian cultures. Du Weiming wrote that the West is the source of modernization, but East Asian modernization has a cultural form quite different from that of West Europe and North America. If the West seriously understands the modernity of East Asia, it will be sharper in seeing the strong and weak points

---

[1] Samuel P. Huntington, et. al., *Culture Matters: How Values Shape Human Progress*, Xinhua Publishing House, 2000, Preface p. 1.
[2] Ibid., p. 14.

of its model to the rest of the world. This will be a big step for the West and other areas of the world towards real exchanges. Without such exchanges, there will be no basic trust and effective cooperation between civilizations. [1] Successful experiences of East Asia are inspiring for other ethnic groups. Culture cannot be simply transplanted but can be learned for reference. After the Asian financial crisis, East Asia has no longer simplistically regarded culture as the cause of economic development, but rather the chance of understanding economic development and the background of improving institutions. The deeper people cognize, the better they can explore the role of culture in economic development.

Another significance of the East Asian identification is that it has enhanced East Asian position in the international arena or collective self-esteem. While the U. S. is making efforts to establish a Pan-American free trade zone and Europe will become a stronger actor, East Asia is able to match them in economic strength, but it lacks mechanization. Only deepened identification can promote strengthened organization and only integrated East Asia can play a bigger role in the world. In the past hundreds of years, the western powers have destroyed the most of civilizations and societies in the world and negated or changed local cultures and morals by means of Christianity, law and trade besides force. The West has bragged itself as the spiritual teacher of other ethnic groups and determined the destiny of them in accordance with its standards. While dominating the world with its hard power, the West has taken precedence in soft power. The rise of East Asian countries will enable East Asia to get its thoughts, cultures, and value systems onto the international stage, to set forth its propositions, to participate in reform of

---

[1] Samuel P. Huntington, et. al. , *Culture Matters: How Values Shape Human Progress*, Xinhua Publishing House, 2000, p. 383.

the international order, establishment of international organizations, adjustment of international mechanisms and distribution of international interests as well as affirmation of its existence with its unique political culture. This has made the West strongly feel the challenge of heterogeneous cultures and the overturn of the rule of its culture. As early as 1980, Roderick MacFarquhar pointed out that in the next century Russian challenge will be military, and Middle East challenge will be economic, while only East Asia will pose an all-round challenge to the West, from the style of economic development to basic values. Indeed, only East Asia, in its high-speed economic growth, clearly put forward "Asian values", which aroused hot debates and will also arouse debates in the future. In my view, the proposal of the "Asian values" itself is of political significance, which will increase rather than decrease.

The development of the current East Asian cultures has undergone two phases. The first phase was from the 1960s to the end of the Cold War, when a new East Asian culture was formed and the "Asian values" were put forward. Since the end of the Cold War, East Asian cultures entered the second phase, in which the East Asian identification has taken shape and developed. This phase may take decades of years. East Asia will strive for its due rights and utter a louder voice in the international political arena. However, this is definitely not Huntington's so-called clash of civilizations. The reason is that the East Asian people have undergone the painful colonial and semi-colonial rule and cultural coercion caused two deviations: strongly resisting all the western culture and blindly worshiping all things of the West. After national independence, people have chosen and learned cultures on their own, thus gradually reducing the two deviations. Western countries have no such experience, which is a past luck to them. For this reason, however, it is difficult for them to understand the excellence and greatness of diversified cultures in the world, which will become their future misfortune. Judging from the present phase, the East Asian identification has just started and is still paving the way for East Asia striving for international position. Even if it achieves this objective in the future, East Asia cannot advocate autocracy repelling other cultures. It is not only because East Asian ethnic groups have suffered from enslavement and are unwilling to impose sufferings on others but also because the values East Asian cultures stress can better contain the essence of human thoughts and cultures.

III. Problems and Prospects of East Asian Identification

East Asian identification remains in its embryonic stage and has to grow, blossom and bear fruit in fighting against hardships. East Asian integration is still very difficult. All the countries have obviously seen the necessity of integration, but the process of realizing it will be one of balancing and coordinating with their political will. Challenges are more in the aspect of security. Disputes over border and territorial waters among countries have not yet been finally settled. Arms expansion does not proceed from the actual needs but rather aims to surpass neighboring countries. What impacts will bilateral or multilateral military alliances have on regional security? Tense relations between ethnic groups and religions and unequal distribution of wealth, which may ferment nontraditional security threats, have also perplexed countries in the region. As many problems cannot be resolved only through bilateral efforts, the countries can only move in the direction of regional integration. The EU is the example of regional integration, but it is not clear what model East Asia will adopt. This depends not only on East Asian further development in politics and economy but also on the depth and characteristics of East Asian cultural identification.

Although East Asian religions are in general modest and plural, extremism is also rising. For example, the emergence of cults, extremist groups relating to the religion, they all have caused social division and instability. East Asian religious diversity may directly or indirectly influence identification. For example, on the anti-terrorism issue, the countries being the most active in supporting the fight against terrorism are Singapore and the Philippines, rather than Islamic countries. In the Southeast Asian Islamic countries, the sentiments of the broad masses of the people have impacts on governmental policy making. Only by prudently dealing with sensitive religious issues, can identification among East Asian countries be promoted.

Most East Asian countries have a lot of ethnic groups. Indonesia has more than 100 ethnic groups, while Myanmar has 135, Vietnam over 60 and Thailand more than 30. With the progress of modernization, the peoples of East Asian countries have enhanced their national self-confidence and have more identification with national states. The generalization of mass media, the consolidation of state power, the industrialization and the urbanization, all have become strong forces pounding at traditional national groups. In nontraditional security threats, some activities are often related to particular ethnic issues. For example, the drug traffickers in the Golden Triangle among Myanmar, Laos and Thailand are mainly Shans in Myanmar, Miaos in Laos and Thailand and Remnants of the Kuomintang. The immature political modernization and the unfinished national integration in East Asian countries may sometimes lead to social clash and even turmoil and even spill over the borders. For instance, in social riots, people of Chinese descent often bear the brunt. Without a correct direction, nationalism in big powers and large countries may cause corrosive of regional identification. Thus it is a major topic for achieving identification to advocate positive nationalism and prevent negative and destructive nationalism.

East Asian cultural identification needs consideration of the integration of cultural diversity and unity. Its long-range objective is to seek universal significance and value of East Asian cultures. At the present stage when western culture dominates, what East Asia demands is cultural tolerance, recognition and respect. However, seeking universality is just denying cultural tolerance. From a static view, the two are not synchronous. East Asia mainly remains in the former, but with the passage of time, the latter will be put on the agenda. If the result of East Asian identification is replacement of the universalization of western culture with that of East Asian culture, this will be evidently unfavorable to world peace and development and will also not be a good deed to the leap of East Asian culture. Therefore, we must bring the East Asian identification within limits, that is, cultural identification should not violate the principle of cultural tolerance, either within the East Asian region or in the whole world. The UNESCO issued a report written by an expert group, pointing out that the mankind needs diversity and also unity. At present, big cultures are the source of diversity, but they have not yet encouraged unity. Unity is not identity and is not based on eliminating differences but rather on integrating these differences into a harmonious whole. Without integration, there will be no growth, evolution and development in the most profound sense. [1]In my view, common values should be formed in the future. That is to say that all cultures contribute their excellent values and turn them into ones accepted universally by the mankind. The dissemination of Western cultural values all over the world is a good model. Other cultures all have the potential of generalization, but they must first undergo upgrade of modernization and then be popularized to the rest of the world.

---

[1] Ervin Laszlo, et. al., *The Multicultural Planet——A Report of A UNESCO International Expert Group*, Social Sciences Document Press, 2001, pp. 230-1.

East Asian identification is still weak and needs overcoming the above-mentioned problems and intensifying efforts to develop identification among the peoples of all the countries. The development of economic interdependence among East Asian countries has laid the material base for the East Asian identification. The identification, however, cannot be naturally increased. Only by making the idea of achieving win-win results through cooperation strike root in the hearts of the people can the original definitions be gradually changed.

In enhancing the East Asian identification, the role of China and Japan is of vital importance. Japan took the lead in realizing the modernization in East Asia. For Japan, due to its traditional strategy of "departing from Asia and joining the West" and a frontrunner of modernization, it considers itself distinct to other East Asian countries. Things now seem to change. Following closer economic integration with East Asian region, Japan starts to be back to East Asia. Japanese Prime Minister Koizumi even said in 2002 during a meeting organized by The Boao Forum for Asia that "a great challenge that faces Asia is to collectively speak to the world and jointly contribute to world prosperity" and asked Asian countries to bind together their individual efforts to create a more organic and expanded regional economic integration. Just as Shiraishi Takashi, Professor of Kyoto University argued, firstly Japan must regain vigor through reform and become a wealthy, stable and reliable country and secondly this kind of results can bring interests to ASEAN countries and even other East Asian countries. The former determines Japan's openness to East Asia and the latter determines Japan's leading role in East Asian community. [1]

Since the beginning of its reform and opening-up, China has

---

[1] Shiraishi Takashi, " 'Japanization' and 'Chinanization' are Key to Formation of East Asian Order", *Chuokoron*, No. 1, 2003.

integrated itself in an all-round way into the world system and constantly promoted its domestic system to dovetail the world market system and international practices. Although China has worldwide interests, it remains a country of the region. However, this does not mean that it is easy for China to cultivate regional identification. China has had the historical Central Kingdom weigh on its mind. Self-centering inclination is unintentionally showed in the people's mentality. The fact that China lacks the experience of being an equal member in the international system has also cast a shadow of worshiping the West and looking down upon the East over the people's mind. Therefore, China needs a long-term education to its people, change of ideas and understanding national interests against the background of regional identification.

In any case, China-Japan relations are of vital importance to East Asia. The region rises when the two countries cooperate and falls when they separate. The economic interdependence between the two countries has been unprecedented, so changes have taken place in mutual definition. But, as to how to get along with each other in the future, they are not prepared in notion and cultural psychology. It needs great efforts for China and Japan to establish a common identification and to reach collective identification with the rest of the East Asian region.